Grammar
Form and Function 2

Second Edition

Milada Broukal

Grammar Form and Function 2, Second Edition

Published by McGraw-Hill ESL/ELT, a business unit of The McGraw-Hill Companies, Inc., 1221 Avenue of the Americas, New York, NY 10020. Copyright © 2010 by The McGraw-Hill Companies, Inc. All rights reserved. No part of this publication may be reproduced or distributed in any form or by any means, or stored in a database or retrieval system, without the prior written consent of The McGraw-Hill Companies, Inc., including, but not limited to, in any network or other electronic storage or transmissions, or broadcast for distance learning.
7 8 9 10 11 12 RMN 18 17 16 15 14 13
ISBN   0-07-719220-6 (Student Book)

Developmental Editor: Regina Velázquez
Contributing Writer: Lisa Varandani
Project Manager: Jenny Hopkins
Publishing Management: Hyphen – Engineering Education
Cover Design: Page2, LLC
Interior Design: Hyphen – Engineering Education

The credits section for this book begins on page 398 and is considered an extension of the copyright page.
Cover photo: Train traveling through a mountain pass in winter: © Donavan Reese/Getty Images.

www.esl.mcgraw-hill.com

The **McGraw-Hill** Companies

Acknowledgements

The publisher and author would like to thank the following educational professionals whose comments, reviews, and assistance were instrumental in the development of the Grammar Form and Function series.

◆ Mary Ahlman, *Coastline Community College,* Fountain Valley, CA

◆ Tony Albert, *Jewish Vocational Services,* San Francisco, CA

◆ Carlos Alcazar, *Newport Mesa Adult School,* Costa Mesa, CA

◆ Ted Andersen, *INTRAX International Institute,* San Francisco, CA

◆ Leslie A. Biaggi, *Miami-Dade Community College,* Miami, FL

◆ Sharon Bidaure, *INTRAX International Institute,* San Francisco, CA

◆ Grace Low Bishop, *Houston Community College,* Houston, TX

◆ Taylor Blakely, *Newport Mesa Adult School,* Costa Mesa, CA

◆ Gerry Boyd, *Northern Virginia Community College,* Annandale, VA

◆ Marcia Captan, *Miami-Dade Community College,* Miami, FL

◆ Sue Chase, *Coastline Community College,* Fountain Valley, CA

◆ Yongjae Paul Choe, *Dongguk University,* Seoul, Korea

◆ Mei Cooley, *INTRAX International Institute,* San Francisco, CA

◆ Laurie Donovan, *Houston Baptist University,* Houston, TX

◆ Elinore Eaton, *INTRAX International Institute,* San Francisco, CA

◆ Emma Fuentes, *INTRAX International Institute,* San Francisco, CA

◆ Sally Gearhart, *Santa Rosa Junior College,* Santa Rosa, CA

◆ Betty Gilfillan, *Houston Community College,* Houston, TX

◆ Frank Grandits, *City College of San Francisco,* San Francisco, CA

◆ Mary Gross, *Miramar College,* San Diego, CA

◆ Martin Guerin, *Miami-Dade Community College,* Miami, FL

◆ Earl Hayes, *City College of San Francisco,* San Francisco, CA

◆ Patty Heiser, *University of Washington,* Seattle, WA

◆ Lillian Johnston, *Houston Baptist University,* Houston, TX

◆ Susan Kasten, *University of North Texas,* Denton, TX

◆ Sarah Kegley, *Georgia State University,* Atlanta, GA

◆ Kelly Kennedy-Isern, *Miami-Dade Community College,* Miami, FL

◆ Elisabeth Lindgren, *INTRAX International Institute,* San Francisco, CA

◆ Wayne Loshusan, *INTRAX International Institute,* San Francisco, CA

◆ Irene Maksymjuk, *Boston University,* Boston, MA

◆ Linda Maynard, *Coastline College,* Garden Grove, CA

◆ Gisele Medina, *Houston Community College,* Houston, TX

◆ Christina Michaud, *Bunker Hill Community College,* Boston, MA

◆ Mike Missiaen, *INTRAX International Institute,* San Francisco, CA

◆ Cristi Mitchell, *Miami-Dade Community College-Kendall Campus,* Miami, FL

◆ Ilene Mountain, *Newport Mesa Adult School,* Costa Mesa, CA

◆ Susan Niemeyer, *Los Angeles City College,* Los Angeles, CA

◆ Carol Piñeiro, *Boston University,* Boston, MA

◆ Michelle Remaud, *Roxbury Community College,* Boston, MA

◆ Diana Renn, *Wentworth Institute of Technology,* Boston, MA

◆ Corinne Rennie, *Newport Mesa Adult School,* Costa Mesa, CA

◆ Jane Rinaldi, *Cal Poly English Language Institute,* Pomona, CA

◆ Alice Savage, *North Harris College,* Houston, TX

◆ Sharon Seymour, *City College of San Francisco,* San Francisco, CA

◆ Larry Sims, *University of California-Irvine,* Irvine, CA

◆ Karen Stanley, *Central Piedmont Community College,* Charlotte, NC

◆ Roberta Steinberg, *Mt. Ida College,* Newton, MA

◆ Margo Trevino, *Houston Baptist University,* Houston, TX

◆ Duane Wong, *Newport Mesa Adult School,* Costa Mesa, CA

Contents

Appendices

WELCOME TO
GRAMMAR FORM AND FUNCTION, SECOND EDITION!

Memorable photos bring grammar to life.

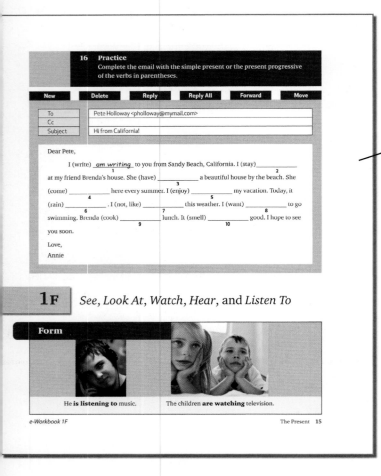

FORM presentations teach grammar structures through clear comprehensive charts, each of which is accompanied by **a full-color photo** that facilitates students' recall of the target grammar structure.

FUNCTION explanations clarify how and when to use grammar structures.

PRACTICE activities guide students from accurate production to fluent use of the grammar.

8 Practice

Use the prompts to write sentences with *as … as* or *not as … as*.

1. autumn/cold/winter

   Autumn is not as cold as winter.

2. the month of September/long/the month of June

   _____

3. in the winter months, California/cold/New York

   _____

4. September/popular/July for vacations in North America

   _____

5. in the fall, plants/grow/fast/in spring

   _____

6. days in summer/short/days in winter

   _____

9 Practice

Many languages have sayings that include a phrase similar to *as … as*. Listen and underline the correct word to finish each saying. Notice that *as* often sounds like "uz." Then work with a partner to explain how the sayings are different in another language that you know.

AUDIO
DOWNLOAD
CD3, 3

1.	a. a feather	b. a car	5.	a. water	b. ink
2.	a. soup	b. sugar	6.	a. grass	b. the sky
3.	a. a mouse	b. a lion	7.	a. a house	b. a bird
4.	a. gold	b. a tomato	8.	a. a dog	b. a child

NEW! LISTENING activities highlight the aural/oral dimension of grammar, further increasing students' ability to use and understand spoken English.

Writing: Write a Friendly Email

Write an email to a friend about your recent experiences.

STEP 1 Think about things in your past and present life you can write about. Write the answers to these questions or others you can think of. Share your answers with a partner.

1. What are you studying?

2. What do you find easy/difficult/interesting?

3. What have you been doing in your free time?

4. Where is the last place you traveled to? What did you do there?

5. What movies have you seen? What kinds of sports have you been doing or have you watched on television?

6. When will you talk to your friend again, or maybe see your friend?

STEP 2 Rewrite your answers in the form of an email.

STEP 3 Evaluate your email.

Checklist
_____ Did you write your friend's email address after "To:"?
_____ Did you include a subject, such as "Hello from school," after "Subject:"?
_____ Did you start with a greeting such as "Dear Rosa"?
_____ Did you put line spaces between your paragraphs?
_____ Did you end with a closing such as "Sincerely," "Your Friend," or "Love,"?
_____ Did you sign your name at the bottom of your email?

STEP 4 Edit your email. Work with a partner or your teacher to edit your sentences. Correct spelling, punctuation, vocabulary, and grammar.

STEP 5 Write the final copy of your email.

146 Unit 6

WRITING assignments guide students to develop writing and composition skills through step-by-step tasks.

ALL-NEW TECHNOLOGY ENHANCEMENTS!

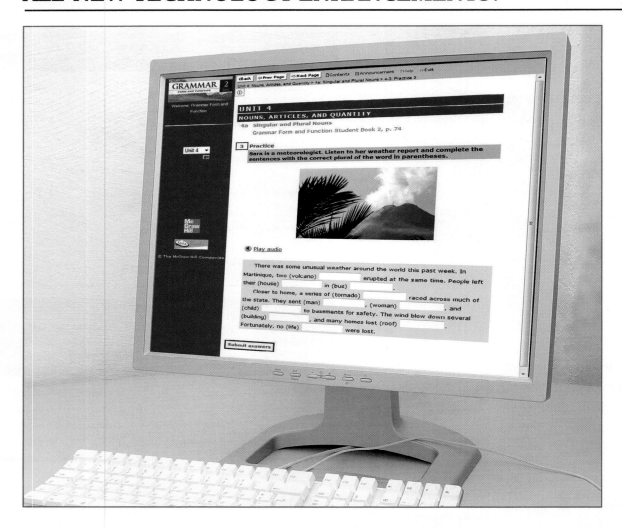

NEW! e-WORKBOOK frees teachers from homework correction and provides students with a wealth of interactive practice, anytime—anywhere.

Add instructional hours to the course, provide homework and additional standardized test-taking exercises, and help learners practice the form and function of each grammar point. Audio segments, photos, and video clips enhance many activities.

To purchase e-Workbooks online, visit: **http://books.quia.com/books.**

NEW! AUDIO DOWNLOAD CENTER offers students the ability to access DOWNLOAD and download MP3 files for all of the listening activities in the Student Book. All Audio Download Center content can be found by visiting **www.esl.mcgraw-hill.com/audio**. To navigate the MP3 files, search for your: Unit Number > Page Number > Activity.

NEW! EZ® Test CD-ROM Test Generator and EZ Test Online enables instructors to access a wealth of grammar items that they can use to create customized tests for each unit. Assessment content is also available at **www.eztestonline.com**.

All-new Internet Activity Worksheets in the Teacher's Manual encourage students to access the Internet to read, research, and analyze information, developing necessary academic skills.

NEW SPECIAL FEATURES

NEW! LISTENING PUZZLES provide audio-based challenges for students to practice new grammar concepts.

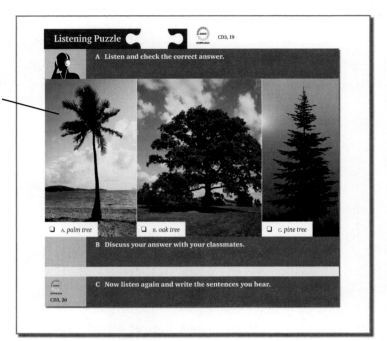

NEW! ACADEMIC READING CHALLENGES recycle key vocabulary and grammar in longer contexts, prompting students to integrate their language and critical thinking skill development.

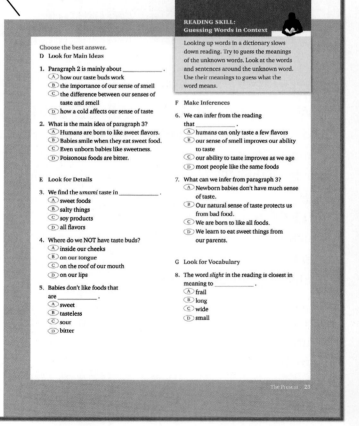

To the Instructor

Series Overview

Form is the structure of a grammar point and what it looks like. Practice of the form builds students' accuracy and helps them recognize the grammar point in authentic situations, so they are better prepared to understand what they are reading or what other people are saying.

Function is when and how we use a grammar point. Practice of the function builds students' fluency and helps them apply the grammar point in their real lives.

Mastery of grammar relies on students knowing the rules of English (form) and correctly understanding how to apply them (function). Providing abundant practice in both form and function is key to student success.

Grammar Form and Function, Second Edition is a three-level, communicative grammar series that helps students successfully learn the rules of essential English grammar (form) and when to apply them and what they mean (function). This new full-color edition ensures academic success and a greater ability to comprehend and communicate with ease through the addition of a robust listening program, new academic readings, new communicative activities, and more opportunities for practice with the e-Workbook.

Components and Unit Organization

Each level of Grammar Form and Function, Second Edition includes:

a **Student Book** with 14 units to present and reinforce the grammar. For each grammar point, the Grammar Form and Function, Second Edition Student Book follows a consistent format:

- **Presentation of Form.** The Student Book presents the complete form, or formal rule, along with several examples for students to clearly see the model. There are also relevant, full-color photos to help illustrate the grammar point.
- **Presentation of Function.** The text explains the function of the grammar point, or how it is used, along with additional examples for reinforcement.
- **Practice.** Diverse exercises practice the form and function together.
- **Application.** Students apply the grammar point in open-ended, communicative activities that integrate all language skills.
- All-new **Listening** and **Listening Puzzle** activities provide students with numerous opportunities to develop their oral/aural and discrimination skills.
- **Pair Up and Talk** encourages students to practice conversation and grammar structures with a partner.
- **Your Turn** invites students to personalize the grammar and language.

- **Read** and **Reading Challenge** activities develop reading and thinking skills.
- **Writing** tasks develop writing and composition skills.
- **Self-Test**. Students take a test to see what they learned and what they still need to work on and practice.

an **e-Workbook** that extends learning, practice, and testing opportunities.

a **Complete Audio CD Program** for teachers that contains all of the listening activities. Each listening activity will include an audio icon with CD and tracking information. The complete audio files are also available for students as **MP3 downloads**.

an **EZ Test® CD-ROM Test Generator** that includes 560 additional testing items that teachers can use and customize to create tests.

a **Teacher's Manual** to make preparation quick. Each unit of this Teacher's Manual includes:

- an overview of each unit to summarize the contents
- **Notes on the Photos** to describe the photos in the Form and Function sections and give background and cultural information
- **Warm-Up Activities** to engage students in the topic and activate the target grammar
- Useful teaching tips and techniques for both new and experienced instructors to provide students with the information they need
- multiple expansion ideas, games, and writing activities to extend and personalize learning
- **Notes on Culture, Notes on Usage, and Notes on Vocabulary** to help instructors clarify, explain, and present the information with ease
- answers to **Frequently Asked Questions** (FAQs) to provide the instructor and students with a deeper understanding of the structure
- answer keys for the exercises and Self-Tests
- **Unit Tests** in a standardized test format and test answer keys to assess understanding and mastery of the unit
- New reproducible **Internet Activity Worksheets** with Internet Activity Procedures to encourage students to expand their online learning and research skills
- new **EZ Test® CD-ROM Test Generator**
- the **Complete Audio CD Program**

Teaching with *Grammar Form and Function, Section Edition*

Leveling and Use

While classes and instructors differ, the Grammar Form and Function, Second Edition Student Books are designed to be used in the following levels:

Grammar Form and Function 1, Second Edition: beginning

Grammar Form and Function 2, Second Edition: intermediate

Grammar Form and Function 3, Second Edition: high-intermediate to advanced

Grammar Form and Function, Second Edition is a flexible series, and instructional hours can vary depending on the needs of the learners. Instructors can greatly expand their instruction and increase their students' exposure to and practice with the language by using all of the activities in the Student Book and the e-Workbook, and by employing the additional suggestions and resources provided in the Teacher's Manual.

Assessment

Students and instructors of the Grammar Form and Function, Second Edition series have numerous opportunities to assess progress. There are two **Self-Tests** for each unit—one at the end of each Student Book unit and another at the end of each e-Workbook unit. The Self-Tests build student confidenWce, encourage student independence as learners, and increase student competence in following standardized test formats.

The Teacher's Manual also includes comprehensive **Tests**. They serve as important tools for the teacher in measuring student mastery of grammar structures. In addition, Grammar Form and Function, Second Edition includes the **EZ Test® CD-ROM Test Generator**. This tool enables instructors to access a wealth of grammar items that they can use and customize to create tests for each unit.

Technology Resources

Grammar Form and Function, Second Edition includes an all-new **e-Workbook**. The e-Workbook can be used to add instructional hours to the course, to provide homework practice and additional standardized testing practice, and to help learners practice the form and function of each grammar point. Color photos, audio segments, and video clips enhance many activities. Students can access the e-Workbook at **http://books.quia.com/books**.

Grammar Form and Function, Second Edition includes reproducible Internet Activity Worksheets that will help students expand their online learning and research skills.

Grammar Form and Function, Second Edition has a wealth of listening activities to encourage communicative competence. The audio icon in the Student Book indicates when audio activities are available and lists the CD or MP3 tracking number. All of the listening activities are available for the instructors on the Complete Audio CD Program that is packaged with the Teacher's Manual. Students can also access and download the **MP3 files** for these activities at the Grammar Form and Function **Audio Download Center**: Go to **www.esl.mcgraw-hill.com/audio**. Select *Grammar Form and Function, 2nd Edition, Level 2*, and download the audio files.

Unit 1
The Present

Dennis **talks** on the phone a lot.

Form

Mike and Lee **work** in the same office. They **read** all the newspapers every morning. Mike **is** a writer. He **writes** about movies for a newspaper. Lee **checks** his work.

1. To form the simple present, use the base form of the verb for most forms. Add *-s* or *-es* to verbs with third person singular subjects (*he*, *she*, *it*, or singular nouns).

2. In negative statements, we use *do not* (*don't*) or *does not* (*doesn't*) plus the base verb.

Affirmative Statements		Negative Statements		
Subject	Verb	Subject	*Do/Does Not*	Base Verb
I		I		
You		You		
We	work.	We	do not don't	
They		They		work.
The computers		The computers		
He/She/It	works.	He/She/It	does not doesn't	
The computer		The computer		

3. When we add *-s* to base verbs, we change the spelling for some verbs.

Singular	Examples		
Add *-s* to most verbs.	walk–walks	get–gets	sing–sings
	leave–leaves	like–likes	run–runs
Add *-es* to verbs that end in *sh, ch, ss, x,* or *o*.	finish–finishes	catch–catches	go–goes
	cross–crosses	relax–relaxes	do–does
If a verb ends in a consonant + *y*, change the *y* to *i* and add *-es*.	try–tries	worry–worries	study–studies
If a verb ends in a vowel + *y*, add *-s*.	pay–pays	play–plays	buy–buys

4. Two verbs are irregular in the simple present: *be* (*am, is, are*) and *have* (*has, have*). Also, *be* forms its negative differently from other verbs.

Affirmative Statements			Negative Statements		
	Subject	**Verb**		**Subject**	**Negative Verb**	
Be	I	am	late.	I	am not 'm not	late.
	You	are		You	are not 're not aren't	
	We			We		
	They			They		
	He/She/It	is		He/She/It	is not 's not isn't	
Have	I	have	a problem.	I	don't have	a problem.
	You			You		
	We			We		
	They			They		
	He/She/It	has		He/She/It	doesn't have	

Function

Dennis **talks** on the phone a lot.
(happens all the time)
Mike **writes** movie reviews on his computer every day. (happens all the time)

1. We use the simple present when we talk about habitual actions and for things that happen all the time or are always true.
    Fish **swim** in the ocean. (always true)
2. We use the negative contracted forms *don't* and *doesn't* in speech and informal writing. We use the full forms *do not* and *does not* in formal writing and in speech to emphasize the negative.

    INFORMAL: I'm sorry. I **don't** have time to help you now.
    FORMAL OR EMPHATIC: The president **does not** want this report to be late.

1 Practice

Complete the sentences with the correct form of the verb in parentheses.
Make the verb negative if the word *not* is in the parentheses.

1. Mike (live) _____lives_____ in New York City.
2. He (have) _____haves_____ an apartment near the office.
3. He (not, take) _doesn't take_ the bus to work.
4. He (walk) _____walks_____ to work.
5. Mike (like) _____likes_____ his job.
6. He (write) _____writes_____ about movies.
7. He (go) _____goes_____ to the movies every day.
8. He (not, go) _doesn't go_ home at 5:00 in the afternoon.
9. Lee (correct) _____corrects_____ his work.
10. Mike and Lee (not, agree) _don't agree_ all the time.

2 Pair Up and Talk

Think of five activities that a friend does all the time. Tell your partner.

My friend Sara teaches art to children. She drives to work. She helps the children.
She likes her job. She sees a movie every weekend.

3 Your Turn

Write three more things you do every day and you don't do every day. Then
talk about them with a partner.

Example

_____I exercise every day._____   _____I don't cook every day._____

_____   _____

_____   _____

_____   _____

4 Practice

Listen and write the missing words. Use the correct *-s* or *-es* spelling of the verb.

1. John (get up) ___*gets up*___ at noon.

2. He (eat) _____ breakfast.

3. He (watch) _____ television.

4. He (meet) _____ his friends for lunch.

5. He (try) _____ to find a job.

6. In the evening, he (go out) _____ with his friends.

7. John (come) _____ home at four o'clock in the morning.

8. On Sundays, he (stay) _____ home.

9. He (wash) _____ his clothes.

10. He (clean) _____ his apartment.

11. He (call) _____ his mother.

12. His mother (worry) _____ about him.

5 Your Turn

Why does John's mother worry about him? Write three reasons. Then share them with a partner.

1. _____

2. _____

3. _____

6 Practice

Work with a partner. Tell your partner what each of the people below do.

Example
A mechanic fixes cars.

a chef   a painter
a doctor   a teacher
a mechanic

1B   Adverbs of Frequency

Form

This is Ann Philips.
She's a host on morning television.
We **often** see her on *Good Morning*.
She **always** gets up early on workdays.
She **usually** arrives at the studio at 4:30 in the morning.

Never, rarely, hardly ever, sometimes, often, frequently, usually, and *always* are adverbs of frequency. They come between the subject and the simple present verb.

```
0% ——————|——————|——————|——————|——————— 100%
never        rarely       sometimes      often        usually      always
             hardly ever                 frequently
```

Subject	Adverb of Frequency	Simple Present	
I	never	eat	Chinese food.
You	rarely	go	to the theater.
He	hardly ever	sees	friends.
She	sometimes	drinks	tea.
It	often	snows	in winter.
You	frequently	clean	your house.
We	usually	get up	early.
They	always	have	breakfast.

Function

Adverbs of frequency tell us how often something happens.

Ann **always** starts the show at 7:00 in the morning.
She **never** gets angry on the show.
She **usually** smiles a lot on the show.

7 Practice

Listen to Ann talk about her workday. Put an *X* to show how often she does each thing.

	0% ——— 50% ——— 100%
1. On weekdays, I get up at 3:30 in the morning.	X
2. I eat breakfast.	
3. I leave the house at 4:15.	
4. I get to the studio at 4:30.	
5. *Good Morning* starts at 7:00.	
6. I leave the studio at 10:00.	
7. I go to the gym after work.	
8. I go shopping after the gym.	
9. My husband and I stay home in the evening.	
10. We go out on weekdays.	
11. We watch television.	
12. I go to bed at 9:00.	

8 Practice

Work with a partner. Use the chart in Practice 7 to talk about Ann's workday.

Example

Ann always gets up early on weekdays.

9 Pair Up and Talk

Which of these do you always do, sometimes do, or never do during the week? Talk about your answers with a partner.

I **always** cook dinner, and I **sometimes** do my homework.

cook dinner	eat breakfast	go to school	play football
do my homework	eat meat	go to the movies	send emails
drive a car	exercise	have lunch	watch television

Form

People **are walking** to their gates.
They **are carrying** suitcases.

1. We form the present progressive with a present form of *be* (*am*, *is*, or *are*) + the *-ing* form of a verb.

Affirmative and Negative Statements

Subject	Form of *Be*	(*Not*)	Verb + *-ing*
I	am		
You	are		
He/She/It	is	(not)	working.
We	are		
They			

Full Forms	Contractions	
Full Form	**Subject + Form of *Be***	**Form of *Be* + *Not***
I am (not)	I'm (not)	*
You are (not)	You're (not)	You aren't
He/She/It is (not)	He's (not) She's (not) It's (not)	He isn't She isn't It isn't
We are (not)	We're (not)	We aren't
They are (not)	They're (not)	They aren't

* There is no contraction for *am not*.

2. When we add *-ing* to a base verb, we change the spelling for some verbs.

Base Verb Ending	Rule	Example	
For most verb endings	Add *-ing*.	start	start**ing**
		play	play**ing**
		study	study**ing**
The verb ends in a consonant + *e*.	Drop *e*, add *-ing*.	live	liv**ing**
		move	mov**ing**
		decide	decid**ing**
The verb ends in a single vowel + a consonant.	Double the consonant, add *-ing*.	stop	stop**ping**
		plan	plan**ning**
		prefer	prefer**ring**
Exceptions Do not double *w* or *x*.		fix	fix**ing**
		show	show**ing**
If a verb has two or more syllables and the stress is not on the last syllable, do not double the consonant.		open	open**ing**
		travel	travel**ing**
		exit	exit**ing**
The verb ends in *ie*.	Change *ie* to *y* and add *-ing*.	tie	t**ying**
		die	d**ying**

Function

A woman **is sitting** on a bench.
A man **is standing** in front of her.
They **are talking**.

1. We use the present progressive to talk about what is happening now.
   I **am sitting**. (happening now)
   I **am looking** for a job. (happening around now)
2. We use contractions in speech and in informal writing. We use full forms in formal writing and when we want to give emphasis to what we are saying.

AUDIO
DOWNLOAD

CD1, 4

10 Practice

Listen and write the *-ing* forms of the missing words. Use the correct spelling.

1. Juan is ___listening___ to a new album.

2. I am _____ for the bus.

3. They are _____ for their English test.

4. I am _____ in the U.S. for another year.

5. Bob is _____ in the ocean.

6. She is _____ her shoelaces.

7. I am _____ to get a new job next year.

8. Joe is _____ the paper in half.

11 Practice

Complete the sentences with the present progressive of the verb.

I love airports. At the moment, I (wait) ___am waiting___ for my plane. I have three
                                                    1
hours. So what am I doing? I (watch) _am watching_ people. Look at that man. He's
                                            2
outside the bookstore. He (look) _is looking_ around. He (not, smile) _isn't smiling_.
                                        3   **4**
He looks worried. Now he (go) _is going_ to the departure gate. Here comes a
                                    5
woman. She (not, walk) _isn't walking_. She (run) _is running_ after the man.
                                6   **7**
She (hold) _is holding_ a passport in her hand. She (shout) _is shouting_ something.
                8   **9**
The man (turn) _is turning_, and now he (smile) _is smiling_. He (put)
                    10   **11**
is putting his arm around her now. They look happy.
    12

12 Pair Up and Talk

Test your memory. Work with a partner. Make three true statements and
three false statements about the photo on page 9. Your partner tells you if
they are true or false without looking at the photo.

YOU: The man is sitting down.
YOUR PARTNER: That's false.

Function

Carla always **starts** work at nine.
Carla **loves** her job.

cubicle

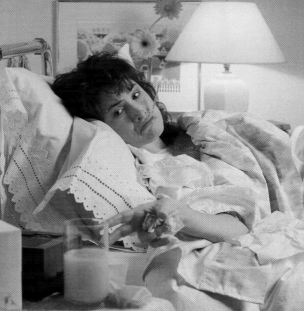

Today, Rose **isn't working**.
Rose **is staying** in bed.

We use the simple present for:	We use the present progressive for:
1. Repeated actions or habits. Rose **gets up** at 7:00 every day.	1. Things that are happening now. She **is trying** to sleep.
2. Things that happen all the time or are always true. She always **stays** home when she's sick. She **gets** tired when she works too much.	2. Things that are happening around this time. She **is drinking** a lot of water.

CD1, 5

13 Practice

Underline the correct verb to complete the conversation. Then listen to check your answers.

Detective Roberts is watching a house. He's talking to Detective Jason on his cell phone.

DETECTIVE ROBERTS: A tall woman with dark hair (comes/<u>is coming</u>) out of the house.
1

DETECTIVE JASON: That's Mrs. Johnson. She (lives/is living) there. She's a
2
housekeeper. It's 8:00. She usually (leaves/is leaving) the house at
3
8:00. She (goes/is going) to the store to do the grocery shopping.
4

DETECTIVE ROBERTS: Wait! A car (stops/is stopping) in front of the house. A man in a
5
uniform (gets/is getting) out. He is tall and thin and has gray hair.
6

DETECTIVE JASON: I know he (doesn't live/isn't living) there.
7

DETECTIVE ROBERTS: He (rings/is ringing) the doorbell. He (looks/is looking) at the
8   9
house carefully. He (goes/is going) to the back of the house. He
10
(jumps/is jumping) over the wall.
11

DETECTIVE JASON: Go get him, Roberts!

Detective Roberts runs after the man and then returns to his car.

DETECTIVE ROBERTS: No luck. He says he (looks/is looking) for the gas meter. He works
12
for the gas company.

14 Practice

Solve the riddle. Complete the sentences with the correct form of the verb in parentheses. Then identify the thing that the paragraph describes.

I usually (stand) ____*stand*____ in the kitchen. I (have) ____*have*____ a door.
1   2
People (open) ____*open*____ the door and (put) ____*put*____ things inside me. Part of
3   4
me (freeze) _____ things for people. Right now, a woman (take) __*is taking*__
5   6
out a bottle of cold water. I am a __*refridgerator*.__
7

12   Unit 1

YOU DON'T KNOW

Every day an old man crosses the village and enters a big, gray house. A soldier watches him do this day after day. One morning the soldier is angry. He stops the old man and asks, "Where are you going?"

"I don't know," replies the old man.

"What do you mean, you don't know?" says the soldier. "Every day I see you walk out of your house at this time, cross the village, and enter the big, gray house. Answer me! Where are you going?"

Again the old man replies, "I don't know."

The soldier gets very, very angry now and takes the man to jail[1]. He pushes him into a cell[2]. Just as the soldier is turning the key, the old man looks at the jail and says, "See! Now I am in jail. *I don't* know. Every day, I don't know — and *you* don't know!"

[1.] *jail = prison*

[2.] *cell = small room in a prison*

1. When does the old man cross the village?   _____
2. Where does he go?   _____
3. What does the soldier do every day?   _____
4. What does the soldier do one morning?   _____
5. What does the old man say?   _____
6. Where does the soldier take the old man?   _____
7. Why does the soldier take the old man to jail?   _____
8. What does the old man say at the jail?   _____

1E | Nonaction or Stative Verbs

Function

Erin **wants** a cupcake.
She **loves** cupcakes with frosting.
Right now, she's **thinking** about eating one.

1. We do not usually use some verbs in the present progressive. We call these nonaction or stative verbs.

CORRECT:	That cake **tastes** good.	INCORRECT:	That cake ~~is tasting~~ good.
CORRECT:	Shirley **wants** a sandwich.	INCORRECT:	Shirley ~~is wanting~~ a sandwich.

Common Nonprogressive Verbs

be	hate	love	smell
believe	have	need	taste
enjoy	hear	prefer	think
feel	know	remember	understand
forget	like	see	want

2. Sometimes we use the verbs *have*, *think*, and others in the present progressive.

Verb	Example	Explanation
Think	He **thinks** it is a good idea.	*Thinks* means "believes."
	She **is thinking** about eating a cupcake.	*Is thinking* refers to her thoughts.
Have	Shirley **has** a cell phone.	*Have* means "possess."
	She **'s having** a good time. She always **has** a good time at parties.	You can use *have* in the present progressive or simple present in certain idiomatic expressions: **have a good/bad time** **have breakfast/lunch/dinner** **have a baby**
Enjoy	They **enjoy** warm weather.	*Enjoy* means "like."
	They **are enjoying** the warm weather.	*Are enjoying* means "take advantage of."
Smell	The flowers **smell** nice.	*Smell* means "have a scent."
	She **is smelling** the flowers.	*Is smelling* means "is sniffing."

16 Practice

Complete the email with the simple present or the present progressive of the verbs in parentheses.

New	Delete	Reply	Reply All	Forward	Move

To	Pete Holloway <pholloway@mymail.com>
Cc	
Subject	Hi from California!

Dear Pete,

　　　　I (write) **am writing** to you from Sandy Beach, California. I (stay) _am staying_
1 　　　　　　　　　　　　　　　　　　　　　　　　　　　　　　　　　　　2
at my friend Brenda's house. She (have) _has_ a beautiful house by the beach. She
　　　　　　　　　　　　　　　　　　　　3
(come) _comes_ here every summer. I (enjoy) _am enjoying_ my vacation. Today, it
　　　　4　　　　　　　　　　　　　　　　　　　5
(rain) _is raining_ . I (not, like) _dont like_ this weather. I (want) _want_ to go
　　　6　　　　　　　　　　7　　　　　　　　　　　　　　　　8
swimming. Brenda (cook) _is cooking_ lunch. It (smell) _smells_ good. I hope to see
　　　　　　　　　　　9　　　　　　　　　　　　　10
you soon.

Love,
Annie

1F   *See, Look At, Watch, Hear,* and *Listen To*

He **is listening to** music.　　　The children **are watching** television.

Function

One man **is looking at** his watch.

1. We use several verbs to express the senses of seeing and hearing. They are different from each other in meaning and in the verb forms that we use with them.

Verbs of Seeing and Hearing			
	Verb	**Meaning**	**Example**
Action Verbs	watch	We *watch* something or someone that is moving. We usually *watch* something that we are paying attention to.	Charles **is watching** television. He **watches** television every evening.
	look at	We *look at* something or someone for a reason.	Susan **is looking at** a painting. She is an art student. She **looks at** paintings carefully.
	listen to	We *listen to* something or someone for a reason.	They **are listening to** music. They **listen to** music often.
Nonaction Verbs (Nonprogressive)	see	We *see* things because our eyes are open.	I **see** the blackboard at the front of the room.
	hear	When we *hear*, we receive sounds with our ears.	I **hear** the music coming from the other room. (I may not be paying attention to it.)

2. We can use action verbs either with the simple present or with the present progressive. But we do not usually use nonaction verbs with the present progressive.

17 Practice

Complete the sentences with the correct verb. Use the simple present or the present progressive.

1. Right now, the students (listen to/hear) __are listening to__ the teacher. She is teaching the present progressive.

2. Tommy (watch/look at) __is watching__ a game on television right now.

3. Susan (watch/look at) __is looking at__ her watch. She wants to know what time it is.

4. The teacher (look at/see) __is looking at__ Bob. She is waiting for an answer.

5. I (look at/see) __am looking at__ the teacher so I can understand better.

6. Tony (listen to/hear) __is listening to__ Susan carefully. She is giving him directions to the bank.

7. Dick turns on the television and (watch/see) __watches__ the news every morning at 7:00.

8. It is 11:00 at night. Tim is in bed. He (hear/listen to) __hear__ a noise in his apartment. He gets up. He (see/look at) __see__ his cat on the kitchen table.

18 Pair Up and Talk

Ask and answer the questions with a partner.

YOU: What are you looking at right now? What do you see?
YOUR PARTNER: I'm looking out the window. I see buildings and students.

1. What are you looking at right now? What do you see?

2. What are you listening to right now? What do you hear?

Form

WOMAN: **Are you taking** the flight to London at 10:00?

MAN: **Yes, I am. Do** you **live** in London?

WOMAN: **No, I don't.** I live in Montreal. **Where do** you **live**?

MAN: I live in Singapore.

1. *Yes/No* questions are questions that we can answer with the words *yes* or *no*.
2. *Wh-* questions begin with a question word like *who* or *what*. We call them *wh-* questions because all except one begin with the letters *wh-*. The question words are *who, whom, what, where, when, why, which,* and *how*. We use *whom* in formal written English.

	Yes/No Questions			Short Answers
	Do/Does	**Subject**	**Base Verb**	
Simple Present	**Do**	I	**need** a haircut?	Yes, you **do**. No, you **don't**.
		you		Yes, I/we **do**. No, I/we **don't**.
		we		Yes, you **do**. No, you **don't**.
		they		Yes, they **do**. No, they **don't**.
	Does	he/she/it		Yes, he/she/it **does**. No, he/she/it **doesn't**.

Yes/No Questions				Short Answers
	Am/Is/Are	Subject	Verb + -ing	
Present Progressive	**Am**	I		Yes, you **are.** No, you **aren't.** OR No, you**'re not.**
	Are	you		Yes, I **am.** No, I**'m not.***
	Is	he/she/it	**leaving** now?	Yes, he/she/it **is.** No, he/she/it **isn't.** OR No, he/she/it**'s not.**
	Are	you		Yes, we **are.** No, we **aren't.** OR No, we**'re not.**
		we		Yes, you **are.** No, you **aren't.** OR No, you**'re not.**
		they		Yes, they **are.** No, they **aren't.** OR No, they**'re not.**

*There is no contraction for *am not*.

3. We do not contract *am, is*, and *are* in short answers.
    CORRECT: Yes, I am. Yes, she is. Yes, they are.
    INCORRECT: Yes, ~~I'm~~. Yes, ~~she's~~. Yes, ~~they're~~.

Wh- Questions					
	Wh- Word	Do/Does	Subject	Base Verb	
Simple Present	**Who/Whom**		you	**like?**	
	What		I	**need?**	
	When	**do**	they	**have**	lunch?
	Where		you	**live?**	
	Why		we	**study**	so hard?
	Which	**does**	he/she/it	**prefer?**	
	How			**make**	that soup?
	Wh- Word	Am/Is/Are	Subject	Verb + -ing	
Present Progressive	**Why**	**am**	I	**doing**	your homework?
	Which book		they	**reading?**	
	What	**are**	we	**working**	on?
	Who/Whom		they	**visiting?**	
	How		you	**doing**	that?
	When	**is**	he/she/it	**leaving?**	
	Where			**going?**	

19   Practice

Complete the conversation with the simple present or the present progressive of the verbs in parentheses. You sometimes need to use short answers. Then listen to check your answers.

WOMAN: Excuse me, (take) _____*are*_____ you _____*taking*_____ the flight to London
                                          1   **2**
             at 10:00?

MAN: Yes, I _____*am*_____ . (live) _____*Do*_____ you _____*live*_____ in London?
                          3   **4**   **5**

WOMAN: No, I _____*don't*_____ . At the moment, I (study) _____*in studying*_____ at Cambridge
                        6   **7**
             University. What about you? (go) _____*Do*_____ you often _____*go*_____
                                                      8   **9**
             to London?

MAN: Yes, I (go) _____*go*_____ there on business.
                            10

WOMAN: Oh. What kind of work (do) _____*do*_____ you _____*do*_____?
                                            11   **12**

MAN: I (work) _____*work*_____ for the marketing department of a company.
                          13
             We publish dictionaries.

20   Practice

Read the postcard. Then answer the questions with complete sentences.

Dear Uncle Joe,
       We are on one of the Greek
islands. It's called Mykonos. We are
staying in a hotel by the beach. We are
having a wonderful time. I'm writing this
postcard from the hotel. Richard is lying
on the beach right now, and Lenny and
Linda are swimming in the sea.

       See you soon,
       Laura, Richard, and the kids

Mr. Joseph Kelly

851 W. 37th St.

New York, NY 10006

1. Who is writing the postcard?

   Laura is writing the postcard.

2. Who is she writing to?

   _____

3. Where are Laura and her family staying?

   _____

4. Where is she writing from?

   _____

5. What are Lenny and Linda doing?

   _____

Listening Puzzle

  CD1, 7

 A Listen and check the correct answer.

❑ _A. blueberry_

❑ _B. pineapple_

❑ _C. strawberry_

B Discuss your answer with your classmates.

CD1, 8

C Now listen again and write the sentences you hear.

A Before You Read

Answer the questions.

1. What are your favorite foods? Do you prefer sweet foods or sour foods?
2. Do you like to try new kinds of food?

B Read

THE SENSE OF TASTE

We have about 10,000 taste buds in our mouths. We find these not just on the tongue, but also on the roof, cheeks, and back of the mouth. By age 70, half of 5 our taste buds disappear.

Our taste buds taste four things: sweet, bitter, sour, and salty. All flavors are a combination of these 10 four. Some experts believe there's a fifth taste group. It is *umami*. We find this taste in soy products. Our sense of taste is not as good as our sense of smell. When we want more detail about the food we eat, we rely 15 on our sense of smell. That is why when we have a cold, we find our food tasteless.

Human beings like sweet things from the moment they are born. Experiments show that unborn babies like the taste of sweetness. 20 Newborn babies give a **slight** smile when you give them something sweet. When you give them something bitter, they make a face. This is a good thing because most poisonous things are bitter.

25 Taste also comes with culture. For example, in Japan, raw seafood is popular, but this is not very popular in North America. Individual tastes vary, too. Some people like one taste, but others don't.

> **DID YOU KNOW ... ?**
> While humans have about 10,000 taste buds, cats have only 473.

C Notice the Grammar

Underline all forms of the present.

Choose the best answer.

D Look for Main Ideas

1. Paragraph 2 is mainly about _____ .
   - Ⓐ how our taste buds work
   - Ⓑ the importance of our sense of smell
   - Ⓒ the difference between our senses of taste and smell
   - Ⓓ how a cold affects our sense of taste

2. What is the main idea of paragraph 3?
   - Ⓐ Humans are born to like sweet flavors.
   - Ⓑ Babies smile when they eat sweet food.
   - Ⓒ Even unborn babies like sweetness.
   - Ⓓ Poisonous foods are bitter.

E Look for Details

3. We find the *umami* taste in _____ .
   - Ⓐ sweet foods
   - Ⓑ salty things
   - Ⓒ soy products
   - Ⓓ all flavors

4. Where do we NOT have taste buds?
   - Ⓐ inside our cheeks
   - Ⓑ on our tongue
   - Ⓒ on the roof of our mouth
   - Ⓓ on our lips

5. Babies don't like foods that are _____ .
   - Ⓐ sweet
   - Ⓑ tasteless
   - Ⓒ sour
   - Ⓓ bitter

READING SKILL:
Guessing Words in Context

Looking up words in a dictionary slows down reading. Try to guess the meanings of the unknown words. Look at the words and sentences around the unknown word. Use their meanings to guess what the word means.

F Make Inferences

6. We can infer from the reading that _____ .
   - Ⓐ humans can only taste a few flavors
   - Ⓑ our sense of smell improves our ability to taste
   - Ⓒ our ability to taste improves as we age
   - Ⓓ most people like the same foods

7. What can we infer from paragraph 3?
   - Ⓐ Newborn babies don't have much sense of taste.
   - Ⓑ Our natural sense of taste protects us from bad food.
   - Ⓒ We are born to like all foods.
   - Ⓓ We learn to eat sweet things from our parents.

G Look for Vocabulary

8. The word *slight* in the reading is closest in meaning to _____ .
   - Ⓐ frail
   - Ⓑ long
   - Ⓒ wide
   - Ⓓ small

Writing: Describe a Person

Write a paragraph about your partner.

STEP **1**   Ask and answer the questions with a partner. Record the answers by checking *Yes* or *No*. Write additional information under *Other Information*.

	Yes	No	Other Information
1. live/in (city)	_____	_____	_____
2. work	_____	_____	_____
3. like/tennis	_____	_____	_____
4. listen/pop music	_____	_____	_____
5. go/movies on weekends	_____	_____	_____
6. speak/(language)	_____	_____	_____
7. play/the piano	_____	_____	_____
8. have/brothers and sisters	_____	_____	_____

STEP **2**   Write sentences about your partner from your notes.

STEP **3**   Rewrite the sentences in the form of a paragraph. Write a title (your partner's name).

> *Kumiko Osawa*
>
> *Kumiko lives in Tokyo. She doesn't work because she's a student.*
> *She likes ...*

STEP **4**   Evaluate your paragraph.

Checklist

_____ Did you indent the first line?

_____ Did you give the paragraph a title?

_____ Did you write the title with a capital letter for each word?

STEP **5**   Edit your work. Work with a partner or your teacher to edit your sentences. Correct spelling, punctuation, vocabulary, and grammar.

STEP **6**   Write your final copy.

Self-Test

1. Many animals _____ their young in the spring.

   A. are having   Ⓐ Ⓑ Ⓒ Ⓓ
   B. have
   C. has
   D. is have

2. Every year, Earth _____ around the sun one time.

   A. travels   Ⓐ Ⓑ Ⓒ Ⓓ
   B. travel
   C. is traveling
   D. does traveling

3. Snow _____ in the Sahara Desert.

   A. sometimes falls   Ⓐ Ⓑ Ⓒ Ⓓ
   B. sometimes is falling
   C. falling sometimes
   D. is falling sometimes

4. Sharks _____ bones.

   A. do not have   Ⓐ Ⓑ Ⓒ Ⓓ
   B. are not having
   C. have not
   D. doesn't have

5. Pandas _____ to eat bamboo.

   A. are preferring   Ⓐ Ⓑ Ⓒ Ⓓ
   B. is preferring
   C. prefer
   D. are prefer

6. At the moment, everybody _____ the football game on television.

   A. is seeing   Ⓐ Ⓑ Ⓒ Ⓓ
   B. is watching
   C. is looking at
   D. does watch

7. We _____ vitamins for good health.

   A. are needing   Ⓐ Ⓑ Ⓒ Ⓓ
   B. need have
   C. have need
   D. need

8. Young children _____ the pictures in books.

   A. always look at   Ⓐ Ⓑ Ⓒ Ⓓ
   B. always looking
   C. look at always
   D. always watch

9. When _____ breakfast?

   A. you usually have   Ⓐ Ⓑ Ⓒ Ⓓ
   B. usually have you
   C. do you usually have
   D. you are usually having

10. _____ French?

    A. All Canadians speak   Ⓐ Ⓑ Ⓒ Ⓓ
    B. All Canadians are speaking
    C. Are all Canadians speaking
    D. Do all Canadians speak

B Find the underlined word or phrase, A, B, C, or D, that is incorrect. Darken the oval with the same letter.

1. Italians <u>usually</u> <u>eats</u> pasta <u>every day</u>
              A   B   C

   <u>of the week</u>.
    D   Ⓐ Ⓑ Ⓒ Ⓓ

2. <u>How many</u> <u>hours</u> does <u>a baby</u> <u>sleeps</u>?
       A   B   C   D

                   Ⓐ Ⓑ Ⓒ Ⓓ

3. <u>People</u> catch <u>sometimes</u> <u>colds</u> <u>in the</u> winter.
      A   B   C   D

                   Ⓐ Ⓑ Ⓒ Ⓓ

4. <u>Do</u> bears <u>eat</u> only meat, or <u>they do</u> <u>eat</u>
     A   B   C   D

   plants, too?
            Ⓐ Ⓑ Ⓒ Ⓓ

5. <u>Why</u> <u>are</u> kangaroos only <u>live</u> <u>in Australia</u>?
     A   B   C   D

                   Ⓐ Ⓑ Ⓒ Ⓓ

6. In India, the cow <u>gives</u> <u>milk</u> <u>and</u> <u>is working</u>
                 A   B   C   D

   on the farm.
            Ⓐ Ⓑ Ⓒ Ⓓ

7. Camels <u>rarely</u> <u>drink</u> <u>often</u> water when
            A   B   C

   they <u>travel</u>.
       D   Ⓐ Ⓑ Ⓒ Ⓓ

8. When <u>do</u> people <u>use</u> computers, they <u>often</u> <u>use</u>
        A   B   C   D

   the Internet to get information.
                   Ⓐ Ⓑ Ⓒ Ⓓ

9. <u>Men and women</u> in Iceland <u>have</u> long lives
        A   B

   because the air <u>has</u> clean and they <u>have</u> good
                C   D

   health care.
            Ⓐ Ⓑ Ⓒ Ⓓ

10. People in Thailand <u>not</u> <u>use</u> chopsticks. <u>They</u>
                     A   B   C

    use <u>spoons</u>.
        D   Ⓐ Ⓑ Ⓒ Ⓓ

Unit 2

The Past

I **was driving** my car
when I **saw** the storm.

Form

Pablo Picasso **lived** in France. He **worked** a lot and **painted** many pictures.

1. To form the simple past of most regular verbs in affirmative statements, add *-ed* to the base verb.
2. In negative statements, use *did not* + a base verb.
3. In questions, use *did* + a subject + a base verb.

Affirmative Statements		Negative Statements		
Subject	**Past Verb**	**Subject**	***Did Not/Didn't***	**Base Verb**
I		I		
You		You		
He/She/It	worked.	He/She/It	did not didn't	work.
We		We		
They		They		

Yes/No Questions			Short Answers	
Did	**Subject**	**Base Verb**	**Yes,**	**No,**
	I		you **did.**	you **didn't.**
	you		I/we **did.**	I/we **didn't.**
Did	he/she/it	**work?**	he/she/it **did.**	he/she/it **didn't.**
	we		you **did.**	you **didn't.**
	they		they **did.**	they **didn't.**

4. We change the spelling of some regular verbs before adding -ed.

Base Verb Ending	Rule	Example	
Most verbs	Add -ed.	start	start**ed**
		obey	obey**ed**
		predict	predict**ed**
The verb ends in a consonant + e.	Add -d.	live	live**d**
		move	move**d**
		decide	decide**d**
The verb ends in a single vowel + a single consonant. **Exceptions:** Do not double w or x. If a verb has two or more syllables and the stress is not on the last syllable, do not double the consonant.	Double the consonant, add -ed.	stop	stop**ped**
		plan	plan**ned**
		prefer	prefer**red**
		fix	fix**ed**
		show	show**ed**
		open	open**ed**
		travel	travel**ed**
		exit	exit**ed**
		color	color**ed**
The verb ends in a consonant + y.	Change y to i and add -ed.	worry	worr**ied**
		study	stud**ied**
The verbs ends in ie.	Add -d.	tie	tie**d**
		die	die**d**

Function

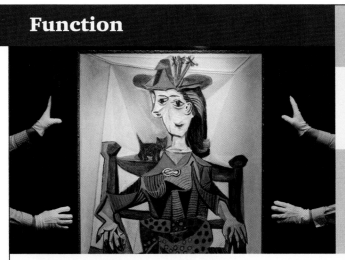

Did Picasso **paint** pictures of women? Yes, he **did**. He **painted** a lot of pictures of women.

We use the simple past to talk about actions and situations completed in the past. We often say when the situation or action happened (for example, *yesterday*, *last night*).

AUDIO DOWNLOAD

CD1, 9

1 Practice

Listen and write the missing words. Use correct spelling.

1. Yesterday, I ___listened___ to the radio.
2. Bob ___waited___ for the movie.
3. I ___studied___ for my test all night.
4. She ___died___ at the age of 86.
5. They ___stayed___ all afternoon.
6. Sam ___made___ the truth. admitted
7. It ___rainned___ last week.
8. The movie ___started___ at 8:00.
9. It ___happend___ this morning.
10. Catherine ___tied___ her shoelaces.
11. She ___opened___ the door.
12. We ___hoped___ to see you.

2 Practice

Complete the sentences. Use the simple past of the verbs in parentheses.

Pablo Picasso was born in Malaga, Spain, in 1881. His first word was *lapiz*

(Spanish for *pencil*), and he (learn) ___learned___ to draw before he (talk)

___talked___ . His father was an artist. Pablo often (watch) ___watched___ him
　　　2　　　　　　　　　　　　　　　　　　　　　　　　　　　　　3

paint pictures. One day, he (finish) ___finished___ one of his father's paintings. His
　　　　　　　　　　　　　　　　　　4

father (not, believe) ___didn't believe___ it. It was wonderful! His father never (paint)
　　　　　　　　　　5

___painted___ again. Pablo was only 13.
　　6

　　　Picasso (travel) ___traveled___ to Paris and became famous. One day, a
　　　　　　　　　　　　7

French minister (visit) ___visited___ Picasso. Some paint (spill) ___spilled___ on
　　　　　　　　　　　8　　　　　　　　　　　　　　　　　　　　9

the minister's trousers by accident. Picasso (want) ___wanted___ to pay to clean
　　　　　　　　　　　　　　　　　　　　　　　　　　　10

them. The minister said, "No, please, Monsieur Picasso, just sign my trousers." Many

people (realize) ___realized___ that Picasso was a genius. His paintings (change)
　　　　　　　　11

___changed___ people's ideas about art. Picasso (die) ___died___ at the age of 91.
　　12　　　　　　　　　　　　　　　　　　　　　　　　　　　13

3 Pair Up and Talk

Ask and answer these questions about Pablo Picasso with a partner.

YOU: Did Picasso paint?

YOUR PARTNER: Yes, he did. He painted a lot of pictures.

1. Picasso/paint
2. Picasso/live/Italy
3. Picasso/become/famous

4. French minister/get mad at/Picasso
5. Picasso/die/young

4 Your Turn

Write a question using the prompts. Write a negative statement. Then write a correct sentence using words from the list. Finally, practice asking and answering the questions with a partner.

Paris   *Hamlet*
radium   the United States

1. Pablo Picasso/live/in London

    Did Pablo Picasso live in London?

    No, he didn't live in London.

    He lived in Paris.

2. Marie and Pierre Curie/discover/penicillin

    _____

    _____

    _____

3. Marilyn Monroe/come/from France

    _____

    _____

    _____

4. Shakespeare/write/*A Tale of Two Cities*

    Did Shakespeare write · · · ·   ?

    _____

    _____

Form

Marie Curie **was** a famous scientist.
Marie **went** to Paris to study.
She **met** Pierre Curie there.

Many common verbs do not end in *-ed* for the simple past. They are irregular. Here is the past form of the verb *go*.

Affirmative Statements		Negative Statements		
Subject	**Past Verb**	**Subject**	*Did Not/Didn't*	**Base Verb**
I		I		
You		You		
He/She/It	**went** to Paris.	He/She/It	**did not** **didn't**	**go** to Paris.
We		We		
They		They		
Yes/No Questions			Short Answers	
Did	**Subject**	**Base Verb**	**Yes,**	**No,**
	I		you **did**.	you **didn't**.
	you		I/we **did**.	I/we **didn't**.
Did	he/she/it	**go** to Paris?	he/she/it **did**.	he/she/it **didn't**.
	we		you **did**.	you **didn't**.
	they		they **did**.	they **didn't**.
Wh- Questions				
Wh- Word	*Did*		**Subject**	**Base Verb**
When			I	**go** to Tokyo?
Where			you	**go** last night?
Why	**did**		he/she/it	**go** out?
Who*			we	**go** out with last week?
How (often)			they	**go** out last week?

* In formal written English, the *wh-* word would be *whom*.

5 Practice

Complete the sentences with the simple past of the verbs in parentheses.

Maria Sklodowska was born in Poland. Maria was a good student. She (want)
__wanted__ to go to college. In those days, women (not, go) _didn't went_ to
1   2
college in Poland. So Maria (leave) ___left___ Poland to go to Paris to study science.
3
Maria (become) __became__ a student at Sorbonne University in Paris. In Paris, she
4
(change) __changed__ her name to Marie. One day, she (meet) ___met___ Pierre
5   6
Curie. They (marry) _married_ one year later. Pierre was also a scientist. Together
7
they (discover) _discovered_ radium. They (win) ___won___ a Nobel Prize for the
8   9
discovery. Three years later, Pierre (die) ___dead died___ in an accident. Marie (give)
10
___gave___ her life to her work. She (die) ___dead died___ in 1934 from cancer.
11   12

6 Practice

**Write questions with the prompts. Then ask and answer the questions about
Marie Curie with a partner.**

1. Marie/study in Poland

   Did Marie study in Poland? No, she didn't.

2. women/go to college in Poland

   Did women go to college in Poland?

3. Marie/study at the university in Paris

   Did Marie study at the university in Paris?

4. Marie/meet Pierre in Paris

   Did Marie meet in Paris?

5. Marie and Pierre Curie/win the Nobel Prize

   Did Marie and Pierre Curie win the Nobel Prize?

6. Pierre/die in an accident

   Did Pierre die in an accident?

buy bought bought

7 Pair Up and Talk

Tell your classmates or your partner about your life. Use the simple past.

I was born in Peru. When I was two, we went to live in Mexico City.

8 Practice

Complete the paragraphs with the simple past of the verbs in parentheses.

A

Elvis Presley was born in 1935 in Mississippi. He (spend) ___*spent*___ a lot

of time with African-American musicians. In 1953, he (pay) ___paid___ to make a

record for his mother's birthday. The owner of the record company (like) ___liked___

it. He (offer) ___offered___ Elvis work. Elvis's first record, in 1954, was a hit.

Teenagers (love) ___loved___ it. They (scream) ___screamed___ when they saw Elvis.

Elvis (record) ___recorded___ 94 gold singles. He (star) ___starred___ in 27 films.

Elvis continued to be famous. His life (end) ___ed___ sadly. He (die)

___died___ at the age of 42. Radio stations (play) ___played___ his songs, and

his fans (cry) ___cried___ .

B

James Dean was born in 1931. His mother (die) ___died___ when he was

young. He (live) ___lived___ with his uncle and aunt on their farm. Later, he (study)

___studied___ acting for two years. Then he (start) ___started___ to work in theater

and the movies. He also (appear) ___appeared___ in a TV commercial. In 1954, he (act)

___acted___ in a play. Some important people from Hollywood (like) ___liked___

him in the play. They (offer) ___offered___ him a movie contract. James Dean (star)

___starred___ in only three films, but he (become) ___became___ popular. He (die)

___died___ in a car crash in 1955.

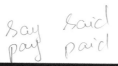
say said
pay paid

9 Read
Read the story. Then write questions for the answers.

THE GOOSE WITH THE GOLDEN EGG

One day, a countryman went to the nest of his goose. There he found a shiny, yellow egg. When he picked it up, it was really heavy as well. He thought someone had played a trick on him. But he took the egg home anyway. When he looked at the egg again at home, he realized it was made of pure gold.

Every morning, the goose laid a golden egg.

The man sold the eggs and soon began to get rich. As he became rich, he became impatient with the goose because she gave him only one golden egg a day.

One day, after he had counted his gold, he wanted to get all the golden eggs at once. So he killed the goose and opened it. But he found nothing.

1. _____ ? He found a shiny, golden egg in the nest.
2. _____ ? He thought someone had played a trick on him.
3. _____ ? He realized it was made of gold.
4. _____ ? The goose laid a golden egg every morning.
5. _____ ? He sold the eggs and began to get rich.
6. _____ ? He became impatient with the goose because she gave him only one golden egg a day.
7. _____ ? He wanted to get all the golden eggs at once.
8. _____ ? He found nothing.

2C The Past Progressive

Form

We **were playing** outside.
The sky **was getting** darker.
Then we saw it. A tornado!
It **was coming** this way!

We form the past progressive with a past form of *be* (*was* or *were*) and a verb + *-ing*.

Affirmative and Negative Statements		
Subject	**Was/Were (Not)**	**Verb + -ing**
I	was was not wasn't	
You	were were not weren't	
He/She/It	was was not wasn't	working.
We	were were not weren't	
They	were were not weren't	

Yes/No Questions			Short Answers	
Was/Were	**Subject**	**Verb + -ing**	**Yes,**	**No,**
Was	I		you **were**.	you **weren't**.
Were	you		I **was**.	I **wasn't**.
Was	he/she/it	working?	he/she/it **was**.	he/she/it **wasn't**.
	we		you **were**.	you **weren't**.
Were	you		we **were**.	we **weren't**.
	they		they **were**.	they **weren't**.

Wh- Questions			
Wh- Word	**Was/Were**	**Subject**	**Verb + -ing**
Who*	was	she	**calling?**
What		I	**saying?**
When		he	**leaving?**
How (fast)		the tornado	**moving?**
Where	were	you	**going** yesterday?
Why		they	**studying** at midnight?
Why		they	**sleeping** in class?

* In formal written English, the *wh-* word would be *whom*.

Function

We use the past progressive to describ[...] the past.
We **were watching** the news [...]

10   Practice
      Listen and wr[...]

[handwritten note:]
3/ were running
5/ weren't watching
6/ were studying
7/ started shouting
8/ was telling

1. Last night, telev[...] people about the tornado.

2. It ___was getting___ closer.   *cading*

3. People _____ for shelter.

4. The tornado ___was destroying___ everything in its way.

5. We _____ television.

6. We _____ in the library.

7. Suddenly, the librarian _____ .

8. She _____ us to run to the basement.

11 Practice

Complete the sentences with the past progressive of the verbs in parentheses.

Amanda Ferguson (drive) _____*was driving*_____ to her mother's house. She

(not, listen) __wasn't listening__ to the radio. She didn't know that a tornado

(come) __was coming__ toward her.

The sky (get) __was getting__ darker and darker, but she thought it was

just an ordinary storm. Suddenly, there was a big noise. It was as dark as night,

and the wind (blow) __was blowing__ very hard. Pieces of houses and trees

(fly) __were flying__ everywhere. Then she knew what

(happen) __was happening__ . She was inside a tornado!

Amanda screamed. Then she saw her mother's house. But she (look)

__was looking__ down at it from 25 feet in the air! Amanda was lucky! The

tornado dropped the car in her mother's backyard. She lived to tell the story.

12 Practice

Listen and put the story in order. Number your answers 1–6.

CD1, 11

___3___ The waves were crashing on the sand.

___6___ A hurricane was coming!

___2___ She noticed that the wind was blowing very hard.

___1___ Susan was walking on the beach.

___5___ When she got back to the house, her husband was covering the windows
with wood.

___4___ Black clouds were coming toward the land very fast.

13   Your Turn

Write *wh-* questions for the answers from Practice 12. Use the *wh-* word in parentheses and the past progressive. Then practice asking and answering the questions with a partner.

1.   (where) _Where was Susan walking?_

Answer: She was walking on the beach.

2.   (how hard) ___was it the wind blowing?___

Answer: It was blowing very hard.

3.   (where) ___was Susan walking___

Answer: On the sand.

4.   (how fast) ___were the clouds coming___

Answer: They were coming very fast.

5.   (when) ___was her husband covering the windows___

Answer: When she got home.

14   Pair Up and Talk

Tell a partner three things that were happening yesterday at each time. Write your partner's answers in the chart.

At 8:00 in the evening, I was sitting on the sofa in my apartment. My brother was watching television.

7:00 in the morning	
1:00 in the afternoon	
8:00 in the evening	

Function

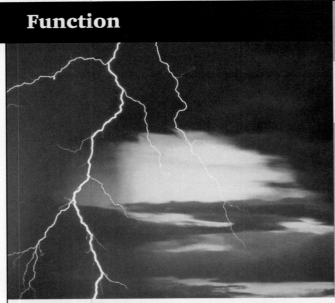

I **was driving** my car when I **saw** the storm.

1. We often use the past progressive and the simple past together in a sentence. The past progressive describes the longer action that was in progress in the past; the simple past describes the shorter action that happened in the middle of the longer action.

    I **was working** when I **heard** the storm.

2. We use the simple past, not the past progressive, to show that one action followed another.

    I **turned off** my computer when I **heard** the storm.

    (First she heard the storm. Then she turned off her computer.)

3. When one action interrupts another, we use *when* before the simple past action or *while* before the past progressive action.

    I was driving my car **when** I saw the storm.

    While I was driving my car, I saw the storm.

4. We can change the order of the parts of a sentence with *when* or *while*.

    When I saw the storm, I was driving my car.

    I saw the storm **while** I was driving my car.

    When we begin a sentence with *when* or *while* plus a subject and a verb, we put a comma between the two parts.

5. We use the past progressive with two actions that continued at the same time in the past. We use *while* to show the actions were happening at the same time.

    While I was driving my car, my husband was trying to call me.

6. Remember, we do not usually use the present progressive with nonprogressive verbs. (See page 14.) The same is true for the past progressive.

    CORRECT: We **saw** the storm.

    INCORRECT: We ~~were seeing~~ the storm.

Complete the sentences with the simple past or past progressive of the verbs in parentheses.

It (rain) **was raining** very hard when the bus (leave) _legt_ the school.
1   2

When we (get) _got_ home, my Aunt Millie and Uncle Ben (tell) _told_
3   4

us to run into their storm cellar underground. When I (look) _looked_ up the
5

road, I (see) _saw_ that a tornado (come) _was coming_ toward our house.
6   7

The tornado (pass) _was passing_ over us while we (try) _was trying_ to get down
8   9

the stairs of the shelter. Everyone (scream) _was screaming_ for help while the tornado
10

(throw) _was throwing_ things on top of us. Suddenly, the wind (become) _became_
11   12

very still. My uncle and sister were hurt, but we all (survive) _were surviving_
13

One of your classmates did not come to school yesterday. He/she had a cold. Imagine what he/she was doing while you were studying at school. Write four sentences about your classmate's activities.

Example

While we were doing exercises in our English class, my classmate was resting in bed.

Form/Function

When young Mozart played, everyone listened.

1. A clause is a group of words with a subject and a verb. Some clauses are main clauses. A main clause can stand alone as a complete sentence. This sentence is a main clause.

   Mozart played for the queen.

2. Time clauses start with words like *when, while, before,* or *after*. Time clauses are dependent clauses. We must use dependent clauses with a main clause.

Main Clause	Time Clause
Everyone listened	**when he played.**
He went to the Sistine Chapel	**while he was in Rome.**
He was playing the piano	**before he was five.**
He wrote music	**after everyone went to bed.**

3. We can put a time clause at the beginning or the end of a sentence. If the time clause comes first, we use a comma after it.

   While he was speaking, he stood up.
   He stood up **while he was speaking**.
   Before he took the money, he counted it.
   He counted the money **before he took it**.

4. In a sentence with a clause starting with *when*, both verbs can be in the simple past.

   When they **asked**, he **sang**.
   (First they asked. Then he sang.)

17 Practice

Complete the sentences with the correct form of the verbs in parentheses.

A

Mozart was born in Austria in 1756. When he (be) ___was___ four years

1

old, he (start) _was ~~started~~_ to play the piano. Before he (be) ___was ~~turn~~___ five, he

2   **3**

(begin) ___began___ to write music. When he (be) ___was ~~being~~___ six, he

4   **5**

(give) ___gave___ concerts all over Europe. Once, he (play) _____ for the

6   **7**

Empress Maria Theresa in Vienna. She (love) ___loved___ Mozart's playing. After he

8

(finish) ___finished___ , he (climb) _was ~~climbing~~_ up on her knee and kissed her.

9   **10** climbed

B

When Mozart (be) _~~was~~ being_ 11, he (write) ___wrote___ an opera.

1   **2**

One time, when he (be) _~~was~~ being_ 14 years old, he (hear) ___heard___ music

3   **4**

in the Sistine Chapel in Rome. When he (get) _was getting_ home, he (remember)

5

remembered everything and (write) ___wrote___ it down exactly.

6   **7**

Mozart always (have) ___had___ money problems when he was an adult. He

8

often (work) ___worked___ all night after everyone was asleep. He (like) ___liked___

9   **10**

to write while he (stand) _was standing_ up. Mozart (die) ___died___ at the age of

11   **12**

35. No one (go) ___went___ to his funeral.

13

18 Pair Up and Talk

Work with a partner. Say three things you did yesterday. Use past time clauses with *when*, *while*, *before*, and *after*. Say two true things and one false thing. Your partner guesses which one is false.

YOU: I ate breakfast before I went to work. While I was at work, I called my mom. After work, I cleaned my kitchen.

YOUR PARTNER: You didn't talk to your mom while you were at work.

YOU: Right!

2F *Used To*

Form

Three hundred years ago, life in North America was very different. People **used to carry** lanterns for light. They **didn't use to have** electricity.

Used to + base verb takes the same form in all persons (positive). We use *use to* for questions and negative forms.

Affirmative Statements		Negative Statements	
Subject	***Used To* + Base Verb**	**Subject**	***Didn't Use To* + Base Verb**
I		I	
You		You	
He/She/It	**used to work** hard.	He/She/It	**didn't use to work** hard.
We		We	
They		They	

Yes/No Questions			Short Answers	
Did	**Subject**	***Use To* + Base Verb**	**Yes,**	**No,**
	I		you **did**.	you **didn't**.
	you		I/we **did**.	I/we **didn't**.
Did	he/she/it	**use to work** hard?	he/she/it **did**.	he/she/it **didn't**.
	we		you **did**.	you **didn't**.
	they		they **did**.	they **didn't**.

Function

We use *used to* when we want to emphasize the fact that a habit or situation no longer exists.

Most people **used to walk** or ride horses. Today they drive cars.

They **used to wash** clothes by hand. Today they have washing machines.

They **didn't use to drink** water because it often wasn't clean. Today people can drink water because it is clean.

19 Practice

Write sentences with the same meaning using *used to* or *did/didn't use to*.

1. Did people wash a lot?

   Did people use to wash a lot?

2. No, people didn't wash very often.

   Did pede use ito idia

3. They didn't have water inside the house.

4. Did people live for a long time?

5. No, most people lived a short life. They didn't have many doctors.

Listening Puzzle

AUDIO DOWNLOAD CD1, 12

A Listen and check the correct answer.

☐ A. *Versailles*

☐ B. *Buckingham Palace*

☐ C. *Neuschwanstein Castle*

B Discuss your answer with your classmates.

AUDIO DOWNLOAD
CD1, 13

C Now listen again and write the sentences you hear.

Reading Challenge

A Before You Read

Answer the questions.

1. Where did the Maya live?
2. Do Mayan people exist today?

B Read

THE MAYA

Between the years 250 and 900, the Mayan people of Central America and Mexico had the greatest civilization in the Americas. There ⁵ were about 14 million Maya at this time. They lived in cities where they built huge pyramids. They had special beliefs. These ₁₀ beliefs controlled the way they lived.

The Maya believed in astrology, and it controlled their lives. They believed in the power of the sun, moon, and stars. They didn't have telescopes, but they knew all about the ₁₅ sky. They had special priests who **predicted** the future by astrology. Everyone listened to the priests and believed them. When a child was born, the parents took the baby to the priest. The priest told the parents the child's destiny. ₂₀ He used the Mayan calendar for this. Each day on the Mayan calendar said what a baby born on that day was going to be. The parents raised the child to be a farmer, a musician, or whatever the calendar said.

₂₅ Mayan cities disappeared around the year 900. We do not know the reason for this. The descendants of the Maya people still exist in Mexico, El Salvador, Guatemala, and Belize. They still have some Mayan priests and use the ₃₀ old Mayan calendar to predict the future.

> **DID YOU KNOW ... ?**
> The Maya invented zero. They also made a calendar that had 365 days in a year.

C Notice the Grammar

Underline all forms of the past.

Choose the best answer.

D Look for Main Ideas

1. Paragraph 1 is mostly about _____ .
   - (A) the people of Central America
   - (B) how and where the Maya lived
   - (C) how the Maya built their pyramids
   - (D) the special beliefs of the Maya

2. What is the main idea of paragraph 2?
   - (A) Mayan priests predicted the future.
   - (B) The Maya studied the sun, moon, and stars.
   - (C) The Maya had their own calendar.
   - (D) Astrology controlled Mayan life.

E Look for Details

3. The Maya _____ .
   - (A) built pyramids in the rainforests
   - (B) invented telescopes
   - (C) did what their priests told them
   - (D) let parents decide their children's occupations

4. Mayan priests _____ .
   - (A) lived in the pyramids
   - (B) used astrology to tell the future
   - (C) were good musicians
   - (D) don't exist today

5. All of the following are true of the Maya EXCEPT
   - (A) They had the greatest civilization in the Americas.
   - (B) They disappeared around the year 900.
   - (C) Their civilization was not in South America and Mexico.
   - (D) They had knowledge of the sun, moon, and stars.

F Make Inferences

6. What can we infer about the Maya from the reading?
   - (A) They were mostly farmers.
   - (B) No Maya survived after the year 900.
   - (C) They didn't know much about the universe.
   - (D) Their disappearance is a mystery.

7. In paragraph 2, we can infer that _____ .
   - (A) Mayan priests had great control over the lives of the Maya
   - (B) the Maya had a lot of freedom in their lives
   - (C) the Maya didn't trust their priests
   - (D) Mayan children had many choices about their futures

G Look for Vocabulary

8. The word *predicted* in the reading is closest in meaning to _____ .
   - (A) made a decision about
   - (B) said what was going to happen
   - (C) took control of
   - (D) believed in

Writing: Describe a Time in the Past

Write a description of your life five years ago.

STEP **1**

Work with a partner. Ask and answer questions about your lives five years ago. The prompts below will help you, or you can use your own ideas.

Example

go out at night a lot

YOU: Did you use to go out at night a lot?

YOUR PARTNER: No, I didn't. I sometimes used to go to concerts or to the theater.

1. go out at night a lot
2. read a lot of books
3. go to the movies
4. live somewhere else
5. watch television

6. drink coffee
7. see your family
8. go to school
9. wear different clothes
10. have a different haircut

STEP **2**

Write the answers to the questions. Then rewrite the answers in paragraph form. Write a title in a few words (My Life Five Years Ago).

My Life Five Years Ago

Five years ago, I used to be very different. I didn't use to go to school, and I used to see my family all the time ...

STEP **3**

Evaluate your paragraph.

Checklist

_____ Did you indent the first line?

_____ Did you give your paragraph a title?

_____ Did you put the title at the top of the page and center it?

STEP **4**

Edit your work. Work with a partner or your teacher to edit your sentences. Correct spelling, punctuation, vocabulary, and grammar.

STEP **5**

Write your final copy.

Self-Test

1. Ed _____ in a rock group, but now he doesn't.

   A. sang   Ⓐ Ⓑ Ⓒ✓ Ⓓ
   B. sung
   C. used to sing
   D. was singing

2. When the earthquake struck, people _____ .

   A. slept   Ⓐ Ⓑ Ⓒ Ⓓ✓
   B. used to sleep
   C. are sleeping
   D. were sleeping

3. Alexander Graham Bell _____ the telephone in 1876.

   A. invent   Ⓐ Ⓑ✓ Ⓒ Ⓓ
   B. invented
   C. used to invent
   D. were inventing

4. It _____ while people were waiting for the bus.

   A. is raining   Ⓐ Ⓑ Ⓒ Ⓓ✓
   B. rains
   C. used to rain
   D. was raining

5. Early colonists _____ to wash a lot.

   A. did not use   Ⓐ✓ Ⓑ Ⓒ Ⓓ
   B. did not used
   C. used not
   D. did use not

6. Why _____ young?

   A. people died   Ⓐ Ⓑ Ⓒ✓ Ⓓ
   B. died people
   C. did people die
   D. people did die

7. _____ have doctors in 1800?

   A. Used they do   Ⓐ Ⓑ✓ Ⓒ Ⓓ
   B. Did they use to
   C. Did they used to
   D. Did use to they

8. The students were taking the test when they _____ the noise.

   A. were hearing   Ⓐ Ⓑ Ⓒ Ⓓ✓
   B. were heard
   C. hear
   D. heard

9. What _____ last night?

   A. you did   Ⓐ Ⓑ Ⓒ✓ Ⓓ
   B. you did do
   C. did you do
   D. you do

10. While the spectators _____ the game, part of the stadium collapsed.

    A. were watching   Ⓐ✓ Ⓑ Ⓒ Ⓓ
    B. watching
    C. watched
    D. was watching

B **Find the underlined word or phrase, A, B, C, or D, that is incorrect. Darken the oval with the same letter.**

1. When van Gogh moved from Holland to
     A   **B**   **C**
   France, he start to paint with bright colors.
        D
   Ⓐ   Ⓑ   Ⓒ   Ⓓ ✓

2. While Marie studying at the university, she
    A   **B**   **C**
   married Pierre Curie.
    D
   Ⓐ   Ⓑ ✓   Ⓒ   Ⓓ

3. Harriet Beecher Stowe worked on her book
                          A
   after everyone was going to bed.
    B   **C**   **D**
   Ⓐ   Ⓑ   Ⓒ ✓   Ⓓ

4. Charles Lindberg flown alone across the
                 A   **B**   **C**
   Atlantic Ocean in 1927.
           D
   Ⓐ ✓   Ⓑ   Ⓒ   Ⓓ

5. Louis Braille invented a system of writing
             A
   for blind people when he was teaching in
    B   **C**   **D**
   a school for them.
   Ⓐ   Ⓑ   Ⓒ ✓   Ⓓ

6. When Franklin D. Roosevelt become president,
    A   **B**
   the United States was suffering from
           C   **D**
   hard times.
   Ⓐ   Ⓑ ✓   Ⓒ   Ⓓ

7. When the Englishman Robert Scott reached
    A   **B**
   the South Pole, he seen the Norwegian flag.
               C   **D**
   Ⓐ   Ⓑ   Ⓒ ✓   Ⓓ

8. When German immigrants arrived in the
    A   **B**
   United States in the 1800s, they were bringing
                  C   **D**
   the hamburger steak with them.
   Ⓐ   Ⓑ   Ⓒ   Ⓓ ✓

9. While he was hiking in the Alps, Georges de
    A   **B**
   Mestral was getting the idea for Velcro®.
           C   **D**
   Ⓐ   Ⓑ   Ⓒ ✓   Ⓓ

10. In ancient Rome, a wife use to wear her gold
                        A   **B**
    ring in public, but at home she wore a ring
                  C   **D**
    made of iron.
    Ⓐ   Ⓑ   Ⓒ ✓   Ⓓ

Unit 3
The Future

If I **go** to the library, **I'll study**.

Form

The astronauts are in the spacecraft. The engines are making a loud noise. Everyone is counting 10, 9, 8, 7, …. In a few seconds, the spacecraft **is going to take off**. It **is going to travel** in space for 40 days. The astronauts **are not going to visit** other planets.

Affirmative and Negative Statements (Full Forms and Contractions)

Subject	Am/Is/Are (Not)	Going To	Base Verb
I	am 'm am not 'm not		
You	are 're are not 're not aren't	going to	leave.
He/She/It	is 's is not 's not isn't		
We	are 're		
They	are not 're not aren't		

Note: We often pronounce *going to* as "gonna."

Yes/No Questions				Short Answers	
Am/Is/Are	**Subject**	*Going To*	**Base Verb**	**Yes,**	**No,**
Am	I			you **are.**	you**'re not.** you **aren't.**
Are	you			I **am.**	I**'m not.**
Is	he/she/it			he/she/it **is.**	he/she/it**'s not.** he/she/it **isn't.**
	we	**going to**	**leave?**	you **are.**	you**'re not.** you **aren't.**
Are	you			we **are.**	we**'re not.** we **aren't.**
	they			they **are.**	they**'re not.** they **aren't.**

Function

1. We use a *be* verb (*am*, *is*, *are*) with *going to* + a base verb to talk about plans for the future.
   The astronaut **is going to do** some experiments in space.
2. We use a *be* verb (*am*, *is*, *are*) with *going to* + a base verb to talk about something in the future that we can see as a result of something in the present.
   The engines are making a loud noise. In a few seconds, the spacecraft **is going to take off**.

1 Practice

Listen and complete the sentences with the *be going to* form of the verb. Remember that *going to* often sounds like "gonna."

AUDIO

DOWNLOAD

CD1, 14

In a minute, the astronauts __are going to enter__ the spacecraft. The air in
₁
the spacecraft is different. The astronauts _are not gonna have_ any weight. They
₂
are going to do everyday things in a different way. They _are not gonna sleep_
₃ ₄
in regular beds. They _are gonna sleep_ in hanging beds. They
₅
are going to fold their arms when they sleep. This holds their arms in place. It
₆
gonna difficult to take a shower. It _is gonna take_ a long time
₇ ₈
because they need special equipment.

2 Practice

What is going to happen in these situations on a spacecraft? Write a question and a negative answer with *be going to*. Use the prompts in parentheses. Then listen to check your answers. Put a check mark next to the sentences that sound like "gonna."

AUDIO
DOWNLOAD

CD1, 15

1. One astronaut misses her family. She picks up a special phone.

   (call, her boss)

   Is she going to call her boss?

   No, she is going to call her family.

2. Today's astronauts have free time. Astronaut Robert Barnes has some music on CDs with him.

   (listen, to a baseball game)

   is he ~~gonna~~ going to~~v~~ a baseball game ?   listen to

   No, he is gonna listen ~~on~~ music on CDs

3. Astronaut Nadia Smith likes to look at the Earth from the window. She has some free time in half an hour.

   (watch, television)

   is she going to watch TV?

   No, she is gonna look at the .....

4. Robert is putting on a special suit. He plans to take a walk in space.

   (take a walk, inside the spacecraft)

   is he going to take a walk inside the spacecraft

   No, he gonna take a walk

5. Nadia feels tired today. She didn't sleep well.

   (rest, tomorrow)

   Is she going to rest ~~to test~~ tomorrow ?

   No, she in gonna tire today

3 Pair Up and Talk

Tell your partner five things you are going to do when you go home today. Then tell the class what your partner is going to do.

I'm going to relax, and then I'm going to do my homework.

3B | *Will*

Scientists want to build colonies in space in the future. The first colony **will be** 240,000 miles (386,242 kilometers) from Earth. Thousands of people **will live** and **work** in the colony.

Affirmative and Negative Statements

Subject	Will (Not)	Base Verb
I		
You	will	
He/She/It	'll	leave.
We	will not	
They	won't	

Yes/No Questions			Short Answers	
Will	Subject	Base Verb	Yes,	No,
	I		you **will**.	you **won't**.
	you		I **will**.	I **won't**.
Will	he/she/it	leave?	he/she/it **will**.	he/she/it **won't**.
	we		you **will**.	you **won't**.
	they		they **will**.	they **won't**.

Function

1. We use *will* + a base verb to make predictions about the future, or what we think will happen.
   People **will live** in space colonies.
   There **won't be** any pollution in space colonies.

2. We often use *probably* with *will*. *Probably* usually comes between *will* and the base verb.

       I'**ll probably see** you tomorrow.

       Olga **will probably call** us tonight.

       She'**ll probably not call** us tomorrow.

       OR   She **probably won't call** us tomorrow.

3. We use *will* when we decide to do something at the moment of speaking.

       A: We need some help here.

       B: OK. I'**ll be** there in 10 minutes.

       A: Which one do you want? The red one or the blue one?

       B: I'**ll take** the red one.

4. We can use verbs like *intend, hope,* and *plan* to express future events and situations. Use the simple present followed by an infinitive (*to* + base verb).

       They **plan** (now) **to build** a colony in space (in the future).

4 Practice

Complete the sentences with *will* or the simple present of the verbs in parentheses.

1.   Space colonies (be)____*will be*____ islands in space.

2.   They (not, be) _____ on planets. They (be) _____ in space.

3.   A space colony (not, have) _____ bad weather.

4.   The people (control) _____ the weather in the colony.

5.   A space colony (look) _____ like a wheel in space.

6.   Scientists (intend) _____ to have more than 10,000 people on the colony.

7.   They (plan) _____ to have animals on the colony.

8.   The colony (not, need) _____ gasoline.

9.   Cars (run) _____ on electricity.

10.   Scientists think it (take) _____ 25 years to build a space colony.

11.   It (cost) _____ hundreds of billions of dollars.

12.   They (hope) _____ to build the colony in this century.

5 Practice

Andy is 18 years old now. What will he be like 10 years from now? Use the prompts and *will* or *won't* to write sentences that Andy could say about himself.

1. I/probably/have a job

   I'll probably have a job.

2. I/be married

   I will be married

3. I/probably/have children

   I"ll probably have children

4. I/not/be/a millionaire

   I won't be a millionaire

5. I/not/look the same as I do now

   I won't look the same as I do now

6. I/probably/have a nice car

   I'll probably have a nice car

7. I/probably/live in an apartment

   I'll probably live in an apartment

8. I/probably/not/live in the city

   I'll probably ~~not~~ won't live in the city

6 Your Turn

What will you be like 10 years from now? Write five sentences about yourself with *will* and *won't*. Use at least two negatives. Then share them with a partner.

Example

In ten years, I will probably have a job.

1) I will have a job   4) I won't smoke
2) I'll have a car   5) I won't ...
3) I'll become millionaire

7 Pair Up and Talk

What do you intend to do tonight? What do you hope to do next week? What do you plan to do next summer? Talk about your answers with a partner.

I intend to call my family tonight.

The Future   57

THE MILKMAID AND HER BUCKET

There is a young girl who is a milkmaid. She is going to the market with a bucket of milk on her head.

"With the money I get from the sale of this milk, I'll buy a red hen," she says. "The hen will lay eggs, and I'll have many chicks. I'll feed them well, and when they grow, they will each lay eggs. Those eggs will hatch, and I'll have more hens. Then I will sell them, and I'll be rich. I'll wear beautiful clothes with diamonds.

Perhaps I'll visit the queen. I'll bring her gifts from China. I'll see the queen with my arms full of treasure. I'll bow low and say, 'For Your Majesty's pleasure!' "

And the milkmaid bows low …

As she bows, the bucket on her head falls down, and all the milk flows out. All her dreams of a hen, chicks, and a new dress also go.

1. Where is the young milkmaid going?
2. What will she do with the sale of the milk?
3. What will she have when the hen lays eggs?
4. What will the chicks do when they grow?
5. What will she do when she has more hens?
6. Who will she visit?
7. What will she do when she sees the queen?
8. What happens to her dreams?

Handwritten answers:
1. She is going to the market
2. She'll buy a red hen
3. She'll have many chicks
4. They will each lay eggs
5. She will sell them
6. She'll visit the queen

3C | *Be Going To* OR *Will*

Function

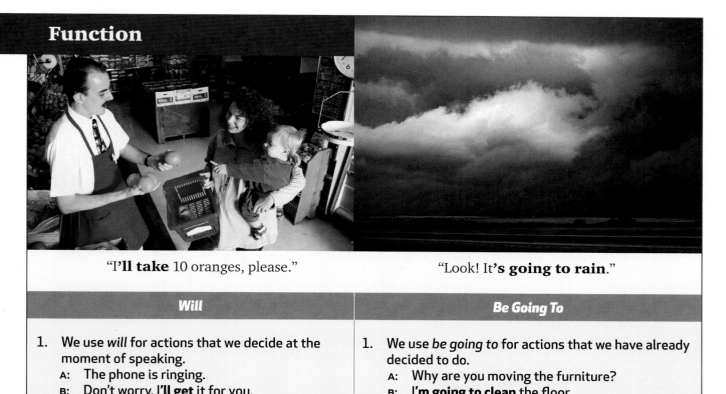

"**I'll take** 10 oranges, please."

"Look! It**'s going to rain**."

Will	Be Going To
1. We use *will* for actions that we decide at the moment of speaking. A: The phone is ringing. B: Don't worry. **I'll get** it for you.	1. We use *be going to* for actions that we have already decided to do. A: Why are you moving the furniture? B: **I'm going to clean** the floor.
2. We use *will* to talk about things that we think or believe will happen in the future. A: It's time for the news on television. B: Let's watch it. I think it **will be** interesting.	2. We use *be going to* to talk about something in the future that will be a result of something in the present. A: I want to watch the news. B: **I'm going to turn on** the television.

9 Practice

Complete the sentences with *be going to* or *will* and the verbs in parentheses.

A: My father is coming to dinner tonight, so I (make) <u>*am going to make*</u> a

       1

special dessert. Oh no! I don't have any sugar. Can you go to the store for me?

B: Sure, I (go) <u>~~am going to go~~</u> . will go

       2

A: Take an umbrella with you. Look at the sky! It (rain) <u>~~will~~ gonna rain</u> .

       3

B: This umbrella is broken. I (take) <u>~~am going to take~~</u> will your umbrella, OK?

       4

10 Practice

Complete the sentences with *will* or *be going to* and the verbs in parentheses.

1. Thanks for lending me this book. I (give)_____'ll give_____ it back to you when I see you again.

2. A: I have a terrible headache.

   B: Wait. I (get) __am going to get__ an aspirin for you.

3. Don't make so much noise. You (wake) ~~are going to wake~~ *will* everybody up.

4. This plant is not growing. It does not look good. I think it (die) ~~will~~ *going to* die .

5. Look at that smoke! That battery (blow up) __gonna blow up__ !

6. Don't worry about the mess. I (clean) __will clean__ it up.

3D The Present Progressive to Express Future Time

Function

John is in a hurry. He**'s giving** a presentation to his boss in 15 minutes, and at 12:00 he**'s leaving** for Texas.

We can use the present progressive to talk about future plans and arrangements when time is indicated somewhere in the sentence.

I**'m leaving** tomorrow at 7:00 in the morning.

We**'re meeting** for dinner before the concert.

11 Practice

Look at Janet's schedule for next week. Then use the present progressive to complete the sentences about her plans.

Schedule

Monday:	Have lunch with John at 1:00.
	Go to gym after work.
Tuesday:	Attend meetings from 8:00 to 4:00.
Wednesday:	Go to the doctor at 1:30.
Thursday:	Pick up dry cleaning at 6:00.
Friday:	Meet Pamela outside the movie theater at 7:00.
Saturday:	Go to Ken and Stella's house for dinner at 7:30.
Sunday:	Play tennis with Mary at 10:00.

1. _____She's having lunch with John_____ at 1:00.
2. _____She's going to the gym_____ after work on Monday.
3. _____She's attending meetings_____ from 8:00 to 4:00 on Tuesday.
4. _____She's going to the doctor_____ at 1:30 on Wednesday.
5. _____She's picking up dry cleaning_____ at 6:00 on Thursday.
6. _____She's meeting Pamela outside the_____ outside the movie theater at 7:00 on Friday.
7. _____She's going to K & Ste's house_____ for dinner at 7:30 on Saturday.
8. _____She is playing tennis with Mary_____ at 10:00 on Sunday.

12 Pair Up and Talk

Work with a partner. Ask and answer questions about your schedule tomorrow.

YOU: What are you doing tomorrow at 10:00?
YOUR PARTNER: I'm going to class.

1. What are you doing tomorrow morning? I'm take
2. What are you doing tomorrow at noon? I'm going to next class
3. Are you going to work tomorrow afternoon? I'm going to home
4. What are you doing at 6:00 tomorrow? Are you going to watch television?
I'm staying at home

Function

School **starts** on January 8th.
The semester **ends** on June 5th.

We use the simple present for the future when it is part of a timetable or planned on a calendar, especially for things such as holidays, appointments, transportation schedules, and brochures.

The flight **arrives** at 10:30 tomorrow.

The train from the airport **leaves** at 11:00.

AUDIO
DOWNLOAD

CD1, 16

13 Practice

Complete the sentences with the simple present or the present progressive of the verbs in parentheses. Then listen to check your answers.

1. This afternoon, I (watch) ___*am watching*___ television. The big game (start)
   ___*start*___ at noon.
   1
   2

2. The final exam (start) ___*starts*___ at 10:00 tomorrow and (end)
   ___*end*___ at 12:00.
   3
   4

3. My flight (arrive) ___*arrive*___ at 3:30 tomorrow, and then I (take)
   ___*'m taking*___ a taxi to the hotel.
   5
   6

4. I (have) ___*'m having*___ dinner with Ben tonight. We (meet)
   ___*'re meeting*___ after work.
   7
   8

5. I (buy) ___*am going to buy*___ a new car this week. Then I (drive)
   ___*'m going to drive*___ to Canada for my vacation.
   9
   10

3F | The Future Conditional

Form/Function

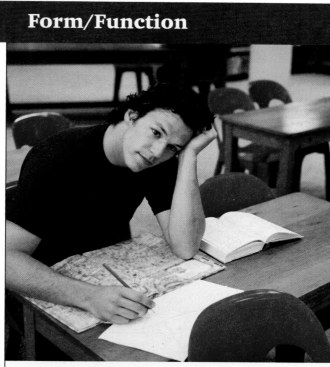

If I **go** to the library, I'**ll study**.
If I **study** hard, I'**ll pass** the test.

1. A conditional sentence has a main clause and a dependent clause that starts with *if*. The *if* clause expresses a condition. The main clause gives the result. Conditional sentences about future events or situations use the simple present in the *if* clause and the future in the main clause.

If Clause — Present	Main Clause — Future
If I **study** hard,	I **will pass** the test.
If you **don't study**,	you **will fail**.
If he **fails**,	his parents **won't give** him any money.
If we **don't go** out,	we'**ll have** more time to study.
If they **don't pass**,	they'**ll repeat** the class.

2. An *if* clause can come before or after the main clause. The meaning is the same. When the *if* clause comes first, we put a comma (,) after it.

    If you don't study, you will fail.
    You will fail **if you don't study**.

3. We use future conditional sentences to talk about events or situations that can possibly happen in the future.

    If I see Yuko tomorrow, I'll borrow her notes.
    If she gets an A, she'll be very happy.

14 Practice

Write sentences about what Katerina hopes will happen in the future.
Use the result of one sentence as the condition of the next. Use results from
the list that make sense.

Katerina

become a dentist	pass her high school exams
earn a lot of money	study dentistry
go to college	study more

Condition

1. If she doesn't go out before the test,
2. *If she studies more,*
3. *If she go to college*
4. _____
5. _____
6. _____

Result

she'll study more.
she'll go to college.
_____
_____
_____
_____

15 Your Turn

Work with a partner. Write four questions about Katerina. Then ask and
answer with a partner.

Example

YOU: What will Katerina do if she goes to college?
YOUR PARTNER: She'll study dentistry.

16 Pair Up and Talk

Work with a partner. Think of three superstitions from your country or
another. Tell them to the class using *if* and the future tense.

In my country, if you see a black cat, you will have bad luck.

3G | Future Time Clauses

Form/Function

We'll walk on Tower Bridge **before we go to Big Ben**.

After we walk on Tower Bridge, we'll go to Big Ben.

1. A future time clause can begin with conjunctions such as *before*, *after*, *as soon as*, or *when*. We usually use the simple present in the time clause. We do not use *will* or *be going to*.

Future Time Clause			Main Clause	
Conjunction	**Subject**	**Simple Present Verb**	**Subject**	**Future Verb**
Before	I	**go** to London,	I	**will get** some British money.
When	she	**goes** to London,	she	**will spend** a lot.
After	they	**visit** the sights,	they	**will go** shopping.
As soon as	we	**arrive**,	we	**will call** you.

2. A future time clause is a dependent clause. It must be used with a main clause.

    CORRECT: **When I get there**, I will call you.

    INCORRECT: ~~When I get there~~.

3. We can put the time clause before or after the main clause. They both have the same meaning. When the time clause comes first, we put a comma after it.

    As soon as we arrive, we'll call you.

    We'll call you **as soon as we arrive**.

17 Practice

Anne and Paul are planning a trip to London. Complete the sentences with the correct form of the verbs in parentheses.

1. They (get) _____*will get*_____ some traveler's checks before they
   (leave) _____*leave*_____ .

2. Anne (make) _____ a list of all the interesting places to visit before
   they (go) _____ .

3. As soon as they (arrive) _____ at their hotel, they
   (call) _____ us.

4. When they (walk) _____ around London, they
   (take) _____ photos.

5. After they (walk) _____ on Tower Bridge, they
   (go) _____ to see Big Ben, the clock.

6. If it (rain) _____ hard, they (visit) _____ a museum.

7. After they (see) _____ Big Ben, they (buy) _____
   tickets to see a play.

8. After they (visit) _____ the sights, they (go) _____
   shopping.

18 Practice

Find the errors in the sentences and rewrite them correctly. If a sentence has no errors, write *No change*.

1. If I get some time off this winter, I go to Arizona for a vacation.

   If I get some time off this winter, I will go

   to Arizona for a vacation.

2. It will be warm, when I get to Phoenix.

   _____

3. As soon as I will arrive, will put on light clothes and walk in the sun.

   _____

4. After I visit sights in Phoenix I will rent a car and drive to the Grand Canyon.

   _____

5. I take a lot of pictures as soon as I will get there.

   _____

19 Your Turn

Write five predictions for the next five years about a famous person or yourself.

Example

Angelina Jolie will have another baby.

20 Pair Up and Talk

Tell your partner three things that you think will happen in your future. Use sentences with future time clauses.

After I finish this course, I'll look for a good job.

Listening Puzzle

   CD1, 17

A Listen and check the correct answer.

❑ *A. Greenland*

❑ *B. Iceland*

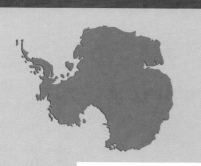

❑ *c. Antarctica*

B Discuss your answer with your classmates.

CD1, 18

C Now listen again and write the sentences you hear.

A Before You Read
Answer the questions.
1. What insect do you think this is?
2. Can one kind of insect look like another kind?

B Read

INSECT MIMICRY

The word *mimicry* means "a copy of something." When we are talking about animals, we use it to describe the likeness of two animals that are not ₅ closely related. These animals usually have bright colors, and one of them has a sting or a nasty taste. The colors are ₁₀ a warning to **predators**. Many animals use mimicry, but we find it most among insects.

If you study the ₁₅ insects in your garden, you'll notice perhaps that many of the flies have black and yellow bands like wasps. Many of the insects that you think are bees will also be flies. This is animal mimicry. Some of these flies will even sound ₂₀ like bees and wasps. Other insects will have the same smell as the insect they are copying.

Why will insects do this? Humans and even many birds know that if they interfere with a bee or a wasp, it will sting them. Therefore, if an ₂₅ insect disguises itself to look like an insect with a sting, a predator will most likely not get near it. There are some flies that even fool the bees. Several species of flies will enter a bee colony and lay their eggs. Some insects mimic others ₃₀ so well that even insect collectors will make a mistake.

> **DID YOU KNOW ... ?**
> Some creatures such as spiders mimic ants because ants have stingers and acid sprays to protect them. Some spiders hold up their front legs to look like ants.

C Notice the Grammar
Underline all forms of the future.

Choose the best answer.

D Look for Main Ideas

1. Paragraph 2 is mainly about _____ .
   - (A) how some insects mimic other insects
   - (B) why flies mimic bees
   - (C) what bees and wasps look and sound like
   - (D) how some insects copy smell

2. What is the main idea of paragraph 3?
   - (A) Many insects can sting.
   - (B) Flies can fool both insects and humans.
   - (C) Insects use mimicry to fool predators.
   - (D) Flies disguise themselves to enter bee colonies.

E Look for Details

3. Which of the following is NOT true of flies?
   - (A) They often mimic insects that sting.
   - (B) Some look like wasps and bees.
   - (C) They can sound like other insects.
   - (D) They learn to sting like bees.

4. Animal mimicry is when _____ .
   - (A) two different animals look alike
   - (B) several different animals act the same way
   - (C) two of the same animals look different
   - (D) several different animals live together

5. Some flies will enter a bee colony to _____ .
   - (A) kill the bees
   - (B) lay their eggs
   - (C) fool their predators
   - (D) avoid humans

Sometimes information is not directly stated in a reading. You have to look at the facts in the reading. Then you make a conclusion. You "infer" the conclusion.

F Make Inferences

6. We can infer from the reading that animals use mimicry to _____ .
   - (A) attack their predators
   - (B) learn new skills
   - (C) attract mates
   - (D) protect themselves

7. What can we infer from the reading?
   - (A) Flies and bees are almost alike.
   - (B) Most animals can mimic other animals.
   - (C) It's easy for humans to know when animals are using mimicry.
   - (D) Some insects look more dangerous than they really are.

G Look for Vocabulary

8. The word *predators* in the reading is closest in meaning to _____ .
   - (A) animals that have bright colors
   - (B) insects that disguise themselves
   - (C) animals that kill and eat other animals
   - (D) animals that have no protection

Writing: Describe a Future City

Write a paragraph about the city of the future.

STEP 1   Work with a partner. Ask and answer questions about the city of the future. Write the answers. These prompts may help you.

1. What kinds of buildings will it have?
2. What kind of transportation will people use?
3. What kind of weather will it have?
4. What kinds of places for sports will it have?
5. How will they control crime?
6. Will there be animals?
7. Will people live and work in the same city?
8. Will there be stores?
9. Will people go to restaurants?
10. Will people go to movies?
11. How clean will the city be?
12. What kind of people will live in this city?

STEP 2   Rewrite your answers in paragraph form. Write a title in a few words (The City of the Future).

The City of the Future

In the city of the future, all of the buildings will be underground. People will ...

STEP 3   Evaluate your paragraph.

Checklist
_____ Did you indent the first line?
_____ Did you give your paragraph a title?
_____ Did you put the title at the top of the page and center it?
_____ Did you capitalize the title correctly?

STEP 4   Edit your work. Work with a partner or your teacher to edit your sentences. Correct spelling, punctuation, vocabulary, and grammar.

STEP 5   Write your final copy.

Self-Test

1. I _____ with the administrator at 3:00 this afternoon.

   A. will going to meet   Ⓐ Ⓑ Ⓒ Ⓓ
   B. going meet
   C. am going to meet
   D. will to meet

2. They _____ to finish the construction next year.

   A. intend   Ⓐ Ⓑ Ⓒ Ⓓ
   B. are going to intend
   C. will intend
   D. intending

3. She'll call me when she _____ at the airport.

   A. will arrive   Ⓐ Ⓑ Ⓒ Ⓓ
   B. is arriving
   C. is going to arrive
   D. arrives

4. People _____ gasoline cars in the future.

   A. won't drive probably   Ⓐ Ⓑ Ⓒ Ⓓ
   B. are going to probably not drive
   C. probably won't drive
   D. are not driving probably

5. The bank _____ at ten o'clock.

   A. will to open   Ⓐ Ⓑ Ⓒ Ⓓ
   B. open
   C. going to open
   D. opens

6. Before I take the test tomorrow, I _____ my notes.

   A. review   Ⓐ Ⓑ Ⓒ Ⓓ
   B. do reviewing
   C. will review
   D. will to review

7. If it snows tomorrow, we _____ problems.

   A. are having   Ⓐ Ⓑ Ⓒ Ⓓ
   B. had
   C. have
   D. will have

8. I leave for Bangkok tomorrow. The conference _____ on Monday.

   A. starts   Ⓐ Ⓑ Ⓒ Ⓓ
   B. going to start
   C. will start
   D. starting

9. In the future, people _____ in underground cities.

   A. will live   Ⓐ Ⓑ Ⓒ Ⓓ
   B. live
   C. are living
   D. going to live

10. Architects _____ the plan will not have any problems.

    A. will hope   Ⓐ Ⓑ Ⓒ Ⓓ
    B. hoping
    C. are hope
    D. hope

1. NASA <u>be</u> <u>planning</u> <u>to send</u> astronauts <u>to</u>
   A   B   C   D
   Mars in this century.

   Ⓐ Ⓑ Ⓒ Ⓓ

2. <u>The scientists</u> <u>will</u> <u>hope</u> <u>to build</u> a space
   A   B   C   D
   station to orbit Earth in the future.

   Ⓐ Ⓑ Ⓒ Ⓓ

3. If <u>the United States</u> <u>will build</u> the space
   A   B
   station, <u>it</u> <u>will be</u> called *The Eagle*.
   C   D

   Ⓐ Ⓑ Ⓒ Ⓓ

4. You <u>won't</u> <u>be able</u> to vote <u>if</u> you <u>will</u> not
   A   B   C   D
   register by tomorrow.

   Ⓐ Ⓑ Ⓒ Ⓓ

5. <u>Scientists</u> <u>are</u> <u>probably</u> be able to predict
   A   B   C
   <u>earthquakes</u> in the future.
   D

   Ⓐ Ⓑ Ⓒ Ⓓ

6. <u>In the future</u>, people <u>are going</u> to the moon <u>for</u>
   A   B   C
   <u>their</u> vacations.
   D

   Ⓐ Ⓑ Ⓒ Ⓓ

7. He <u>is going to</u> celebrate <u>after</u> he <u>will get</u> a good
   A   B   C
   score <u>on</u> the test.
   D

   Ⓐ Ⓑ Ⓒ Ⓓ

8. Scientists <u>think</u> <u>transportation</u> <u>is</u> much faster
   A   B   C
   <u>in the future</u>.
   D

   Ⓐ Ⓑ Ⓒ Ⓓ

9. In the future, <u>people</u> <u>are driving</u> <u>electric</u> <u>cars</u>.
   A   B   C   D

   Ⓐ Ⓑ Ⓒ Ⓓ

10. The store <u>is opening</u> <u>at</u> 10:00 every <u>morning</u>
    A   B   C
    except <u>on</u> Sundays.
    D

    Ⓐ Ⓑ Ⓒ Ⓓ

Unit 4

Nouns, Articles, and Quantity

Giraffes are tall.

4A | Singular and Plural Nouns

Form/Function

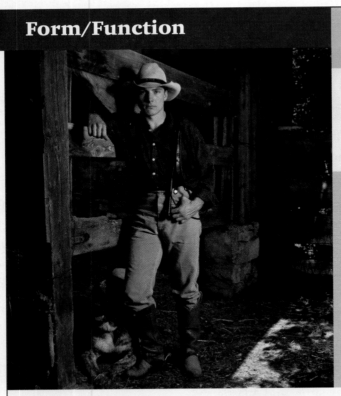

Ben works on **a farm**. He has **a dog** and **a horse**. He takes care of **the cows**, **chickens**, and **sheep**.

1. Nouns name people, places, and things.
2. Singular nouns refer to one thing. Plural nouns refer to two or more things. All nouns have a singular form. Many nouns also have plural forms, but some do not.

Singular Nouns

3. We often use the articles *a* or *an* in front of a singular noun. We use *a* with nouns that start with a consonant sound. Some consonant sounds are spelled with the letters *b, c, d, f, g, h, j, k, l, m, n, p, q, r, s, t, v, w, x, y*, and *z*.

    a hat   **a** dog   **a** farmer   **a** neighborhood

    a university (the *u* in *university* starts with a *y* sound)

We use *an* when a word begins with a vowel sound. Some vowel sounds are spelled with the letters *a, e, i, o*, and *u*.

    an animal   **an** eye   **an** ice cream   **an** uncle   **an** hour (the *h* in *hour* is silent)

4. *A* and *an* have the same meaning. They mean "one."

Plural Nouns

5. Many nouns have plural forms. We do not use the articles *a* and *an* before plural nouns.
6. We form the plural of most nouns by adding -*s* to the singular form. Sometimes there are other spelling changes.

Regular Plural Nouns

Rule	Singular Noun	Plural Noun
Add -s to most nouns.	horse	horse**s**
Add -es to nouns ending in s, ss, sh, ch, and x.	bus	bus**es**
	glass	glass**es**
	dish	dish**es**
	watch	watch**es**
	box	box**es**
Nouns ending in a consonant + y: change y to i and add -es.	country	countr**ies**
	party	part**ies**
Nouns ending in a vowel + y: add -s.	boy	boy**s**
Nouns ending in f or fe: change f or fe to -ves.	life	li**ves**
	leaf	lea**ves**
Exceptions:	belief	belief**s**
	chief	chief**s**
	roof	roof**s**
Nouns ending in o: Some add -es.	echo	echo**es**
	hero	hero**es**
	tomato	tomato**es**
Some add -s.	piano	piano**s**
	radio	radio**s**
	zoo	zoo**s**
Some can add either -s or -es.	zero	zero**s**/zero**es**
	volcano	volcano**s**/volcano**es**

7. Some nouns have irregular plural forms.

Irregular Plural Nouns

Singular	Plural	Singular	Plural
man	**men**	fish	**fish**
woman	**women**	sheep	**sheep**
child	**children**	deer	**deer**
tooth	**teeth**	species	**species**
foot	**feet**	ox	**oxen**
mouse	**mice**	person	**people**
goose	**geese**	moose	**moose**

Complete the sentences with *a* or *an*.

1. I took my nephew to _____ *a* _____ zoo last weekend.

2. We saw _____ an _____ elephant and her baby.

3. There was _____ a _____ zebra and _____ an _____ antelope.

4. We spent almost _____ an _____ hour watching the monkeys.

5. We saw _____ a _____ hippopotamus in _____ a _____ lake.

6. It was _____ a _____ huge animal!

7. There was _____ an _____ exhibit of snakes, and my nephew loved it.

8. We met _____ a _____ guide there. He learned about snakes at _____ a _____ university in Florida.

9. My nephew wanted to hold _____ a _____ snake, and the guide said yes.

10. I let him do it. I'm _____ a _____ good uncle, aren't I?

11. We had _____ an _____ ice-cream cone before we left.

2 Practice

Underline the nouns in the sentences. Write *S* if a noun is singular. Write *P* if it is plural.

1. There were a lot of <u>men</u>, <u>women</u>, and <u>children</u> in the <u>park</u>.
   P   *P*   *P*   *S*

2. It was beautiful. The <u>leaves</u> were changing <u>color</u>.
   P   *S*

3. There were <u>geese</u> on the <u>lake</u>.
   P   *S*

4. A <u>man</u> and a <u>woman</u> were in a <u>boat</u> on the <u>lake</u>.
   S   *S*   *S*   *S*

5. <u>They</u> were paddling the <u>boat</u> with their <u>feet</u>.
   P   *S*   *P*

6. I could see lots of <u>fish</u> in the <u>lake</u>.
   P   *S*

7. Some <u>kids</u> were listening to their <u>radio</u> and <u>dancing</u>.
   P   *S*

8. Others were riding their <u>bicycles</u>.
   P

9. It was a beautiful <u>day</u> for a walk in the park.
   S

3 Practice

Listen to the plurals of the following words. Then write the plural words under the correct headings.

CD1, 19

baby	child	half	leaf	piano	thief
bird	city	hero	mouse	potato	tomato
bush	dress	key	ox	radio	wolf *chó sói*
category	foot	knife	peach	sandwich	
cherry	fox	lady	photo	sheep	

-s	-es	-ies	-oes	-ves	Irregular
birds	*bushes*	*babies*	heroes	knives	feet
radios	dresses	categories	potatoes	halves	oxen
halfs	foxes	cherries	tomatoes	wolves	sheep
keys	sandwiches	cities		leaves	chicken
mouses	peaches	ladies		thieves	mice
photos					

4 Practice

Listen and write the missing words. Be careful to use the correct spelling.

CD1, 20

DON: Did you go shopping yesterday?

CARLA: Yes, I did. I bought a lot of things because they were on sale.

DON: Oh, what did you buy?

CARLA: I bought two ___*dresses*___ , two _____ , and three _____ .
                         1   2   3

DON: Did you buy anything for the house?

CARLA: Yes, I bought two beautiful _____ , six _____ , six
                                      4   5

_____ , and six _____ .
        6   7

DON: Wow! You sure bought a lot of things!

5 Your Turn

Look around the classroom. Write the plural names of things you see. Then compare with a partner. Who found the most things?

___*chairs*___ _____ _____ _____

_____ _____ _____ _____

4B Nouns as Subjects, Objects, and Objects of Prepositions

Form/Function

Sheep eat grass.
Lambs are baby sheep.
The lambs are lying on the grass.

1. A noun can be the subject of a sentence. The subject names the thing or person that does the action in a sentence.
2. A noun can be the object of a verb. The object names the thing or person that receives the action of the verb.
3. A noun can be the object of a preposition. The object of a preposition is a noun or pronoun that follows a preposition. A preposition and the words following it are prepositional phrases.

They are lying **on** the **grass**.

preposition

Grass is the object of the preposition *on*.

subject

Lambs eat **grass**.

object

The lambs went **down** the **hill**.

The dog ran **after** the **lambs**.

He chased them **toward** the **pond**.

The lambs did not go **into** the **water**.

Then the farmer saw a coyote **at the bottom of** the **hill**.

That night, the dog got steak **with** its **dinner** and slept **beside** the **fireplace**.

down *buried*

6 Practice
Underline and label the subject (S), verb (V), and object (O) of each sentence.

           S V O
1. The farm has cows.
2. The cows give milk.
3. The family drinks the milk.
4. The farm has chickens.

5. The chickens lay eggs.
6. Don has a dog.
7. The dog follows Don.
8. His brother has a cat.

7 Practice
Label the subject (S), verb (V), preposition (P), object (O), and the object of the preposition (OP).

           S V P OP
1. Ben lives on a farm.
2. Ben wears a hat on the farm.
3. Ben works on the farm with his brother and father.
4. His mother cooks the food for the family.
5. His mother grows vegetables in a garden behind the farmhouse.
6. The family eats the vegetables from the garden.

7. The family drinks milk from the cows on the farm.
8. The family eats eggs from the chickens in the yard.
9. Ben drives his truck to the town on Saturdays.
10. Ben takes his dog with him in the truck.

8 Practice
Listen and underline the correct answer.

CD1, 21

1. a. Terry   b. in   c. office
2. a. he   b. drinks   c. coffee
3. a. Lois   b. uses   c. at
4. a. It   b. on   c. desk
5. a. sits   b. next to   c. Terry
6. a. They   b. are   c. friends

Form/Function

Fresh **air** is good for your **health**.
Sunshine is good for you, too.

1. Count nouns are nouns that we can count (*one book, two books, three books*, etc.). They can be singular or plural (*a chair, two chairs*).
2. We put *a* or *an* before singular nouns.
3. We cannot count noncount nouns. They have no plural.
4. We do not use the articles *a* or *an* with noncount nouns.
5. Some nouns that are usually noncount can also be count nouns, but the meaning is different.

NONCOUNT NOUN:	She makes salad dressing with olive **oil**.
COUNT NOUN:	She uses several **oils** in her cooking. (*Oils* = kinds of oil)
NONCOUNT NOUN:	Brazil produces a lot of **coffee**.
COUNT NOUN:	Can I buy you a **coffee**? (*A coffee* = a cup of coffee)

Here are some common noncount nouns in categories.

Categories	Examples of Noncount Nouns		
	beef	glass	pasta
	bread	gold	plastic
	butter	ham	pork
	chalk *chalk board*	ice cream	silk
Solids	cheese	iron	soap
	chicken	margarine *fake butter*	steel
	"cole" coal *than old*	meat	wood
	cotton	nylon	wool
	fish	paper	yogurt

Liquids	blood	juice	soup
	coffee	milk	tea
	gasoline	oil	vinegar *giấm*
	honey	shampoo	water
Powders and Grains *phấn* *ngũ cốc*	cereal	flour	salt
	corn	pepper	sand *cát*
	dust	rice	sugar
Gases *khí*	air	oxygen	smog
	fog	pollution	smoke
	hydrogen	smell	steam *hơi nc*
Names of Categories	clothing	fruit	mail
	email	furniture	money
	food	jewelry	traffic
School Subjects and Languages	biology	Korean	music
	Chinese	literature	science
	history	math	Spanish
Weather	darkness	light	sunshine
	frost	rain	thunder
	hail	sleet	weather
	ice	snow	wind
Physical Forces	electricity	light	speed
	gravity	magnetism	weight
Abstract Nouns (things we cannot touch)	advice	health	love
	beauty	help	luck
	crime	homework	peace
	education	information	poverty
	fun	innocence *k'có tội*	progress
	guilt *có tội*	insurance	time
	happiness	kindness	wealth
	hate	knowledge	work

wine   *used to*

9 Practice

Listen to the words. Underline *count* or *noncount*.

AUDIO
DOWNLOAD

CD1, 22

1. count   <u>noncount</u>   3. count   noncount   5. count   noncount

2. <u>count</u>   noncount   4. count   noncount   6. count   <u>noncount</u>

10   Pair Up and Talk

Work with a partner. Make a list of five foods that are count nouns and five foods that are noncount nouns. Then talk about which foods are good for you and which foods are bad for you. Do you agree?

YOU: Eggs are good for you.

YOUR PARTNER: Butter is bad for you.
                     Salt

11   Practice

Complete the sentences with the singular or plural of the nouns in parentheses.

My new living room looks nice. There are no (rug) ___*rugs*___ on the floor.

The floor is made of (wood) ___*wood*___ . There is a lot of (light) ___*li*___ in
                              2   **3**

the room from the two big (window) ___*windows*___ . I have two big
                                         4

(armchair) ___*armchairs*___ . They are covered in blue (cotton) _____ .
              5   **6**

The (furniture) ___*furniture*___ is all new and modern. I have two small (table)
                        7

___*tables*___ made of (glass) ___*glass*___ , and two (lamp) ___*lamp*___ .
    8   **9**   **10**

12   Practice

Work with a partner. Write as many nouns as you can for the categories below. The pair with the most correct is the winner.

Things you see on a farm	Things you wear	What things are made of
animals	*shirts*	*flours*
fences	*shoes*	*cloths*
plants	*hats*	*Rices*

4D | *A, An,* and *Some*

There are **a** pair of glasses, **some** paper, **a** lamp, and **some** books on the desk.

1. We use *a* or *an* in front of singular count nouns.

   a book   **an** orange

2. We use *some* in front of noncount nouns. We don't use *a* or *an* in front of noncount nouns.

   CORRECT: I need **some** milk to make this cake.

   INCORRECT: I need ~~a milk~~* to make this cake.

3. We also use *some* with plural count nouns.

   a book   **some** books

* It is possible to say "a milk," but the meaning is "a serving of milk."

13 Practice

What does Pete carry with him? Complete the sentences with *a, an,* or *some*.

I have _____*a*_____ wallet. In the wallet, there is _____*some*_____ money,
          1   **2**
and there are _____*a*_____ business cards. I also have _____*an*_____ identification
          3   **4**
card, _____*a*_____ checkbook, and _____*some*_____ credit cards. In my pocket,
          5   **6**
I have _____*a*_____ pen, _____*some*_____ keys, _____*a*_____ cell phone,
          7   **8**   **9**
and _____*an*_____ address book.
          10

14 Practice

Nancy always carries a lot of things in her bag. Complete the sentences with *a*, *an*, or *some*.

She has _____ a _____ hair brush, _____ a _____ coin purse, _____ a _____
         1   2   3

wallet, _____ a _____ pack of tissues, _____ a _____ bottle of water, _____ some _____
        4   5   6

pens, _____ an _____ apple, _____ an _____ umbrella, _____ a _____ notepad,
       7   8   9

_____ some _____ paper clips, _____ a _____ calendar, and _____ Some _____ jewelry.
     10   11   12

15 Pair Up and Talk

Someone takes you to a restaurant. You can eat whatever you want. Don't think about diet or the price. Tell your partner what you want to eat and drink. Then listen to what your partner wants to eat and drink.

I want a big steak with some fries. I want some hot bread with some cheese. Then I'll have some ice cream with some strawberries and whipped cream.

4E   *Some, Any, Much, Many, A Little, A Few, and A Lot Of*

Form/Function

A: Did you see **any** crocodiles in the river?

B: Yes, we saw **a few**.

	Affirmative	Negative
Count Nouns	There are **many** kangaroos.	There aren't **many** kangaroos.
	There are **a lot of** snakes.	There aren't **a lot of** snakes.
	There are **some** big towns.	There aren't **any** big towns.
	There are **a few** trees.	There aren't **many** trees.
Noncount Nouns	There is **a lot of** sunshine.	There isn't **much** sunshine.
	There is **some** rain.	There isn't **any** rain.
	There is **a little** snow.	There isn't **much** snow.

16 Practice

Ted and Julia went to Australia. Their friend Mary is asking Ted about their vacation. Underline the correct expression in parentheses. Then listen to check your answers.

CD1, 23

MARY: Did you see a lot of wild animals? How about koala bears?

TED: No, we didn't see (<u>any</u>/some) koala bears, but we saw (a little/<u>a lot of</u>) kangaroos.
　　　　　　　　　　　　1　　　　　　　　　　　　　　　　　　　　　　　　2
They were everywhere.

MARY: Did you stay in the cities or did you go to the countryside?

TED: We didn't spend (a few/<u>any</u>) time in the city. We drove into a desert area called
　　　　　　　　　　　　3
the outback. You don't see (<u>any</u>/a few) people for hours, and of course there isn't
　　　　　　　　　　　　　　　　4
(a few/<u>any</u>) traffic. There is (<u>a lot of</u>/any) sunshine, and there aren't
　　5　　　　　　　　　　　　　　　　6
(a few/<u>any</u>) trees. There isn't (<u>much</u>/a few) water in this area. Someone took us to a
　　7　　　　　　　　　　　　　　8
river where we saw (<u>a few</u>/any) crocodiles. I was really scared!
　　　　　　　　　　　　9

17 Pair Up and Talk

What kinds of things do you take on a long trip? Work with a partner. Talk about the things you pack in your suitcase. Use *much, many, a lot of, a little,* and *a few.*

I take a lot of T-shirts. I usually take a little water and a few snacks. I don't take many credit cards, and I don't take much jewelry.

4F   *Few*, *A Few*, *Little*, and *A Little*

Form/Function

The restaurant has **few** umbrellas outside.   There are **a few** umbrellas on the beach.

1. We use *few* and *a few* with plural count nouns (*books*, *tables*, etc.).

    A few means "not many, but enough." It has a positive meaning.

    > I have **a few** apples. I can make an apple pie.

    Few means "almost none." It has a negative meaning.

    > There are **few** apples. We must get some more.

2. We use *little* and *a little* with noncount nouns (*milk*, *time*, etc.)

    A little means "not much, but enough."

    > I have **a little** time. I can finish this exercise.

    Little means "almost none." It has a negative meaning.

    > I have **little** time. I must hurry.

18   Practice

Complete the sentences with *a few*, *few*, *a little*, or *little*.

1. Stella knew ____*little*____ English before she took ____*a few*____ courses.

2. I like to listen to __*a little*__ music when I drive.

3. There is ____*a little*____ time before the train leaves, so we can buy ____*a few*____ magazines and things from the store.

4. There's ____*little*____ food left in the refrigerator. I'll go to the supermarket and get ____*a few*____ things.

5. My mother sent me ____*a little*____ money, so I am going to buy ____*a few*____ things I need.

THE TOWN MOUSE AND THE COUNTRY MOUSE

A town mouse once visited a relative in the country. For lunch, the country mouse offered him some beans, some cheese, and some bread. It was all he had, but there was much food.

The town mouse didn't like the country food. He had a little of this and a little of that. Then he said, "Cousin, how can you eat such poor food as this? But of course you cannot expect anything better in the country. Come to my town and see."

The two mice went to the mansion of the town mouse. In the dining room, there were leftovers from a big dinner. There were figs, honey, desserts, and a lot of fine food to eat.

Suddenly, they heard a loud noise. "What's that?" said the country mouse. "It's only the dogs of the house," answered the town mouse. Just then the door flew open and two huge dogs ran in. The mice ran. "Goodbye, Cousin," said the country mouse.

"What's wrong?" asked the town mouse.

The country mouse replied, "I prefer to have my beans and bread in peace than cakes and honey in fear."

1. _____ ? The country mouse offered him some beans, some cheese, and some bread.

2. _____ ? He had a little of this and a little of that.

3. _____ ? He took his cousin to the dining room of the mansion.

4. _____ ? They heard the loud noise of the dogs of the house.

5. _____ ? The country mouse liked to eat in peace.

Form/Function

A: What's in the grocery bags?

B: There's **a bag of** tortilla chips, **a loaf of** bread, **a bunch of** carrots, **a pound of** apples, and many other things.

1. We can use units of measure such as *a cup of coffee* or *a glass of water* to express quantities of noncount nouns and count nouns.
2. Count nouns following the units of measure (*two slices of pie, ten loaves of bread, three bottles of juice, five cans of beans*) are plural.
3. Here are some units of measure.

a bag of chips	a head of lettuce	a sheet of paper
a bar of soap	a jar of jam	a slice of cake
a bottle of water	a loaf of bread	a tube of toothpaste
a box of chocolates	a package of spaghetti	two pounds of apples/cheese
a bunch of bananas	a piece of fruit	ten gallons of gasoline
a can of tomatoes/soup	a piece of information	two cartons of milk
a carton of milk/juice	a roll of toilet paper	two cups of tea

20 Practice

Pam wrote a note for Pete. Complete the note on page 89 with the following quantity words.

a bag of	a can of	a loaf of	a tube of	cartons of	sheets of
a bar of	a jar of	a pound of	bottles of	pounds of	

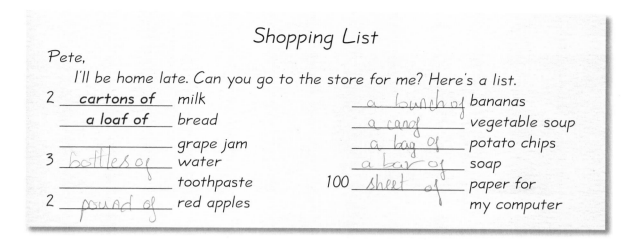

Shopping List

Pete,

I'll be home late. Can you go to the store for me? Here's a list.

2 __cartons of__ milk

__a loaf of__ bread

_____ grape jam

3 __bottles of__ water

_____ toothpaste

2 __pound of__ red apples

__a bunch of__ bananas

__a cand__ vegetable soup

__a bag of__ potato chips

__a bar of__ soap

100 __sheet of__ paper for my computer

CD1, 24

21 Practice

Listen and underline the correct item for each quantity.

1. a. toothpaste   b. lettuce   c. <u>cereal</u>
2. a. chicken soup   b. chips   c. bread
3. a. spaghetti   b. cheese   c. coffee
4. a. potatoes   b. water   c. soap
5. a. cheese   b. chocolate   c. bread
6. a. fruit   b. toilet paper   c. juice

22 Pair Up and Talk

Work with a partner. Look at the following shopping list. Ask and answer questions with *how much* or *how many* for each item. Answer with quantity expressions such as numbers, *some*, *a lot of*, *a few*, and *a little*.

YOU: How much soap do you need?

YOUR PARTNER: Not much. Just two bars.

Shopping List

apples	juice	oranges	margarine
bread	lettuce	potatoes	yogurt
chips	light bulbs	rice	soap

Nouns, Articles, and Quantity   **89**

Form/Function

My uncle**'s** name is Jim.
He's in the photo, and that's
Jim**'s** son, Tommy.

1. We use *'s* (apostrophe + *s*) or *'* (apostrophe) to talk about things that belong to people.

Singular Possessive Noun	Plural Possessive Noun
My uncle**'s** name is Jim. (one uncle)	My uncles**'** names are Jim and Ken. (more than one uncle)
It's the boy**'s** bag. (one boy)	They are the boys**'** bags. (more than one boy)

2. We add *'s* or just *'* for names and nouns that end in *-s*.
   This is James**'s** friend. OR This is James**'** friend.
   That is the boss**'s** car. OR That is the boss**'** car.
3. We use *'s* with irregular plurals.
   These are children**'s** books.
   They sell women**'s** clothes.

23   Practice
Listen and write the missing words. Use *'s* or *'* to show possession.

CD1, 25

RITA: Where did you take this photo?

LAURA: At my ___friend's___ house. My ___friend's___ name is Carla. That day was the
                    1   **2**

___twins'___ birthday party. This is Cindy, my ___brother's___ wife. And that is
         3   **4**

___Cindy's___ sister.
         5

RITA: Who are the two boys?

e-Workbook 4H

LAURA: The _____boys'_____ names are Ken and Dave. They are _____Sandy's_____ sons.
6   7

And that's the _____boys'_____ teacher, Mrs. Parkinson.
8

24 Practice
Rewrite these questions using the possessive nouns.

1. What's the first name of your father?

    What's your father's first name?

2. What are the names of your friends?

    What are your friend's name?

3. What's the name of your mother?

    What's your mother's name?

4. In class, what are the colors of the shirts of the women?

    In class, what are the colors of the women's shirts?

5. What are some of the favorite movies of your classmates?

    What are some your classmates' favorite movies?

6. What's the telephone number of your doctor?

    What's your doctor's telephone number

7. What are the colors of the shoes of the men in class?

    What are the colors of the men's shoes in the class?

25 Your Turn
Write answers to the questions in Practice 24.

1. My _father's first name is Frank._

2. My _____friend name is Hien_____

3. My _____women's mother's name is Lien_____

4. In class, the _____women's color is Black_____

5. _____

6. _____The doctor's telephone number is . . . ._____

7. _____The color shoes's the men is brow_____

4I | *A, An,* or *The*

Function

There is **a** woman outside. She is sitting on **a** truck. **The** truck is big and old. **The** woman is young.

1. We use *a* or *an* when we talk about a person or a thing (singular count noun) for the first time. We use *the* when we talk about it for the second time.

    There is **a** woman outside. **The** woman is sitting on **a** truck.

2. We use *a* or *an* when we talk about a general, not a specific, person or thing.

    I spent **a** year in Mexico City.

3. We use *the* when the person we are speaking to knows which person or thing we are talking about.

    TED: Where's Bill?

    ANNIE: He's in **the** house.

    (Both Ted and Annie know which house they are talking about.)

4. We use *the* with count nouns (singular and plural) and noncount nouns.

    She has a truck. **The** truck is old. (singular count noun)

    I ate two cookies. **The** cookies were delicious. (plural count noun)

    We had some coffee. **The** coffee was good. (noncount noun)

26   Practice

Complete the sentences with *a*, *an*, or *the*.

A

Kelly had _____*a*_____ pain in her back, so she went to _____a_____ new
                    1   **2**

doctor that her friend recommended. _____The_____ doctor gave her _____a_____
                                              3   **4**

tablet to take every day. After _____a_____ few days, _____the_____ pain went away.
                                      5   **6**

B

I gave Lucy _____a_____ gift for her ninth birthday. It was _____a_____ box
                 1   **2**

of paints. Now she spends _____an_____ hour or more every day painting. She wants
                                3

to be _____an_____ artist one day. Yesterday, she painted _____a_____ picture of
            4   **5**

_____a_____ woman. _____The_____ painting is very good.
      6   **7**

C

I live in _____an_____ apartment in Boston. It is _____an_____ old apartment
                1   **2**

building in _____the_____ center of _____the_____ city. There is _____an_____
                  3   **4**   **5**

elevator and _____a_____ doorman at _____the_____ entrance of the building. I have
                   6   **7**

_____a_____ view from my kitchen window.
      8

D

Yesterday was _____a_____ very bad day. I had a lot of work at _____the_____
                    1   **2**

office. On the way back, I missed _____a_____ train and took _____a_____ taxi.
                                        3   **4**

When I arrived home, there was _____a_____ message from a friend on my answering
                                     5

machine. She told me to meet her at _____the a_____ restaurant at seven. She gave
                                          6

me _____the_____ name of the restaurant and its address. I went to _____the_____
         7   **8**

restaurant, but she wasn't there. I waited for _____an_____ hour and came back home.
                                                     9

I was hungry, tired, and in _____a_____ bad mood.
                                 10

4J | Generalizations

Giraffes live in Africa.
Giraffes are tall.
Giraffes have long necks.
Giraffes eat leaves.

1. We do not use *the* or *a/an* when we talk about something in general.
   Giraffes are tall.
   Diamonds are expensive.
2. We use *the* when we talk about specific things.
   The giraffes that we saw at the zoo were young.
   The diamond in your ring is beautiful.

27   Practice
Complete the sentences with *the* or X (no article).

1. Drinkable ___X___ water is more expensive than ___X___ salt in some places.

2. ___The___ water that we drink in this city is bad. I buy ___X___ water in bottles.

3. Which is more important for you, ___X___ love or ___X___ money?

4. I love ___X___ photographs, and I really like ___the___ photographs you took of Rome.

5. Do you know that ___X___ glass is made from ___X___ sand?

6. In this city, ___the/X___ museums are closed on Mondays, but ___the___ Museum of Science is open this Monday for a special exhibit.

7. It's true that ___X___ life is very difficult without ___X___ electricity.

8. Vegetarians don't eat ___X___ meat, but some eat ___X___ eggs and ___X___ cheese.

28 Practice

Complete the sentences with *the*, *a*, *an*, or *X* (no article).

John gave Linda_____X_____ flowers for her birthday. It was hot outside.
__The__ flowers looked terrible by the time he gave them to her. He also bought
_____X_____ chocolates for her. He put _____the_____ chocolates in _____the_____
car, and they were warm and soft when she opened them. Then he took her to
_____a_____ movie. _____The_____ movie was a horror film. John forgot Linda didn't
like _____X_____ horror movies. At the end of _____the_____ movie, John heard
_____a_____ scream. He thought it was _____a_____ woman in _____the_____
movie, but it was Linda.

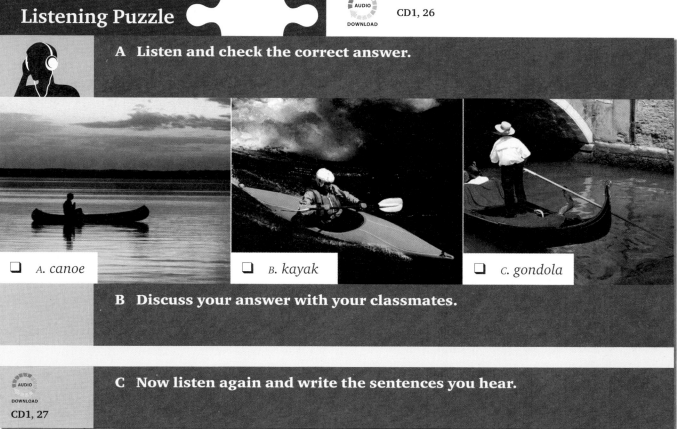

Reading Challenge

A Before You Read

Answer the questions.

1. Where do you think the Inuit live?
2. How do you think they travel today?

B Read

THE INUIT

DID YOU KNOW ... ?
The Inuit language has about 70 different kinds of words for *snow*.

The Inuit are the people who live in the Arctic Circle. This covers the coldest parts of the world such as Siberia, Alaska, Canada, and 5 Greenland. The old name for the Inuit was "Eskimo." However, this meant "eater of raw meat," and many Inuit didn't like this 10 name. They changed it to "Inuit," which means "people" in their language. One person is called an "Inuk."

In the past, the life of the Inuit was different. Men traveled and hunted for food. They 15 traveled on the snow on sleds. These sleds were pulled by dogs. The Inuit made clothes from fur and skins of animals. They lived in tents or houses made of snow called igloos.

Today, the way of life of the Inuit is 20 changing. Hunting is still important for the Inuit people, but they do not hunt as often. People still use dogsleds, but they also use snowmobiles. These run on gasoline and can go much faster than a dogsled. They buy most of 25 their clothing from shops now. These are made from **synthetic** materials. The Inuit today live in towns in houses made of wood. They build igloos only when they go out to hunt.

The Inuit in Canada wanted their own land. 30 In 1999, the Canadian government gave them a piece of land in the north of Canada. Their new land is called Nunavut. Their language, Inukitut, is the language of this new country.

C Notice the Grammar

Underline the nouns.

Choose the best answer.

D Look for Main Ideas

1. What is the main topic of paragraph 1?
   - (A) The Inuit live in the Arctic Circle.
   - (B) The Inuit changed their name.
   - (C) The coldest parts of the world are in the Arctic Circle.
   - (D) Several countries are in the Arctic Circle.

2. Paragraph 3 is mostly about _____ .
   - (A) the changes occurring in Inuit life
   - (B) the importance of hunting to the Inuit
   - (C) what Inuit clothing is made from
   - (D) how dogsleds and snowmobiles are different

E Look for Details

3. What does the word *Inuit* mean?
   - (A) hunters
   - (B) eaters of raw meat
   - (C) those who live in the cold
   - (D) people

4. Canada gave the Inuit their own _____ .
   - (A) land
   - (B) language
   - (C) money
   - (D) name

5. Life has changed in all the following ways for the Inuit EXCEPT _____ .
   - (A) they now use snowmobiles as well as dogsleds
   - (B) they now wear clothes made of synthetic materials
   - (C) they no longer hunt
   - (D) they don't live in igloos any more

Skimming is reading a passage quickly to get the main idea. Look at the title, the beginning, the end, photos or drawings, and the first sentence in each paragraph.

F Make Inferences

6. What can we infer about the Inuit people in the past?
   - (A) They needed lots of government help.
   - (B) They relied on nature for survival.
   - (C) They didn't like the areas they lived in.
   - (D) They had advanced technology.

7. We can infer from the reading that the Inuit _____ .
   - (A) don't want to change their old ways
   - (B) will soon lose their native language
   - (C) are using modern technology but are keeping some traditions
   - (D) have become completely modernized

G Look for Vocabulary

8. The word *synthetic* in the reading is closest in meaning to _____ .
   - (A) made of soft fibers
   - (B) made from things found in nature
   - (C) made by machine only
   - (D) not made from natural materials

Writing: Write a Friendly Letter

Complete a letter to a friend about a vacation.

STEP 1
Work with a partner. Think of a famous vacation place. It may be anywhere in the world. Ask and answer questions about this place. Write your answers. Answer the questions using *some, any, a lot of, much, many, a,* **and** *the*. **Ask questions like these:**

What kinds of things did you see?   What kinds of things did you eat?

What photos did you take?   What gifts or souvenirs did you buy?

STEP 2
Rewrite your answers as a paragraph to complete a letter like this one.

> *August 18, 20XX*
>
> *Dear Hamid,*
>   *You were right. Alex and I had a fantastic time at the pyramids in Egypt. Everyone should go there at least once. When we were there, we saw _____.*
>   *Thanks again for your advice. I'm telling all of my friends that they must visit the Egyptian pyramids. It was the best vacation I've ever had.*
>
> *Your friend,*
> *Julio*

STEP 3
Evaluate your paragraph.

Checklist

_____ Did you include the date at the top of the letter?

_____ Did you start with a greeting such as "Dear Hamid"?

_____ Did you indent your paragraphs?

_____ Did you describe your experiences on your vacation?

_____ Did you use articles and quantifying words like *many, much, some, any, a, an,* and *the*?

_____ Did you end with a closing and sign your name at the bottom of your letter?

STEP 4
Edit your work. Work with a partner or your teacher to edit your sentences. Correct spelling, punctuation, vocabulary, and grammar.

STEP 5
Write your final copy.

Self-Test

1. There is _____ at this time.

   A. many traffic   Ⓐ Ⓑ Ⓒ Ⓓ
   B. a lot of traffic
   C. lot of traffic
   D. traffics

2. Did you see _____ kangaroos in Australia?

   A. much   Ⓐ Ⓑ Ⓒ Ⓓ
   B. a
   C. a little
   D. any

3. We need _____ from the supermarket.

   A. a loaf of bread   Ⓐ Ⓑ Ⓒ Ⓓ
   B. a piece of bread
   C. a bread
   D. a packet of bread

4. There are _____ tourists in small towns.

   A. few   Ⓐ Ⓑ Ⓒ Ⓓ
   B. any
   C. little
   D. much

5. The price of a _____ of lettuce is going up again.

   A. piece   Ⓐ Ⓑ Ⓒ Ⓓ
   B. bar
   C. bunch
   D. head

6. It's bedtime. Can you turn off _____ ?

   A. a light   Ⓐ Ⓑ Ⓒ Ⓓ
   B. the light
   C. light
   D. lights

7. I have _____ on me.

   A. a money   Ⓐ Ⓑ Ⓒ Ⓓ
   B. few money
   C. a little money
   D. a few money

8. These are _____ toys.

   A. the children's   Ⓐ Ⓑ Ⓒ Ⓓ
   B. the children
   C. the childrens'
   D. the childrens

9. In this town, there is _____ .

   A. an university   Ⓐ Ⓑ Ⓒ Ⓓ
   B. a university
   C. the university
   D. university

10. In _____ , the police don't carry guns.

    A. some country   Ⓐ Ⓑ Ⓒ Ⓓ
    B. some countries
    C. some country's
    D. some countries'

B Find the underlined word or phrase, A, B, C, or D, that is incorrect. Darken the oval with the same letter.

1. Everyday <u>life</u> is <u>difficult</u> without <u>an</u>
        A   **B**   **C**

   <u>electricity</u>.
     D   Ⓐ Ⓑ Ⓒ Ⓓ

2. There <u>are</u> <u>a lot</u> <u>of</u> <u>sheeps</u> in New Zealand.
        A   **B** **C** **D**

               Ⓐ Ⓑ Ⓒ Ⓓ

3. Could <u>you</u> please <u>give</u> me <u>some</u> <u>advices</u>?
        A   **B**   **C**   **D**

               Ⓐ Ⓑ Ⓒ Ⓓ

4. He needs <u>any</u> <u>help with</u> <u>his</u> <u>homework</u>.
           A   **B**   **C**   **D**

               Ⓐ Ⓑ Ⓒ Ⓓ

5. <u>The grass</u> looks <u>green</u> today because <u>we got</u>
      A   **B**   **C**

   <u>any</u> rain this week.
    D   Ⓐ Ⓑ Ⓒ Ⓓ

6. <u>A</u> <u>pollution</u> is a problem in many large <u>cities</u>
   A **B**   **C**

   <u>in the United States</u>.
        D   Ⓐ Ⓑ Ⓒ Ⓓ

7. <u>Some</u> people <u>say</u> that <u>the money</u> cannot
     A   **B**   **C**

   buy <u>happiness</u>.
       D   Ⓐ Ⓑ Ⓒ Ⓓ

8. California has <u>a good weather</u>, but <u>there are</u>
                A   **B**

   <u>a lot of</u> <u>earthquakes</u>.
     C   **D**   Ⓐ Ⓑ Ⓒ Ⓓ

9. <u>Vegetarians</u> don't eat <u>meats</u>, and some don't
     A   **B**

   eat <u>eggs</u> or <u>cheese</u>.
      C   **D**   Ⓐ Ⓑ Ⓒ Ⓓ

10. Could I have <u>some</u> <u>informations</u> about
                 A   **B**

    <u>the courses</u> <u>for next semester</u>?
       C   **D**

                     Ⓐ Ⓑ Ⓒ Ⓓ

Unit 5
Pronouns

She's looking at **herself** in the mirror.

5A Subject and Object Pronouns
(**I**, **You**, **He**, **She**, **It**, **We**, and **They**; **Me**, **You**, **Him**, **Her**, **It**, **Us**, and **Them**)

5B Possessive Adjectives and Possessive Pronouns
(**My**, **Your**, **His**, **Her**, **Its**, **Our**, and **Their**; **Mine**, **Yours**, **His**, **Hers**, **Its**, **Ours**, and **Theirs**)

5C Reflexive Pronouns
(**Myself**, **Yourself**, **Himself**, **Herself**, **Itself**, **Ourselves**, **Yourselves**, and **Themselves**)

5D *Another*, *The Other*, *Other*, *Others*, and *The Others*
(**I drank another coffee. He ate the other cookie.**)

5E *One* and *Ones*
(**I like this one. She wants the other ones.**)

5F Indefinite Pronouns
(**Something**, **Somebody**, **Anything**, **Anybody**, **Everything**, **Everybody**, **Nothing**, and **Nobody**)

✦ Listening Puzzle: Extreme Sports

✦ Reading Challenge: George Washington Carver

✦ Writing: Write a Personal Description

✦ Self-Test

5A Subject and Object Pronouns

Form

> At the moment, **he** doesn't agree with **her**, and **she** doesn't agree with **him**.

1. Many sentences in English have a subject, a verb, and an object. The subject and the object can be nouns.

Subject (Noun)	Verb	Object (Noun)
Mike	plays	**football** very well.
Helena and Joe	love	**their children.**

2. We can replace nouns with pronouns.

Subject (Pronoun)	Verb	Object (Pronoun)
He	plays	**it** very well.
They	love	**them.**

3. Pronouns used as subjects are sometimes different from pronouns used as objects.

Subject Pronouns	Object Pronouns
I	me
you	you
he	him
she	her
it	it
we	us
they	them

4. A pronoun can refer to a noun or to a noun phrase (a noun + a group of words related to the noun).

Subject (Noun)	Verb	Object (Noun Phrase)	Subject (Pronoun)	Verb	Object (Pronoun)	
Lisa	drives	an old black car.	She	bought	it	last year.

5. We use object pronouns after prepositions.

Subject	Verb	Prepositional Phrase (Noun Phrase Object)	Subject (Pronoun)	Verb	Prepositional Phrase (Pronoun Object)
We	listened	to the math teacher.	We	listened	to him.

6. Remember to use the correct pronoun forms.

CORRECT:	My friends and I went to the mall.
INCORRECT:	My friends and ~~me~~ went to the mall.
CORRECT:	Sam saw my friends and me at the mall.
INCORRECT:	Sam saw my friends and ~~I~~ at the mall.
CORRECT:	I went to the mall with you and him.
INCORRECT:	I went to the mall with you and ~~he~~.

1 Practice

Complete the sentences with subject or object pronouns. Underline the word that each pronoun refers to.

1. Eddy likes <u>football</u>, but I don't like _____it_____ .

2. As for me, _____ like tennis, but Eddy doesn't like _____ .

3. Eddy's favorite movie star is Brad Buff, but I don't like _____ very much.

4. His favorite actress is Tina Lewis, but I don't like _____ .

5. My favorite movie stars are Mira Raintree and Joshua Darkly, but Eddy doesn't like _____ .

6. My friends and _____ are going shopping, but Eddy doesn't want to come with _____ .

7. Eddy likes _____ , but I don't like him. Why do I talk about _____ so much?

2 Practice

Complete the sentences with subject and object pronouns.

A

I am a student at a university. I am studying computer science. _____*It*_____
                                                                        1

is a good major. My friend Tom is taking the same courses with _____*me*_____ .
                                                                        2

_____ do our homework together in the library. I like the library. _____
        3   **4**

is a quiet place. Tom and _____*I*_____ have our final examinations next week, so we
                              5

are studying a lot.

B

I work for Mr. Kim on Saturdays. I help _____ in his store, and he pays
                                              1

_____ money. I am saving _____ to buy my girlfriend a necklace.
        2   **3**

_____ is going to be a surprise for _____ .
        4   **5**

C

My mother can't find her glasses. _____*she*_____ is looking for _____*them*_____ all
                                          1   **2**

over the house. She says she put _____*them*_____ on the table in the kitchen, and now
                                         3

_____*they*_____ are not there. She says she can't drive without _____*them*_____
       4   **5**

3 Pair Up and Talk

Ask and answer questions about two gifts you gave or received recently.

YOU:	What did you get from your father on your birthday?
YOUR PARTNER:	I got a computer from him. I love it.
YOU:	What did you give your sister for her birthday?
YOUR PARTNER:	I gave her some chocolates. She ate them in one day!

Possessive Adjectives and Possessive Pronouns

Form/Function

A: Is this **your** key?
B: No, it isn't **mine**.

Possessive Adjectives	Possessive Pronouns	Possessive Adjectives	Possessive Pronouns
my	mine	its	its*
your	yours	our	ours
his	his	their	theirs
her	hers		

*We rarely need to use the possessive pronoun *its*.

1. We put a possessive adjective before a noun. We use a possessive pronoun alone. There is no noun after it.

   This is **my** key. It's **mine**.
   That is **their** car. It's **theirs**.
   Their car is blue. **Mine** is red.

2. We use possessive adjectives and possessive pronouns to show that something belongs to somebody.

   Excuse me, is this **your** pen? OR Excuse me, is this pen **yours**?

3. Be careful when using *its/it's* and *their/they're*. They are pronounced the same, but their meanings are different.

Word	Meaning	Example
its	Possessive form of *it*	It's a great car, but I don't like **its** color.
it's	Contraction of *it is*	Where's the car? **It's** in the garage.
their	Possessive adjective of *they*	**Their** car has a flat tire.
they're	Contraction of *they are*	**They're** getting it fixed now.
there	Shows location	The car is in the garage. It's safe **there**.
	Shows existence	**There** is a problem with my car.

4 Practice

Underline the correct word. Then listen to check your answers.

CD1, 28

A

PAOLO: Is this (<u>your</u>/yours) wallet?
1

LILLIAN: No, it's not (mine/my). I thought it was (your/yours).
2   3

PAOLO: No, I have (my/<u>mine</u>) in my pocket. Maybe (its/it's) Ingrid's.
4   5

LILLIAN: If it is (her/hers), she will be very worried. She went to the airport with
6

(her/hers) husband. (They're/Their) going to Canada to visit
7   8

(her/hers) parents.
9

B

(Our/Ours) television is not working. (Our/Ours) neighbors have an extra television, and
1   2
(they're/there) going to give (it/its) to (us/we). We have to fix (our/ours) or get a new one.
3   4   5   6
(They're/Their) expensive, you know. Our neighbors don't mind, so we may watch
7
(theirs/their) for a long time.
8

C

The Parkers are (our/ours) neighbors. (They're/Their) very rich. They have two cars in
1   2
(theirs/their) garage, and the Porsche parked in front of (our/ours) house is (their/theirs),
3   4   5
too. Everybody thinks (its/it's) (our/ours), but (our/<u>ours</u>) is an old Honda. We park it in
6   7   8
front of (our/ours) other neighbor's house. We like to leave it (their/there).
9   10

5 Pair Up and Talk

Talk about your favorite things or people. Use pronouns and possessive adjectives, but do not say the name. Your partner guesses.

YOU: I first saw it on TV. Its color is red. I bought it in July.
YOUR PARTNER: It's your car.
YOU: Right!

5C Reflexive Pronouns

Form

She's looking at **herself** in the mirror.

Subject Pronouns	Reflexive Pronouns	Subject Pronouns	Reflexive Pronouns
I	myself	it	itself
you (singular)	yourself	we	ourselves
he	himself	you (plural)	yourselves
she	herself	they	themselves

Function

1. We use reflexive pronouns as objects when the subject and the object of the verb or preposition refer to the same person or thing.

Subject	Verb	Object
She	hurt	**herself**.
The machine	can't work	by **itself**.

2. Reflexive pronouns often come after these verbs and phrases.

be proud of	enjoy	take care of
behave	help*	talk to
burn	hurt	teach
cut	introduce	work for

* If you *help yourself to something*, it means "serve yourself something." For example, "Help yourself to the potatoes."

I cut myself while I was shaving.
Did you enjoy yourself at the party?
Sue taught herself how to cook.

3. We use the reflexive pronoun with the preposition *by* when we mean "alone" or "without any help."

    Lillian painted the bathroom **by herself**.

    He sits **by himself** for hours.

4. We do not usually see reflexive pronouns with verbs such as *dress*, *wash*, and *shave*. But we can use these verbs with a reflexive pronoun if we want to show that someone did something unusual or with a lot of effort.

    I got up, **dressed**, and went to work.

    Timmy is only three years old, but he can **dress himself**.

6 Practice

Complete the sentences with the correct reflexive pronoun.

1. A: What a beautiful dress! Where did you buy it?

    B: I made it __*myself.*__

2. A: Who painted your house?

    B: We painted it __ourselves__

3. A: Could you wash this shirt for me?

    B: No, you'll have to wash it __yourselves__

4. A: Did Pablo get some help with his homework?

    B: No, he did it __himself__

5. A: Tom and I are going to Min's party.

    B: OK. Enjoy __yourselves__

6. A: Do you want me to turn off the iron?

    B: No, it will turn _____ off automatically.

AUDIO
DOWNLOAD

CD1, 29

7 Practice

Johnnie is five and Jenny is seven. They are alone in the kitchen. Listen and underline the correct answer to complete each sentence.

1. a. himself   b. themselves
2. a. himself   b. herself
3. a. myself   b. himself
4. a. herself   b. yourself
5. a. himself   b. herself
6. a. ourselves   b. themselves

8 Read

Read the story. Then write answers to the questions.

THE MAN AND HIS TWO WIVES

In the old days, when men could have many wives, a middle-aged man had two wives. One wife was old and one wife was young. Each wife loved him very much and wanted to see him like herself.

Now the man's hair was turning gray. The young wife didn't like this because it made him look too old for her husband. So every night she used to comb his hair and pick out the gray hairs. But the older wife saw her husband growing gray with great pleasure because she didn't want to be mistaken for his mother. So every morning she used to arrange his hair and pick out as many black hairs as she could.

The result was that the man soon found himself to be completely bald[1].

[1] bald = without hair on the head

1. How old was the man?
2. What was the difference between the two wives?
3. What did each wife like to see the husband as?
4. Why didn't the young wife like his gray hair?
5. What did she do?
6. Why did the older wife like his gray hair?
7. Which hairs did she pick out?
8. How did the man find himself to be in the end?

_____
_____
_____
_____
_____
_____
_____
_____

5D Another, The Other, Other, Others, and The Others

Form

These cookies are good.
Can I have **another**?

1. We use *another* and *the other* as adjectives before nouns.

	Adjective	Noun
Oliver ate	**another**	cookie.
Melanie ate	**the other**	cookie.

2. We use *another* and *the other* as pronouns.

	Pronoun
Jorge ate	**another**.
Toshi ate	**the other**.

3. We use the adjective *other* (with no -*s*) with a plural noun.

	Adjective	Noun
There are	**other**	**cookies** in the box.
I like		**kinds** of cookies.

4. We use the pronoun *others* (with -*s*) when there is no noun that follows.

	Pronoun	
There are	**others***	on the plate.

* others = other cookies

Function

1. *Another* means one "more of the same thing (or the same group) we had before."

   These cookies are good. Can I have **another**? (one more of the same cookies)
2. *The other* means "the one that is left of the same thing."

   There are two pieces of chocolate left. I'll take one and you take **the other**.
3. *Other* and *others* mean "several more of the same group. *The others* means the ones left of the same group."

   There are **other** cookies in the box.

   There are **others** in the box.

   These cookies have nuts in them. **The others** have coconut.

9 Practice
Complete the sentences with *another* or *the other*.

1. One country in Europe is France. ___*Another*___ is Italy.
2. There are two countries I want to visit. One is France, and ___other___ is Italy.
3. Paris is a city in Europe. Rome is ___another___ city in Europe.
4. In France, people speak French. Belgium is ___another___ country where people speak French.
5. There are three European countries where people speak French. One is France, ___another___ is Belgium, and ___the others___ is Switzerland.
6. Paris is a beautiful city in Europe. Prague is ___another___ beautiful city in Europe.

10 Practice
Complete the sentences with *other*, *others*, or *the others*.

1. Baseball is a popular sport. ___*Others*___ are basketball and football.
2. There are three popular team sports at this school. One is baseball. ___the other___ are basketball and football.
3. Some sports are team sports like football. ___Others___, like tennis, are not team sports.
4. There are many kinds of water on the earth. Oceans are one kind. Some _____ kinds are seas, lakes, and rivers.

11   Practice
Complete the sentences with *another*, *other*, *the other*, *others*,
or *the others*.

1. Our teacher was absent today, so ___*another*___ teacher came in her place.

2. I wasn't happy because I like our usual teacher, but all of ___the other___ students in my class were happy.

3. Our usual teacher always gives us homework, but ___the other___ teacher didn't.

4. Some students talk a lot in class. ___others___ don't, and a few rarely talk.

5. After we finished our exercises in class, she gave us a few ___another___ to do for homework.

6. A few of us understood the lesson, but some ___others___ didn't.

7. Some students always ask the teacher questions. All of ___the others___ keep quiet.

8. Most teachers tell students to write their essays on the computer. ___Another___ teachers want hand-written essays. Some teachers will accept both.

5E   *One* and *Ones*

Form/Function

| MAN: | Do you like this red shirt? |
| WOMAN: | No, I like this **one**. |

1. We use the pronoun *one* in the singular and *ones* in the plural so that we do not repeat the noun.
    Do you like the red tie?
    No, I like the blue **one** (tie).
    I never wear brown shoes. I always wear black **ones** (shoes).

2. *One/Ones* and *some/any* are indefinite (like the article *a*). *It* and *they/them* refer to something definite (like the article *the*).

> I don't have a passport. I need **one**.
> I don't have any envelopes. I need **some**.
> I have my passport. I received **it** yesterday.
> I have envelopes. I bought **them** yesterday.

AUDIO

DOWNLOAD

CD1, 30

12 Practice

Complete the sentences with *one, ones, some, it,* or *them*. Then listen to check your answers.

1. I'm sorry, but I broke this glass. I dropped _____ *it* _____ .
2. I'm making a sandwich. Would you like _____ one _____ , too?
3. If you need change for the parking meter, I have _____ some _____ .
4. She bought some cookies and ate all of _____ them _____ .
5. I am throwing away the old magazines and keeping the new _____ ones _____ .
6. We need to call a taxi. I'll call for _____ one _____ .

5F Indefinite Pronouns

Form

This is strange. There's **something** wrong. The door is open.
I don't hear **anything**, and there isn't **anybody** in the house.

	Affirmative Sentences	Negative Sentences	Questions
People	someone/somebody	anyone/anybody	anyone/anybody
	no one/nobody		no one/nobody
	everyone/everybody		everyone/everybody
Things	something	anything	anything/something
	nothing		nothing
	everything		everything
Places	somewhere	anywhere	anywhere/somewhere
	everywhere		everywhere

1. We use *someone/somebody* (a person), *something* (a thing), and *somewhere* (a place) in affirmative statements.

   I met **somebody** new today. He lives **somewhere** near the airport.

2. Indefinite pronouns are always singular.

   Nobody wants to miss the sale next week. **Everything** in the store is on sale.

3. We use *anyone/anybody*, *anything*, and *anywhere* for questions and negative statements.

   Is there **anybody** here? I can't hear **anything**.

4. We can use *no one/nobody*, *nothing*, and *nowhere* in place of *not anyone/anybody*, *not anything*, and *not anywhere*.

   There isn't **anybody** in the house. OR There is **nobody** in the house.

5. We use the adjective *every* with singular count nouns.

   Every student must take the test. (*Every student* means "all the students.")

6. We use the pronouns *everyone/everybody*, *everything*, and the adverb *everywhere* in affirmative statements and questions. We use a singular verb with these pronouns.

   Is everybody there?

   Yes, **everybody is** here, but **everything is not** ready for the party.

Function

1. Unlike the other pronouns, indefinite pronouns do not take the place of a noun or a noun phrase.

2. We use indefinite pronouns with *some* and *any* to talk about an unknown person, place, or thing.

   I saw **someone** take your jacket. (I don't know who took it.)

   I put my glasses **somewhere**, and now I can't find them. (I don't know where I put them.)

3. We use indefinite pronouns with *every* to talk about all people, places, or things that we are talking about.

   We invited **everyone** to the party.

   They didn't buy **everything** they wanted.

13　Practice
Underline the correct word in parentheses.

BEN:　I lost my grammar book yesterday. I left it (<u>somewhere</u>/anywhere).
1

LEE:　Did you look in the classroom?

BEN:　Yes, I did. It wasn't there. It isn't (everywhere/anywhere).
2

LEE:　Did you ask (anyone/nobody)?
3

BEN:　Yes, I asked my teacher, and I asked (everyone/anyone) in my class.
4

LEE:　Don't worry. You can share a book with (someone/anyone) in the class tomorrow.
5

BEN:　But I don't want to share a book with (anyone/someone). I want my book. I have all
6

the answers in it.

Listening Puzzle

AUDIO DOWNLOAD　CD1, 31

A　Listen and check the correct answer.

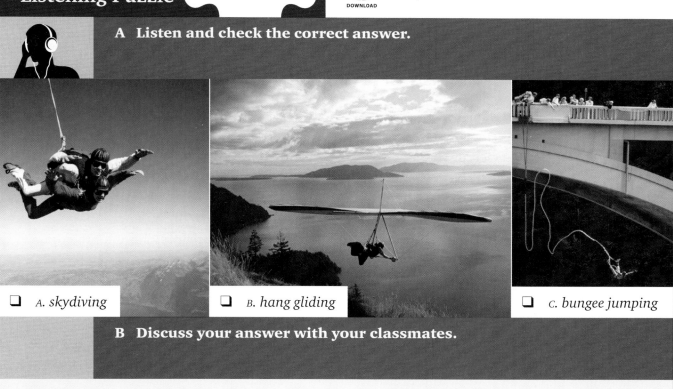

❑　*A. skydiving*

❑　*B. hang gliding*

❑　*C. bungee jumping*

B　Discuss your answer with your classmates.

AUDIO DOWNLOAD
CD1, 32

C　Now listen again and write the sentences you hear.

Reading Challenge

A Before You Read

Answer the questions.

1. George Washington Carver was a scientist. What other famous scientists do you know?
2. Look at the photo. What kind of scientific research do you think he did?

B Read

GEORGE WASHINGTON CARVER

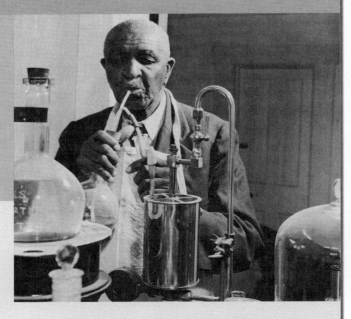

George Washington Carver was born a slave in 1861, but soon his parents died. Susan and Moses Carver were his owners, and they raised George. Slaves often took
5 the names of their owners, so George Washington's last name was Carver. The law stopped slavery in 1865, but George continued to
10 live with the Carvers. The Carvers taught him to read and write. At age 12, George left the Carvers and started life on his own.

George went to high school and then to college. He worked and saved money to go
15 to school. He studied agriculture at Iowa Agricultural College. He was the only black student there, and everybody admired him for his research on plants. After he graduated, the college asked him to teach there. Carver taught
20 at the college and continued with his research.

> **DID YOU KNOW ... ?**
> George Washington Carver invented peanut butter.

A few years later, Carver decided to teach at Tuskegee Institute. This was a poor black agricultural school in Alabama. He didn't get a high salary, and he didn't have a laboratory
25 to work in, but he liked it there. He taught agriculture and showed farmers how to grow new **crops** to make more money.

He found more than 300 uses for the peanut. He became known as the "peanut man." He
30 received many prizes for his work. He also found more than 100 uses for the sweet potato.

Carver became famous all over the world, but he continued to work at Tuskegee Institute. When he died in 1943, he left all his savings to
35 Tuskegee Institute.

C Notice the Grammar

Underline all possessive adjectives and indefinite pronouns.

Choose the best answer.

D Look for Main Ideas

1. What is the main idea of paragraph 1?
   - (A) Susan and Moses Carver taught George Washington Carver to read and write.
   - (B) George Washington Carver was born a slave.
   - (C) The Carvers raised George Washington Carver in their home.
   - (D) Carver lived on his own at an early age.

2. Paragraph 4 is mainly about _____ .
   - (A) the prizes that Carver won
   - (B) the gift that Carver left to Tuskegee Institute
   - (C) the things that Carver accomplished
   - (D) why Carver was known as the "peanut man"

E Look for Details

3. When did slavery end?
   - (A) when Carver was born
   - (B) in 1865
   - (C) when Carver was 12
   - (D) after Carver died

4. At Tuskegee Institute, Carver _____ .
   - (A) worked in a laboratory
   - (B) was the only black student
   - (C) made a lot of money
   - (D) taught agriculture

5. What did Carver do after he graduated?
   - (A) He worked at Tuskegee Institute.
   - (B) He found many uses for the peanut.
   - (C) He left Tuskegee Institute.
   - (D) He taught at Iowa Agricultural College.

READING SKILL:
Scanning

Scanning is reading quickly to find a specific piece of information like a date or place. We move our eyes quickly over the passage. It is not necessary to read the whole passage carefully.

F Make Inferences

6. What can we infer about Susan and Moses Carver?
   - (A) They were kind people.
   - (B) They liked to read.
   - (C) They were slaves, too.
   - (D) They were old.

7. Carver went to teach at Tuskegee Institute. What can we infer from that?
   - (A) Tuskegee Institute was very famous.
   - (B) Carver liked to help poor black people.
   - (C) Carver wanted to do research on plants.
   - (D) Tuskegee was a better school than Iowa Agricultural College.

G Look for Vocabulary

8. The word *crops* in the reading is closest in meaning to _____ .
   - (A) plants used as food
   - (B) flowers
   - (C) wheat products
   - (D) green vegetables

Writing: Write a Personal Description

Write a description of your best friend.

STEP **1** Think about your best friend. Write the answers to the following questions. Then think of other things to say about your friend. Share your answers with a partner.

1. What is your friend's name?
2. Does your friend have any brothers or sisters?
3. What does your friend do?

4. What does your friend like?
5. What does your friend dislike?
6. What do you do together?
7. Why do you like your friend?

STEP **2** Rewrite your answers in paragraph form. Write a title in a few words (My Best Friend).

My Best Friend

My best friend's name is Isabel. She has two sisters. She loves them very much. Isabel takes care of herself ...

STEP **3** Evaluate your paragraph.

Checklist

_____ Did you indent the first line?

_____ Did you give your paragraph a title?

_____ Did you put the title at the top center of the page?

STEP **4** Edit your work. Work with a partner or your teacher to edit your sentences. Correct spelling, punctuation, vocabulary, and grammar.

STEP **5** Write your final copy.

Self-Test

A Choose the best answer, A, B, C, or D, to complete the sentence. Darken the oval with the same letter.

1. Is this _____ suitcase?

   A. hers   Ⓐ Ⓑ Ⓒ Ⓓ
   B. her
   C. her's
   D. she's

2. Oh no! Our teacher is giving us _____ test this week.

   A. other   Ⓐ Ⓑ Ⓒ Ⓓ
   B. the another
   C. another
   D. another one

3. SUE: I like your shoes.
   PAM: These are _____ I bought in Italy.

   A. the one   Ⓐ Ⓑ Ⓒ Ⓓ
   B. the ones
   C. others
   D. ones

4. There isn't a drugstore _____ !

   A. anywhere   Ⓐ Ⓑ Ⓒ Ⓓ
   B. anything
   C. nothing
   D. somewhere

5. I don't have my credit card. I left _____ at the store.

   A. one   Ⓐ Ⓑ Ⓒ Ⓓ
   B. them
   C. it
   D. some

6. I left _____ homework at home.

   A. mine   Ⓐ Ⓑ Ⓒ Ⓓ
   B. my
   C. myself
   D. me

7. The children enjoyed _____ at Disney World, but their parents didn't.

   A. theirselves   Ⓐ Ⓑ Ⓒ Ⓓ
   B. theyselves
   C. them
   D. themselves

8. There _____ to park on this street.

   A. is anywhere   Ⓐ Ⓑ Ⓒ Ⓓ
   B. isn't somewhere
   C. isn't nowhere
   D. isn't anywhere

9. I need a quarter. Do you have _____ ?

   A. one   Ⓐ Ⓑ Ⓒ Ⓓ
   B. quarter
   C. it
   D. a

10. That is _____ .

    A. ours car   Ⓐ Ⓑ Ⓒ Ⓓ
    B. our car
    C. car ours
    D. ourselves car

B Find the underlined word or phrase, A, B, C, or D, that is incorrect. Darken the oval with the same letter.

1. <u>Some</u> teachers can remember all of <u>the</u>
   A   B
   <u>student</u> <u>names</u>.
   C   D

   Ⓐ Ⓑ Ⓒ Ⓓ

2. If you don't like <u>your</u> job, <u>you can</u> look for
                      A   B
   <u>other</u> <u>one</u>.
   C   D

   Ⓐ Ⓑ Ⓒ Ⓓ

3. <u>Nobody</u> mentioned <u>the</u> problem
   A   B
   <u>to</u> <u>ourselves</u>. *themselves*
   C   D

   Ⓐ Ⓑ Ⓒ Ⓓ

4. We took <u>our</u> little sister with <u>us</u> because she
           A   B
   doesn't like to stay home <u>by</u> <u>ourself</u>.
                             C   D

   Ⓐ Ⓑ Ⓒ Ⓓ

5. I didn't buy <u>the</u> shirt because I have <u>one</u>
                A   B
   just like <u>her</u> in <u>another</u> color.
             C   D

   Ⓐ Ⓑ Ⓒ Ⓓ

6. Only two of the <u>questions</u> on <u>the</u> exam
                   A   B
   were easy. <u>Others</u> were <u>difficult</u>.
              C   D

   Ⓐ Ⓑ Ⓒ Ⓓ

7. There are two very popular <u>cities</u>
                             A
   <u>in the United States</u>. <u>One</u> is New York,
   B   C
   and <u>another</u> is San Francisco.
       D

   Ⓐ Ⓑ Ⓒ Ⓓ

8. In a multiple choice question, <u>one</u> of the
                                  A
   <u>choices</u> is correct, and <u>others</u> <u>are</u> incorrect.
   B   C   D

   Ⓐ Ⓑ Ⓒ Ⓓ

9. We looked at <u>my</u> old <u>videos</u> last night, and we
                A   B
   enjoyed <u>themselves</u> <u>a lot</u>.
           C   D

   Ⓐ Ⓑ Ⓒ Ⓓ

10. <u>Our friend</u> is in the hospital because he burned
    A
    <u>himself</u> by accident, so <u>we</u> visited <u>himself</u>
    B   C   D
    last night.

    Ⓐ Ⓑ Ⓒ Ⓓ

Unit 6

The Present and Past Perfect

Carrie **has been waiting** for 45 minutes.

6A The Present Perfect
(I have visited the United States.)

6B *For* and *Since*
(I have lived here since 2007. I have studied English for three years.)

6C *Ever* and *Never*
(Have you ever been to the White House? No, I have never been.)

6D *Already*, *Yet*, and *Just*
(I've just gotten my grades. They haven't left yet.)

6E The Simple Past OR The Present Perfect
(I have been to Hollywood. OR I went there in 2006.)

6F The Present Perfect Progressive
(I've been waiting since yesterday.)

6G The Present Perfect OR The Present Perfect Progressive
(I have just arrived. OR I have been working since nine o'clock.)

6H The Past Perfect
(I bought a car when I had saved enough money.)

6I The Past Perfect Progressive
(He had been teaching for 20 years.)

✦ Listening Puzzle: Races

✦ Reading Challenge: Penicillin

✦ Writing: Write a Friendly Email

✦ Self-Test

6A The Present Perfect

Form

Jim and his mother, Sofia, are in New York. They **have visited** many places. They **have seen** the Statue of Liberty. They **have gone** up to the top of the Empire State Building, and **they've been** to Central Park.

1. We use the past participle verb form in the present perfect. The past participle form of regular verbs is the same as the simple past form.

Simple Past Form	Past Participle
washed	washed
finished	finished

2. The past participle of irregular verbs is often different from the simple past form.

Simple Past Form	Past Participle	Simple Past Form	Past Participle
ate	eaten	saw	seen
came	come	spoke	spoken
did	done	took	taken
drank	drunk	was	been
knew	known	went	gone

3. We form the present perfect with *have* or *has* + the past participle of the verb.

Affirmative and Negative Statements		
Subject	**Have/Has (Not)**	**Past Participle**
I You	**have** **'ve** **have not** **'ve not** **haven't**	
He/She/It	**has** **'s** **has not** **'s not** **hasn't**	**arrived.**
We They	**have** **'ve** **have not** **'ve not** **haven't**	

Yes/No Questions			Short Answers	
Have/Has	**Subject**	**Past Participle**	**Yes,**	**No,**
Have	I		you **have.**	you **haven't.**
	you		I/we **have.**	I/we **haven't.**
Has	he/she/it	**arrived?**	he/she/it **has.**	he/she/it **hasn't.**
Have	we		you **have.**	you **haven't.**
	they		they **have.**	they **haven't.**

Wh- Questions				
Wh- Word	*Have/Has*	**Subject**	**Past Participle**	
Who*	**has**	she	**spoken**	to?
What	**have**	you	**made**	for lunch?
Where	**have**	they	**been?**	
Why	**has**	the music	**stopped?**	
How many **(movies)**	**have**	we	**seen**	this year?
How long	**have**	you	**been**	ill?

*In formal written English, the *wh-* word would be *whom*.

Function

1. We use the present perfect for an action or situation that happened at some unspecified time in the past. The exact time is not important. The action or situation has importance in the present.

    They**'ve been** to New York. (We're talking about their experiences as of *now*.)

    I**'ve washed** the car. (It's clean *now*.)

    He **hasn't done** his homework. (We're talking about the situation *now*.)

2. We can also use the present perfect to talk about actions that were repeated in the past. The exact time is not stated or important.

    We**'ve taken** two tests this month.

    I**'ve been** to New York three times.

3. We often use the present perfect with the time expressions *for, since, just, already, yet, recently,* and *how long.*

    Lin **has lived** here **since** 1999.

    I **have known** you **for** three years.

---

1 Practice

Complete the postcard that Jim wrote to his friend Brian. Use the present perfect of the verbs in parentheses.

Dear Brian,

    We (be) __have been__ in New York for four days.
             1
We (go) _____ to the Empire State Building,
          2
we (see) _____ the Statue of Liberty, and
          3
we (walk) _____ in Central Park. We (eat)
          4
_____ great food, and we (buy) _____
  5   6
tickets for a Broadway show. We still (not, visit)

_____ the Metropolitan Museum of Art,
  7
but we are going there tomorrow. Mom (come)

_____ back from shopping, so I'll close now.
  8
Jim

Mr. Brian Shih

4125 E. 25th Rd.

Phoenix, AZ 86000

_____

2 Practice

Listen and underline the correct answer to each question.

CD2, 2

1. a. <u>Yes, they have.</u> b. No, they haven't.
2. a. Yes, they have. b. No, they haven't.
3. a. Yes, they have. b. No, they haven't.

4. a. Yes, he has. b. No, he hasn't.
5. a. Yes, they have. b. No, they haven't.
6. a. Yes, they have. b. No, they haven't.

3 Pair Up and Talk

Work with a partner. Ask and answer questions with the prompts about what Sofia and Jim have done in New York.

Sofia and Jim/arrive in New York

YOU: Have Sofia and Jim arrived in New York?

YOUR PARTNER: Yes, they have.

1. they/walk/in Central Park
2. they/see/the Statue of Liberty
3. they/go/to the Empire State Building
4. they/eat/good food

5. they/buy/tickets for a Broadway show
6. they/visit/the Metropolitan Museum of Art

4 Practice

Complete the conversation with *wh-* or *yes/no* questions in the present perfect. Then listen to check your answers.

CD2, 3

SUE: I haven't seen Sofia and Jim all week. Where are they?

PETE: You didn't know? They've gone away on vacation.

SUE: Really! <u>*Where have they gone?*</u>
                                          1

PETE: They've gone to New York.

SUE: How long _____
                                                2

PETE: They've been in New York for four days now.

SUE: _____ in any interesting restaurants?
                                                3

PETE: Oh, yes. They've eaten in Chinese, Korean, Greek, and Indian restaurants.

SUE: _____
                                                4

PETE: No, but they're going to visit the Metropolitan Museum of Art tomorrow.

The Present and Past Perfect   **125**

5 Practice

Armando's roommate, Daniel, is a problem. Complete the dialogue with the present perfect of the verbs in parentheses. Then listen to check your answers.

CD2, 4

ARMANDO: Daniel, I'm sorry, but it's time for you to find another place to live.

DANIEL: Why? What's wrong?

ARMANDO: What's wrong? You (be) __*have been*__ a terrible roommate.

1

For example, today you (eat) _____ my food and you (break)

2

_____ my CD player.

3

DANIEL: Don't be so sensitive, Armando. I'll replace those things for you.

ARMANDO: That's not all. You (not, pay) _____ the rent for two months. You

4

(insult) _____ my sister, and you (try) _____ to steal my

5   6

girlfriend. I (be) _____ very patient, but now I want you to go.

7

DANIEL: Well, OK. I'll leave if you want. But … um, I (spend) _____ all my

8

money. Could you lend me $500?

6 Practice

Complete the conversation with the present perfect of the verbs in parentheses. Then ask a partner what he or she has done today.

MARCO: What things (do) __*have*__ you __*done*__ up to now?

1   2

TINA: Lots of things. I (wash) _____ the dishes, and I (make)

3

_____ the bed. I (go) _____ shopping. What about you?

4   5

MARCO: I (do) _____ my homework, and I (clean) _____ my room.

6   7

And … oh, yes. I (have) _____ lunch.

8

7 Pair Up and Talk

Think of five things to do or places to see in the town where you are now. Ask your partner what he or she has done in your town.

YOU: Have you been to the cathedral?

YOUR PARTNER: Yes, I have. Have you been to the zoo?

YOU: No, I haven't. Have you visited the art museum?

6B | *For* and *Since*

Function

This house has been here **since** 1925.
My grandmother has lived here **for** 50 years.

1. We use *for* with the present perfect when we are talking about a period or length of time that started in the past and continues to the present.

   I've lived here **for** three years.

2. We use *since* with the present perfect when we are talking about a point of time in the past such as a date, a month, or a day.

   I've worked here **since** August.

   She's been sick **since** Tuesday.

8 Practice
Some of these time expressions are used with *for*. Others are used with *since*.
Put them in the correct list.

2003	about a week	I moved here	six hours
30 seconds	eight o'clock	I was a child	ten minutes
a long time	Friday evening	last summer	two months

I have been here for...

a long time
30 seconds
about a week
six hours
ten minutes
two month

I have been here since...

2003
last summer
Friday evening
eight o'clock
I move here
I was a child

9 Practice

Complete the sentences with *for* or *since*.

1. Rob has had his car _____*for*_____ a year, but he wants to sell it.

2. He's had problems with it _____ the day he bought it.

3. It has made a funny noise _____ several weeks.

4. He has taken it to a mechanic six times _____ June.

5. He has run an ad in the newspaper every day _____ a week.

6. So far, he hasn't had a response _____ he ran the ad.

10 Pair Up and Talk

Work with a partner. Ask questions with *how long* and the verbs.
Your partner answers the questions using *for* or *since*.

YOU: How long have you lived in this country?
YOUR PARTNER: I have lived here for eight months.

be	know	own	study
have	live	speak	work

6C   *Ever* and *Never*

Form/Function

A: Have you **ever** seen the Taj Mahal?
B: No, **never**.

1 We can use *ever* in questions, often with the present perfect. It means "at any time up to now."

2 In present perfect questions, *ever* comes between the subject and the past participle.

Have you **ever** been to China?

3. We often use *never* (at no time) when we give a negative answer.

No, I've **never** been to China.

AUDIO DOWNLOAD

CD2, 5

11 Practice

Interview the famous movie star La La Labore. Write questions with the prompts and give short answers. Then listen to check your answers.

1. ever be/married _____*Have you ever been married?*_____

    Yes, ___*I have.*___ I've been married eight times.

2. ever be/to Hollywood _____

    Yes, _____ I've been there many times.

3. ever drive/a Ferrari _____

    No, _____ I never drive. I have a chauffeur.

4. ever give/an interview on television _____

    Yes, _____ I've given interviews to famous journalists.

5. ever write/a book _____

    No, _____ Other people write about me.

6. ever sing/in a movie _____

    No, _____ I can't sing.

12 Pair Up and Talk

Work with a partner. Ask questions with *have you ever* and the prompts.

YOU: Have you ever flown in a helicopter?
YOUR PARTNER: Yes, I have. OR No, I never have. OR No, never.

drive a truck	hold a snake	speak to a famous person
fly in a helicopter	meet a millionaire	take a photo of a lion
go to Hawaii	play baseball	tell a lie
have the flu	sleep in a tent	travel by boat

THE FOX AND THE CROW

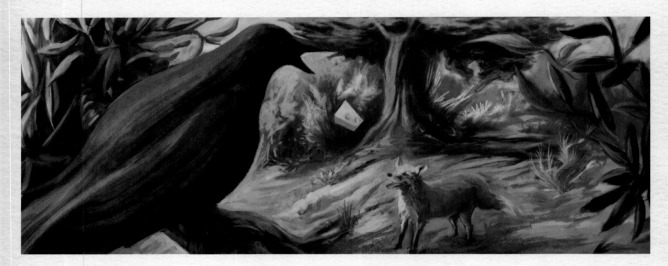

A big black crow is sitting high up in the trees. In her beak is a piece of cheese. A clever fox comes along and thinks, "Mm, that cheese looks good. It will be easy to get some."

"Oh, Crow," calls the fox. "How well you look today. Your feathers are so glossy and your eyes are so bright. I feel sure you can sing better than the other birds; let me hear one song from you, and I will call you Queen of Birds."

The crow has never heard anyone say such a compliment. So she opens her beak and begins to sing. But as she does this, the piece of cheese falls into the the fox's mouth.

"Oh, no!" says the crow. "You've stolen my dinner."

"No, I haven't," says the fox. "It's a fair trade! You've gotten the compliments, and I've gotten the cheese!"

1. _____ ?   The fox has seen a crow high up in the trees.
2. _____ ?   The crow has a piece of cheese.
3. _____ ?   The fox says he wants the crow to sing, and he will call her Queen of Birds.
4. _____ ?   The fox really wants the crow to sing because he wants the cheese to fall down.
5. _____ ?   The crow begins to sing because she has never heard anyone say such a compliment.
6. _____ ?   The piece of cheese falls into the fox's mouth.
7. _____ ?   It is a fair trade for the fox because the crow got the compliments, and he got the cheese.

6D | *Already, Yet, and Just*

Form/Function

They've **just** gotten married.
They've **already** had a ceremony.
They haven't gone on their honeymoon **yet**.

1. We use *yet* in negative sentences to say that something has not happened, but we think it will. *Yet* comes at the end of the sentence.

   The plane hasn't arrived **yet**.

2. We also use *yet* in questions to ask if something we expect to happen has happened.

   Has the plane arrived **yet**?

3. We use *just* if the action is very recent. *Just* comes before the past participle.

   I've **just** spoken to Tony.

4. We use *already* to say something happened before now or before it was expected to happen. *Already* comes before the past participle.

   I've **already** told you how to get there.

14 Practice

A Carlos and Rosa are in San Francisco on vacation. It's their last day. Read this list of things they want to do today. They have already done some of these things, but they haven't done others yet. A check mark (✔) shows what they have already done.

1. ✔ get postcards
2. write postcards
3. have lunch
4. ✔ visit the Museum of Modern Art
5. ✔ see a show

6. buy souvenirs
7. ask the hotel for the bill
8. ✔ pack the suitcases
9. go to the post office
10. call the airline

1. <u>*They've already gotten postcards.*</u>
2. <u>*They haven't written postcards yet.*</u>
3. _____
4. _____
5. _____
6. _____
7. _____
8. _____
9. _____
10. _____

15   Your Turn

Write a list of things you do every day. Then write sentences about things you've recently done and things you haven't done yet today.

Example

exercise	*I've already exercised.*
eat breakfast	*I've just eaten breakfast.*
do my homework	*I haven't done my homework yet.*

1. _____
2. _____
3. _____
4. _____
5. _____

16   Pair Up and Talk

Work with a partner. Read each other's lists from Practice 15. Ask and answer questions about what you've done and haven't done.

YOU: Have you exercised yet?

YOUR PARTNER: Yes, I've already exercised.

Function

Antonia Beck **has been** to Turkey.
She **went** there in 2001.

1. We use the simple past when we are talking about the past. We use it for actions that happened in the past. We can state the specific time of the action.
   She **went** to Turkey in July 2001. After a month, she **went** to Athens.
2. We use the simple past for an action that started and finished in the past.
   George **had** a headache for two hours this morning. (He's doesn't have a headache now.)
3. We use the present perfect for an action that happened in the past. The action has importance in the present. The specific time is unimportant, and we cannot state it.
   CORRECT: Antonia **has been** to Turkey.
   INCORRECT: Antonia **has been** to Turkey ~~in 2001~~.
4. We use the present perfect for an action that started in the past and is still continuing in the present.
   George **has had** a headache for two hours. (He still has a headache.)

AUDIO
DOWNLOAD

CD2, 6

17   Practice
Complete the sentences with the simple past or present perfect of the verbs in parentheses. Then listen to check your answers.

1.   A: I (see) _____ saw _____ Karen yesterday.

     B: Oh, really? I (not, see) _____ her for weeks.

2.   A: What (do) _____ you _____ last Saturday?

     B: I (stay)_____ at home.

3. A: (write) _____ you _____ your essay yet?

   B: Yes, I (finish)_____ it an hour ago.

4. A: (be) _____ you _____ to the United States?

   B: Yes, I (go) _____ to Miami last summer.

18   Pair Up and Talk

Antonia Beck has made a lot of business trips in the last few years.
Work with a partner to ask and answer questions about which cities
she has visited and when she went there. Use the simple past and the
present perfect.

YOU: Has she been to New York?
YOUR PARTNER: Yes, she has. She went there in May 2005.

Student A	Student B
Question	Answer
1. New York	yes/May 2005
2. Bangkok	yes/March 2004
3. Paris	no
4. Tokyo	yes/August 2007
5. Chicago	yes/May 2007
6. Seoul	no

Student B	Student A
Question	Answer
7. Boston	yes/May 2006
8. Mexico City	yes/January 2008
9. Istanbul	no
10. Cairo	yes/April 2006
11. Jakarta	yes/December 2005
12. Rio de Janeiro	no

6F The Present Perfect Progressive

Form

Carrie **has been waiting** for 45 minutes.

We form the present perfect progressive with *have/has* + the past participle of *be* (*been*) + verb + *-ing*.

Affirmative and Negative Statements			
Subject	**Have/Has (Not)**	**Been**	**Verb + -ing**
I	have (not) 've (not) haven't		
You		been	waiting.
He/She/It	has (not) 's (not) hasn't		
We	have (not) 've (not) haven't		
They			

Yes/No Questions				Short Answers	
Have/Has	**Subject**	**Been**	**Verb + -ing**	**Yes,**	**No,**
Have	I			you **have.**	you **haven't.**
	you			I/we **have.**	I/we **haven't.**
Has	he/she/it	been	waiting?	he/she/it **has.**	he/she/it **hasn't.**
Have	we			you **have.**	you **haven't.**
	they			they **have.**	they **haven't.**

We use the present perfect progressive to talk about an action that began in the past and continues into the present. We can use the present perfect progressive to show how long an activity has been in progress. We use the time words *for* and *since* for this.

She **has been waiting for** 45 minutes.

She **has been talking** on the phone **since** six o'clock.

19 Practice

Complete the sentences with the present progressive or present perfect progressive of the verbs in parentheses.

A A: You look busy. What have you been doing?

B: I (write) *have been writing* my research paper.
   1

A: How long (work) _____ you _____ on it?
   2   3

B: I (work) _____ on it since January.
   4

B At the moment, I (sit) _____ in class. I (sit) _____
   1   2
here for 20 minutes. We (learn) _____ about the present perfect
   3
progressive since the beginning of this class.

20 Practice

Write answers using the present perfect progressive and a time expression with *for* or *since*.

1. How long have you been going to this school?

   I have been going to this school since September.

2. How long have you been learning English?

   _____

3. How long have you been using this book?

   _____

4. How long have you been sitting in this classroom today?

   _____

5. How long have you been learning the present perfect?

_____

6. How long have you been doing this exercise?

_____

21 Pair Up and Talk

Work with a partner. Ask and answer questions about your lives with *how long* + the present perfect progressive. Use the list of verbs for ideas.

YOU: How long have you been living in your house?
YOUR PARTNER: I've been living there for six months.

live   stay   study   work

6G The Present Perfect OR The Present Perfect Progressive

Function

Karen **has been talking** on the phone for two hours.
She **has made** four telephone calls.

1. We use the present perfect for an action that has just finished or that was finished at some unstated point in the past.
   He **has just missed** the bus.
   I **have missed** the bus, but I won't be late.
2. We use the present perfect to talk about a repeated action.
   She **has made** four telephone calls.
3. We use the present perfect progressive for an action that started in the past and continues into the present.
   Mr. Black **has been teaching** for nine years.

4. We use the present perfect progressive to emphasize the duration of the action.

   She **has been talking** on the phone for two hours.

5. With some verbs that take place over time, like *live*, *stay*, *study*, *teach*, and *work*, we can use either the present perfect or the present perfect progressive.

   He **has taught** for nine years.

   OR He **has been teaching** for nine years.

22 Practice

Complete the sentences with the present perfect or the present perfect progressive of the verbs in parentheses.

1. Carlos and Rosa are planning to buy a house. They
   (look) _____*have been looking*_____ for a house for a month.
   They (look) _have looked_ at five houses, but they
   (not, find) _haven't find_ one that they like yet.

2. My grandfather (paint) _____ for ten years
   now. He (paint) _____ more than fifty
   paintings.

3. I (learn) _____ to drive for four months.
   I (take) _have took_ the driving test three times
   now and (not, pass) _haven't passed._ yet.

4. John (write) _____ on his computer for an
   hour. He (already, send) _____ five email
   messages to his friends.

5. Karen (drive) _____ for three hours now.
   She (drive) _____ almost 200 miles.

6. I (read) _____ this book for two weeks
   now, but I (not, finish) _____ yet.

7. Jerry (work) _____ on a math problem for
   half an hour, and he (not, find) _____ the
   answer yet.

8. I (cook) _____ for hours, and I (just, burn)
   _____ the cake.

23 Practice

Complete the sentences with the present perfect or the present perfect progressive of the verbs in parentheses.

New	Delete	Reply	Reply All	Forward	Move

To:	Sarah_Perkosz@mymail.com
From:	Tim_Perkosz@ westcollege.edu
Subject:	Summer Vacation

Dear Sarah,

I (mean) __*have been meaning*__ to write you for weeks, but you know how it is.
                        1
Everything is fine here at home. I (just, finish) _____ my second year at
                                                        2
college, and I (get) _____ good grades. I (decide) _____ to
                            3   **4**
get a job for the summer and save some money. So far, I (help) _____ Mom
                                                                        5
with the shopping and the cooking.

Dad (sell) _____ the old car! He (buy) _____ a new
                    6   **7**
one of the same make and color, of course! I (not, drive) _____ it yet. Mom
                                                                    8
is busy with redecorating the house. It (be) _____ a mess here. The painters
                                                    9
(work) _____ as fast as they can, and I hope they will be done soon. The
            10
house will look great by the time you come to visit.

I hope you (work) _____ hard!
                            11
See you soon.

Your brother,

Tim

6H | The Past Perfect

Form

Candice was sad because her friends **hadn't asked** her to go biking with them.

We form the past perfect with *had* + the past participle of the verb.

Affirmative and Negative Statements		
Subject	***Had (Not)***	**Past Participle**
I You He/She/It We They	**had** **'d** **had not** **hadn't**	**left**.

Yes/No Questions			Short Answers	
Had	**Subject**	**Past Participle**	**Yes,**	**No,**
Had	I	**left?**	you **had.**	you **hadn't.**
	you		I/we **had.**	I/we **hadn't.**
	he/she/it		he/she/it **had.**	he/she/it **hadn't.**
	we		you **had.**	you **hadn't.**
	they		they **had.**	they **hadn't.**

Function

1. We use the past perfect for a past action that happened before another past action.
2. We use the past perfect for the first action in time and the simple past for the second action.

            1st Action   **2nd Action**

    When he **had saved** enough money, he **bought** a car.

3. The past perfect verb can come after the simple past verb. The verb forms tell you which action happened first.

            2nd Action   **1st Action**

    He **bought** a car when he **had saved** enough money.

24 Practice

Rob's mother- and father-in-law are coming to stay for a few days. Listen to a conversation between Rob and his wife, Linda. Check *yes* or *no* to show what things they had already done by the time their guests arrived.

CD2, 7

		yes	no				yes	no
1.	She cleaned the house.	☐	✔	5.	He developed photos.		☐	☐
2.	She washed the dishes.	☐	☐	6.	He rented movies.		☐	☐
3.	She changed the sheets.	☐	☐	7.	He did the laundry.		☐	☐
4.	He bought food.	☐	☐	8.	He made dinner.		☐	☐

25 Practice

Ask and answer questions about what Rob and Linda had done by the time their guests arrived. Use the answers in Practice 24.

YOU: Had Linda cleaned the house?

YOUR PARTNER: No, she hadn't cleaned the house yet.

6I The Past Perfect Progressive

Form

Bob Blake was hot and nervous. He **had been waiting** for his boss for two hours.

We form the past perfect progressive with *had been* + verb + *-ing*.

Affirmative and Negative Statements		
Subject	**Had (Not)**	**Been + Verb + -ing**
I	**had** **'d**	**been working.**
You		
He/She/It	**had not** **hadn't**	
We/ They		

Yes/No Questions			Short Answers	
Had	**Subject**	**Been + Verb + -ing**	**Yes,**	**No,**
Had	I	**been working?**	you **had.**	you **hadn't.**
	you		I/we **had.**	I/we **hadn't.**
	he/she/it		he/she/it **had.**	he/she/it **hadn't.**
	we/ they		you **had.**	you **hadn't.**
			they **had.**	they **hadn't.**

Function

1. We use the past perfect progressive as the past of the present perfect progressive.
2. The past perfect progressive emphasizes the duration of an action that started and finished in the past, usually before another action in the past.

Past Perfect Progressive	Present Perfect Progressive
He **had been waiting** for me for an hour. (He isn't waiting now.)	He **has been waiting** for me for an hour. (He is still waiting now.)

3. We also use the past perfect progressive to show the cause of an action that happened in the past.

          Result   **Cause**

Her eyes were tired. She **had been working** on the computer for hours.

---

26   Practice

What had they been doing? Complete the sentences using the verbs from the list and the past perfect progressive.

dream   lie   run   wait   walk

1. Sophie's feet ached. She *had been walking* in her new shoes for hours.

2. Louis was angry. He _____ for Kim for 45 minutes.

3. Carmen woke up in the night. She was frightened. She _____ .

4. Ted was hot and out of breath when he came in. He _____ in the park.

5. Tony came in from the beach looking very red. He _____ in the sun.

Listening Puzzle

 AUDIO DOWNLOAD   CD2, 8

A Listen and check the correct answer.

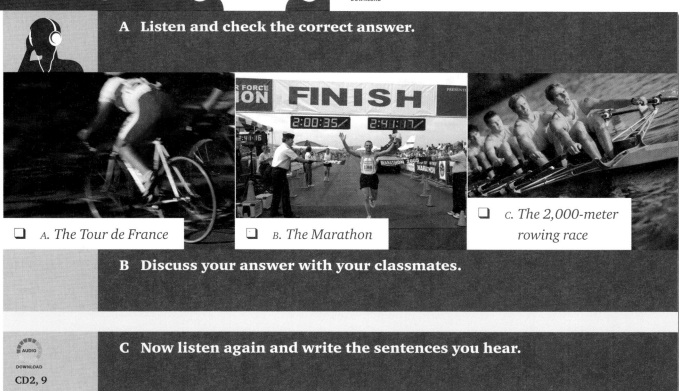

☐ A. *The Tour de France*   ☐ B. *The Marathon*   ☐ C. *The 2,000-meter rowing race*

B Discuss your answer with your classmates.

C Now listen again and write the sentences you hear.

CD2, 9

Reading Challenge

A Before You Read

Answer the questions.

1. What drug do you take when you have a bad infection?
2. What did people do in the past when they had infections?

B Read

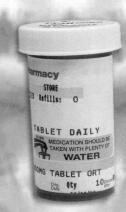

PENICILLIN

For thousands of years, people have used many folk remedies to cure infections. Egyptians used moldy bread crumbs together with animal fat as 5 medicine. Even 500 years ago, people kept moldy bread to put on a wound to stop infection. They didn't know that 10 the moldy bread contained what is now a modern medicine—penicillin.

Penicillin has often been described as a miracle drug, and that is exactly what it was when it was discovered. Before the discovery of 15 penicillin, people had died from minor injuries and diseases.

The discovery of penicillin was almost an accident. In 1928, Alexander Fleming, a Scottish scientist in London, England, was growing 20 some bacteria for an experiment. His assistant forgot to cover the dish where the bacteria was growing. Some mold fell on the dish and killed the bacteria. Fleming found the part of the mold that killed the bacteria and called it 25 penicillin. Later, two other scientists, Howard Florey and Ernest Chain, worked on what Fleming had found. They discovered how to turn the penicillin into a drug. Fleming, Florey, and Chain received the Nobel Prize in 1943 30 for their discovery. Penicillin was first given to a patient with an infection in 1940, and the patient survived. Other scientists worked with Florey and Chain to **mass produce** penicillin. Since mass production of penicillin began in 35 1943, it has saved the lives of millions of people around the world.

> **DID YOU KNOW … ?**
> The U.S. now makes 95 percent of the world's penicillin and exports it.

C Notice the Grammar

Underline all forms of the perfect.

Choose the best answer.

D Look for Main Ideas

1. What is the main idea of paragraph 1?
   - Ⓐ Many people died before penicillin was discovered.
   - Ⓑ People have used folk remedies for thousands of years.
   - Ⓒ Penicillin is a miracle drug.
   - Ⓓ Penicillin has been used to cure infection for many years.

2. The main topic of paragraph 2 is _____ .
   - Ⓐ the importance of penicillin
   - Ⓑ how penicillin was discovered
   - Ⓒ the first human test of penicillin
   - Ⓓ when penicillin was first mass produced

E Look for Details

3. Howard Florey and Ernest Chain _____ .
   - Ⓐ discovered penicillin
   - Ⓑ found what part of mold killed bacteria
   - Ⓒ discovered how to turn penicillin into a drug
   - Ⓓ mass produced penicillin on their own

4. How did moldy bread help wounds in the past?
   - Ⓐ It stopped the bleeding.
   - Ⓑ It stopped infection.
   - Ⓒ It made the patient calm.
   - Ⓓ It put bacteria in the wound.

5. What did Fleming's assistant do?
   - Ⓐ He didn't cover a dish of bacteria.
   - Ⓑ He dropped mold into a dish of bacteria.
   - Ⓒ He dropped a dish of bacteria into a dish of mold.
   - Ⓓ He put some mold into a dish of bacteria.

READING SKILL:
Extensive Reading

Extensive reading is reading long texts, like books. It will improve your reading skills and vocabulary. Don't try to understand every word. Read for the main ideas and important details.

F Make Inferences

6. What can we infer from paragraph 1?
   - Ⓐ Folk remedies have always worked as well as modern medicine.
   - Ⓑ Folk remedies often caused people to die from minor injuries.
   - Ⓒ Ancient people had modern medical knowledge.
   - Ⓓ Some folk remedies worked, but people didn't know why.

7. We can infer from the reading that _____ .
   - Ⓐ once penicillin was discovered, it was easy to turn it into a widespread cure
   - Ⓑ the discovery of penicillin was more important than any later research on it
   - Ⓒ the discovery of penicillin was only the beginning of a long and difficult process
   - Ⓓ Fleming's work was more important to medicine than that of Florey and Chain

G Look for Vocabulary

8. The phrase *mass produce* in the reading is closest in meaning to _____ .
   - Ⓐ make for a large number of people
   - Ⓑ make quickly
   - Ⓒ make for a small number of individuals
   - Ⓓ make only once

Writing: Write a Friendly Email

Write an email to a friend about your recent experiences.

STEP **1**   Think about things in your past and present life you can write about.
Write the answers to these questions or others you can think of.
Share your answers with a partner.

1. What are you studying?
   _____

2. What do you find easy/difficult/interesting?
   _____

3. What have you been doing in your free time?
   _____

4. Where is the last place you traveled to? What did you do there?
   _____

5. What movies have you seen? What kinds of sports have you been doing
   or have you watched on television?
   _____

6. When will you talk to your friend again, or maybe see your friend?
   _____

STEP **2**   Rewrite your answers in the form of an email.

STEP **3**   Evaluate your email.

Checklist
_____ Did you write your friend's email address after "To:"?
_____ Did you include a subject, such as "Hello from school," after "Subject:"?
_____ Did you start with a greeting such as "Dear Rosa"?
_____ Did you put line spaces between your paragraphs?
_____ Did you end with a closing such as "Sincerely," "Your Friend," or "Love,"?
_____ Did you sign your name at the bottom of your email?

STEP **4**   Edit your email. Work with a partner or your teacher to edit your sentences.
Correct spelling, punctuation, vocabulary, and grammar.

STEP **5**   Write the final copy of your email.

Self-Test

1. I _____ since 10:00 when the doorbell rang.

   A. was sleeping   Ⓐ Ⓑ Ⓒ Ⓓ
   B. have been sleeping
   C. slept
   D. had been sleeping

2. Sandy _____ a new computer last week. She likes it.

   A. bought   Ⓐ Ⓑ Ⓒ Ⓓ
   B. had bought
   C. was buying
   D. had been bought

3. Sam has lived in San Francisco _____ three years.

   A. since   Ⓐ Ⓑ Ⓒ Ⓓ
   B. for
   C. already
   D. yet

4. She _____ .

   A. has just arrived   Ⓐ Ⓑ Ⓒ Ⓓ
   B. just arrive
   C. has just arrive
   D. arrived just

5. I _____ my homework.

   A. have done already Ⓐ Ⓑ Ⓒ Ⓓ
   B. did already
   C. have already done
   D. have done since

6. I _____ .

   A. haven't finished yet   Ⓐ Ⓑ Ⓒ Ⓓ
   B. didn't finished yet
   C. haven't yet finished
   D. didn't yet finish

7. After he _____ , he called a taxi.

   A. has packed   Ⓐ Ⓑ Ⓒ Ⓓ
   B. was packing
   C. pack
   D. had packed

8. I _____ such a strange story in my life.

   A. never heard   Ⓐ Ⓑ Ⓒ Ⓓ
   B. have never heard
   C. heard never
   D. have heard never

9. I _____ you since December.

   A. haven't saw   Ⓐ Ⓑ Ⓒ Ⓓ
   B. haven't seen
   C. didn't see
   D. not see

10. We _____ our trip to Thailand for a month. We have almost finished, and we are leaving next week.

    A. are planning   Ⓐ Ⓑ Ⓒ Ⓓ
    B. planned
    C. have been planning
    D. had planned

B Find the underlined word or phrase, A, B, C, or D, that is incorrect. Darken the oval with the same letter.

1. Have you yet learned all the irregular
   A   B   C D
   past participles?
   Ⓐ Ⓑ Ⓒ Ⓓ

2. Have you study English when you were in
   A   B   C   D
   high school?
   Ⓐ Ⓑ Ⓒ Ⓓ

3. We have been studying the past for the
      A   B   C
   beginning of the semester.
                    D
   Ⓐ Ⓑ Ⓒ Ⓓ

4. Picasso has painted hundreds of paintings
            A
   before he died in 1973.
   B   C   D
   Ⓐ Ⓑ Ⓒ Ⓓ

5. My friend had not been working since the
                 A   B   C   D
   company closed down two months ago.
   Ⓐ Ⓑ Ⓒ Ⓓ

6. The Science Museum had been closed for five
   A   B   C   D
   days because of repairs, but it will open again
   next Monday.
   Ⓐ Ⓑ Ⓒ Ⓓ

7. Have you seen ever the Statue of Liberty
   A   B   C
   in New York?
   D
   Ⓐ Ⓑ Ⓒ Ⓓ

8. How many verb forms did you studied
   A   B   C   D
   up to now?
   Ⓐ Ⓑ Ⓒ Ⓓ

9. Have you see a kangaroo when you were in
   A   B   C   D
   Australia last winter?
   Ⓐ Ⓑ Ⓒ Ⓓ

10. Have you been to London before you were
    A   B   C
    there last month?
          D
    Ⓐ Ⓑ Ⓒ Ⓓ

Unit 7

Questions and Phrasal Verbs

Where do lions live?

Form

A: **Does** Andy fight fires?
B: **Yes**, he does.

1. When forms of the verbs *be*, *have*, and *do* are used with other verb forms such as the base form, the *-ing* form, or the past participle, they are auxiliary (helping) verbs.

   He **is wearing** a firefighter's uniform. (*Is* is an auxiliary verb.)
   Does he **fight** fires? (*Does* is an auxiliary verb.)
   He **has fought** many fires. (*Has* is an auxiliary verb.)

2. Modal verbs such as *can*, *should*, and *will* are also auxiliary verbs.

   He **should** be careful on the job!

3. Auxiliary verbs are used to form tenses, questions, and negative statements.

4. There are 17 common auxiliary verbs in English that we use to make questions. Auxiliary verbs are also used to make short answers.

5. In *yes/no* questions, the auxiliary verb is the first word in the question, then the subject, then the verb.

Yes/No Questions				Short Answers	
Auxiliary Verb	Subject	Base Verb or Base Verb + -ing or Past Participle		Yes,	No,
Am	I	**disturbing**	you?	you **are.**	you **aren't.**
Is	it	**raining**	hard?	it **is.**	it **isn't.**
Are	they	**studying**	English?	they **are.**	they **aren't.**
Was	she	**studying**	English last year?	she **was.**	she **wasn't.**
Were	you	**trying**	to call me?	I **was.**	I **wasn't.**
Do	they	**like**	country music?	they **do.**	they **don't.**
Does	this school	**have**	a language lab?	it **does.**	it **doesn't.**
Did	it	**rain**	last night?	it **did.**	it **didn't.**
Have	they	**finished**	their work?	they **have.**	they **haven't.**
Has	Anne	**come**	home yet?	she **has.**	she **hasn't.**
Had	they	**eaten**	yet?	they **had.**	they **hadn't.**
Can	you	**swim**	well?	I **can.**	I **can't.**
Could	you	**ride**	a bike as a child?	I **could.**	I **couldn't.**
Will	they	**be**	here on time?	they **will.**	they **won't.**
Would	you	**go**	outside in a storm?	I **would.**	I **wouldn't.**
Should	you	**see**	a doctor?	I **should.**	I **shouldn't.**
Must	we	**stand**	in this line?	we **must.**	*

* In this meaning, the negative short answer with *must* is "No, we don't have to."

1 Practice
Match the questions with the short answers.

_g_ 1. Have you had lunch yet?   a. Yes, it is.

_____ 2. Do you work in the city?   b. No, you can't.

_____ 3. Is it raining outside?   c. Yes, I do.

_____ 4. Did you take the test yesterday?   d. No, they aren't.

_____ 5. Can I borrow your car?   e. No, it wasn't.

_____ 6. Was the test difficult?   f. No, I didn't.

_____ 7. Are your parents coming?   g. Yes, I have.

2 Practice

Listen and underline the best answer.

CD2, 10

1. a. <u>No, it isn't.</u>   b. No, it can't.

2. a. No, he wasn't.   b. No, he isn't.

3. a. Yes, they have.   b. Yes, they do.

4. a. No, he wasn't.   b. No, he didn't.

5. a. No, she wasn't.   b. No, she couldn't.

6. a. Yes, it did.   b. Yes, it does.

7. a. Yes, they can.   b. Yes, they have.

8. a. Yes, there were.   b. Yes, there are.

3 Practice

What kind of person are you? Complete the questions with the correct auxiliary verb. Then answer by checking *Yes* or *No*.

		yes	no
1. ____*Are*____ you shy?		_____	_____
2. _____ you like sports?		_____	_____
3. _____ you worry a lot?		_____	_____
4. _____ you clean and tidy?		_____	_____
5. _____ you cry when you watch a sad movie?		_____	_____
6. _____ you get angry quickly?		_____	_____
7. _____ friends very important to you?		_____	_____

4 Pair Up and Talk

Ask your partner five *yes/no* questions. Use your own ideas or the ones in the list.

YOU: Do you have a lot of friends?

YOUR PARTNER: Yes, I do.

friends   music   school   sports

7B | Questions with *Wh-* Words

Form

A: **Where** do polar bears live?
B: They live in the Arctic.
A: **What** do they eat?
B: They eat seals and fish.
A: **When** do they have young?
B: In the spring.

1. We call words that start questions "*wh-* words" because most of them start with the letters *wh*.
2. When the verb in a *wh-* question is the simple present or past form of *be* (*am, is, are, was,* or *were*), we make questions by putting the verb before the subject.

Wh- Word	Present or Past of *Be*	Subject
Who	is	she?
Where	are	those students?
Why	were	you late?

3. For questions with all other verbs and tenses, we put an auxiliary verb before the subject.* The verb can be a base verb, an *-ing* verb, or a past participle.

Wh- Word	Auxiliary Verb	Subject	Verb
Who**	can	you	see?
What	did	he	do?
When	does	she	arrive?
Where	have	you	lived?
Why	are	they	leaving?
How	did	your team	win?

*When *who* or *what* is the subject of the question, we do not change the word order. See section 7c on page 156.

**In formal written English, the *wh-* word would be *whom*.

Function

We use *wh-* words to ask for information about something.

1. We use *who(m)** to ask about a person.
   Who(m) were you calling?   I was calling Jill.
   Who took my dictionary?   Tom took your dictionary.
2. We use *what* to ask about a thing.
   What is she studying?   She's studying engineering.
3. We use *when* to ask about dates and times.
   When is the test?   It's on Monday at 9:00 A.M.
4. We use *where* to ask about places.
   Where do you live?   I live on Lemon Street.
5. We use *why* to ask for reasons.
   Why are you leaving?   I have to catch a train.
6. We use *how* to ask for the way something happened.
   How did you get here?   I took the bus.

* In formal written English, *whom* is the object form of *who*. We usually use *who* for both subjects and objects in speech and informal writing.

5 Practice

Who is the person? Read the answers and write questions with the words in parentheses. Say who the person is. Then listen to check your answers.

CD2, 11

A

1. Question: <u>When was she born?</u>
   Answer: She was born in 1961. (when)

2. Question: _____
   Answer: She married a prince. (who)

3. Question: _____
   Answer: She was famous for her fashionable clothes. (what)

4. Question: _____
   Answer: She died in 1997 in a car accident. (when)

5. Question: _____

   Answer: The accident happened in Paris. (where)

The person is _____

B

1. Question: _____

   Answer: He was born in 1975. (when)

2. Question: _____

   Answer: He was born in Florida, in the United States. (where)

3. Question: _____

   Answer: He started to play golf when he was three. (when)

4. Question: _____

   Answer: He studied economics in college. (what)

5. Question: _____

   Answer: He is famous because he is already one of the best players of all time,
   even though he is young. (why)

The person is _____

6 Your Turn

Write a quiz about the country you live in now. Write five questions with *what,
when, where, who*, and *why*. Ask your partner the questions.

Example

What is the name of the ocean in the west?

Where do most people live?

1. _____

2. _____

3. _____

4. _____

5. _____

7C | Questions with *Who* and *What* as the Subject

Form

What happened?
My boss slipped on a banana peel.

Who dropped the banana peel?
I did.

When *who* or *what* is the subject of a question, the word order is the same as in statements. If *who(m)* or *what is* the object of the question, the word order is in the question form.

Who/What as Subject	*Who(m)/What* as Object
Who met you?	Who(m) did you meet?
What happened?	What did you see?

7 Practice

Write questions with *who* or *what*. The underlined word is the answer.

1. Pete saw <u>Karen</u> at the store yesterday.
   <u>*Who did Pete see at the store yesterday?*</u>

2. <u>Pete</u> saw Karen at the store yesterday.

   _____

3. Karen was buying <u>fresh strawberries</u>.

   _____

4. <u>Karen</u> was buying fresh strawberries.

_____

5. <u>Karen</u> invited a friend for dinner yesterday.

_____

6. Karen invited <u>a friend</u> for dinner yesterday.

_____

8 Practice

A Listen and write the missing words on the lines.

CD2, 12

There was an accident this ___*morning*___ . It was 10:00, and it was raining. Bob saw a
                                    1

_____ jogger crossing the street. Then he _____ a loud bang. A white
        2   **3**

truck had suddenly stopped, and a red _____ had crashed into the back of the
                                            4

truck. Bob _____ 911 for the police and an ambulance. At about 10:15, the
                5

_____ and ambulance came. A police officer asked him _____ .
        6   **7**

B Complete the questions about the story with _who_ or _what_.

1. ___*Who*___ saw the accident?

2. _____ caused the accident? The rain or the jogger?

3. _____ called 911?

4. _____ made the loud bang?

5. _____ happened to the driver of the white truck?

6. _____ happened to the jogger?

7. _____ happened to the driver of the red car?

8. _____ came at 10:15?

9. _____ asked questions?

10. _____ answered questions?

C With a partner, ask and answer the questions in part B. Use information from the story when possible. If not, use your imagination.

YOU: Who saw the accident?

YOUR PARTNER: Bob saw it.

7D Questions with *Which* and *What*

Form/Function

Which woman has straight hair?

Which woman has very long hair?

1. We use *what* or *which* to ask about people, places, and things.
2. We use *what* when the choices are not limited.
   What sports do you like?
   What authors do you like?
3. We use *which* when the choices are limited.
   Which is your favorite, swimming or tennis?
   Which author do you prefer, Agatha Christie or Stephen King?
4. When using *which*, we can say *which*, *which* + a noun, or *which one*.
   Which do you prefer, Christie or King?
   Which author do you prefer, Christie or King?
   Which one do you prefer, Christie or King?
5. We can use *which* with singular or plural nouns.
   Which places did you visit?
   Which place was your favorite?

9 Pair Up and Talk
Work with a partner. Look at the photo of the two women above. Ask and answer questions with *which* or *what* about the women. Use the words in the list or your own ideas. You can answer using *The one on the right/left, Neither one,* or *Both of them.*

YOU: Which woman has very long hair?
YOUR PARTNER: The one on the right.

a green shirt	very long hair	glasses	smiling
a sleeveless shirt	dark hair	laughing	straight hair

10 Practice
Complete the questions with *what* or *which*. Then listen to check your answers. Now practice the conversation with a partner.

AUDIO
DOWNLOAD

CD2, 13

NINA: ____*Which*____ countries did you visit in Europe?
           1

CLAUDIA: I went to France and Italy.

NINA: _____ did you like better?
           2

CLAUDIA: I loved France.

NINA: _____ did you buy?
           3

CLAUDIA: I bought some clothes and perfume.

NINA: _____ country had the best clothes, France or Italy?
           4

CLAUDIA: Italy had the best clothes.

NINA: _____ one had the most perfumes?
           5

CLAUDIA: France had the most perfumes. Tourists buy them tax free.

NINA: _____ cities did you visit in France?
           6

CLAUDIA: I went to Paris, Lyon, Nice, and Cannes.

NINA: _____ city was the most beautiful?
           7

CLAUDIA: Paris, of course.

NINA: _____ is a good time to visit Paris?
           8

CLAUDIA: Anytime is good. I prefer spring.

NINA: _____ month, April or May?
           9

CLAUDIA: I prefer May; it's warmer.

NINA: _____ country was cheaper, France or Italy?
           10

CLAUDIA: They are about the same. My company paid for the trip; it was for business, you see.

Questions with *How*

Form/Function

How long is the blue whale?
It's about 100 feet long (30.5 meters).
How much does it weigh?
It weighs more than 100 tons (90 metric tons).
How big is its mouth?
Its mouth can be 20 feet long (6 meters).

1. We can use *how* alone, without a word such as *much* or *many*.

Use	Example
We use *how* to ask about the way someone is or the way someone does something.	**How** did she sing? She sang beautifully. **How** do I look? You look very handsome.
We use *how to* ask about a means of transportation.	**How** did you get here? By plane./I flew. By car./I drove. By train./I took the train. On foot./I walked.

2. We can use *how* with an adjective or an adverb.

Use	Example
We use *how* + adjective/adverb to ask about qualities of things or how things are done.	**How old** are you? I'm 22. **How tall** is he? He's five feet eight. **How quickly** can you come? In five minutes.
We use *how often* to ask about the frequency that something happens.	**How often** do you have English class? I have class three times a week. **How often** do you go to the gym? I usually go every day.

We can also say *how many times a day/week/ month/year* to ask about frequency.	**How many times a week** do you have English class? I have class three times a week. **How many times a month** do you go to the movies? I go once or twice a month.
We use *how much* and *how many* to ask about the amount of something.	
We use *how much* with noncount nouns.	**How much** money do you need? I need a lot of money. **How much** time do we have? Not much.
We use *how many* with count nouns.	**How many** questions are there on the test? Fifty. **How many** sisters and brothers do you have? Just one sister.
We use *how far* to ask about the distance from one place to another.	**How far** is the school from your house? It's about ten blocks. **How far** is New York from Los Angeles? About 3,000 miles (4,828 kilometers).
We use *how long* to ask about a period of time.	**How long** have you been waiting? Not long. Just a few minutes. **How long** did you stay in Houston? We stayed for one week.
We often ask and answer a question about length of time with *it takes* + time.	How long **does it take** to fly there? **It takes** about six hours. How long **did it take** to write this essay? **It took** about three hours. How long **will it take** for the rice to cook? **It will take** about 20 minutes.
We can also say *how many minutes/hours/days/ weeks/months/years* to ask about length of time.	**How many** years is this passport good for? Ten years.

3. We use *how about* to suggest something. We often use it in response to a statement or question.

Statement or Question	How About	Noun/Pronoun/Gerund*
I don't know what to make for dinner.		**spaghetti**?
What would you like to do tonight?		**going** to a movie?
I need someone to go to the party with me.	How about	**me**?
We're cleaning the apartment.		**giving** us some help?

* A gerund is a verb + *-ing* that is used as a noun.

What about means the same thing as *how about*.

What about going to a movie?   OR   **How about** going to a movie?

11 Practice

Work with a partner. Use the prompts to ask and answer the questions about whales with *how, how big, how many/much, how fast, how long,* or *how often.*

Example

STUDENT A: How does a whale breathe?

STUDENT B: It blows water high into the air and takes in fresh air.

Questions	Answers
1. ___How___ does a whale breathe?	1. It blows water high into the air and takes in fresh air.
2. _____ does it come to the surface to breathe?	2. It comes to the surface every 15 minutes.
3. _____ is the blue whale's heart?	3. Its heart is the size of a small car.
4. _____ can it swim?	4. It can swim 30 miles (48 kilometers) an hour.
5. _____ milk does a baby whale drink?	5. It drinks 100 gallons (378 liters) of its mother's milk each day.
6. _____ weight does the baby whale gain?	6. A baby whale gains eight pounds (3.6 kilograms) each hour!

12 Practice

Complete the conversation with *how, how long, how many/much, how often,* and *how far*. With a partner, talk about where this conversation is taking place. Who is the man? Who is the woman?

1. MAN: Passport please. ____How____ are you today, ma'am?

   WOMAN: I'm fine, thanks. And you?

2. MAN: Fine. _____ did you stay out of the country?

   WOMAN: Not long. About three weeks.

3. MAN: _____ countries did you visit?

   WOMAN: Two countries. England and France.

4. MAN: _____ friends do you have in Europe?

   WOMAN: I have one friend in Oxford and one in Paris.

5. MAN: _____ have you known these friends?

   WOMAN: I have known both for eight years.

6. MAN: _____ gifts did you buy?

   WOMAN: I bought about seven gifts.

   MAN: Can I see them?

13 Practice

Write questions for which the underlined words are the answers.
Use *wh-* words: *who, what, where, when, why, which,* and *how.*

1. Lions live in <u>Africa and Asia</u>.

   Where do lions live?

2. Lions live in groups. There are <u>about 6 to 30 lions</u> in a group.

   _____

3. <u>The male lion</u> is the largest member of the cat family.

   _____

4. A male lion can weigh <u>up to 520 pounds (240 kilos)</u>.

   _____

5. The male lion sleeps for <u>about 20</u> hours a day.

   _____

6. The job of the male lion is <u>to make sure other lions do not come near the home of his family</u>.

   _____

7. Sometimes the male lion makes a loud roar. You can hear the sound <u>five miles</u> away.

   _____

8. <u>The female lion</u> kills other animals for food.

   _____

14   **Practice**
Write questions for which the underlined words are the answers.
Use *wh-* words.

1. Bob is <u>an accountant</u>.

   What is Bob?

2. He lives <u>near Boston, in the United States</u>.

   _____

3. He travels to work <u>by subway</u>.

   _____

4. His wife's name is <u>Donna</u>.

   _____

5. They have <u>two</u> children.

   _____

6. The girl is <u>three</u> and the boy is <u>nine</u>.

   _____

7. Bob plays football and baseball. He prefers <u>football</u>.

   _____

8. He watches football on television <u>because he doesn't have time to play</u>.

   _____

9. <u>His son</u> watches it with him.

   _____

10. He usually watches <u>cartoons</u> with his daughter.

    _____

15   **Pair Up and Talk**
Work with a partner. Make suggestions to visit three places in your city.
Suggest the days and times you can both go. Use *How about* and *What about*
to make suggestions.

YOU:	Where would you like to go on Saturday?
YOUR PARTNER:	How about the park?
YOU:	OK. That's a good idea. What time?
YOUR PARTNER:	What about 10:30?
YOU:	OK.

Form

John is your brother, **isn't he?**

1. Tag questions are short questions at the end of a sentence. We form tag questions with the auxiliary verb from the first part of the sentence. The subject of the tag question at the end is always a pronoun—we do not repeat the noun. When we write, we always use a comma before the tag question.

   CORRECT: John is your brother, **isn't he?**

   INCORRECT: John is your brother, isn't ~~John~~?

2. We make a tag question in the same way we make a regular question, but when the first part of the sentence is positive, the tag question is negative.

   He is a farmer, **isn't he?**

3. When the first part of the sentence is negative, the tag question is positive.

   He isn't a businessman, **is he?**

4. When the verb in the first part of the sentence is in the simple present or the simple past of any verb except *be*, we use the auxiliaries *do*, *does*, or *did* in the tag question. When the first part of the sentence uses *be*, we use *be* again in the tag.

Affirmative Verb, Negative Tag		Negative Verb, Affirmative Tag	
Main Sentence	**Tag**	**Main Sentence**	**Tag**
She **likes** music,	**doesn't she?**	He **doesn't like** fish,	**does he?**
You **are** a student,	**aren't you?**	You **didn't do** it,	**did you?**
She**'s** learning English,	**isn't she?**	He **wasn't** nice to you,	**was he?**
We **had** fun,	**didn't we?**	We **didn't have** fun,	**did we?**

Note: With the subject and verb *I am*, the tag question is *aren't I* or *am I not*.

CORRECT:	I'm late, **aren't I?**
INCORRECT:	I'm late, ~~amn't I?~~
CORRECT (very formal):	I'm late, **am I not?**

Function

1. We use tag questions when we want to check something we have said in the first part of the sentence.

    He lives in Utah, **doesn't he**? (The speaker is not sure and uses a tag question to check.)

2. We also use tag questions when we ask for agreement.

    The food is good, **isn't it**? (The speaker expects the answer *Yes*.)

    You aren't angry, **are you**? (The speaker expects the answer *No*.)

16   Practice

Complete the conversation with the correct tag questions and short answers.

TINA: You went to Brazil, __*didn't you?*__
1

JENNY: Yes, I _____
2

TINA: You speak Portuguese, _____
3

JENNY: No, I _____
4

TINA: It was difficult to get around, then, _____
5

JENNY: No, it __wasn't__ I spoke English.
6

TINA: A lot of people speak English there, __don't they__
7

JENNY: Many people in hotels and restaurants do.

TINA: Rio is beautiful, __isn't he__
8

JENNY: Yes, __he is__
9

TINA: You had gone there before, __hadn't you__
10

JENNY: Yes, a long time ago. You've been to Brazil, __haven't you__
11

TINA: No, I __haven't__
12

166   Unit 7

7G Phrasal Verbs

Form

Julie is **sitting down** on a chair. She is **waiting for** the meeting to begin.

1. Many verbs in English consist of more than one word. These verbs have a verb plus a particle (an adverb such as *up* or *down*). These are phrasal verbs.

2. Sometimes we can guess the meaning of a phrasal verb.

    She walked into the room and **sat down**.

    When the president came into the room, everyone **stood up**.

    The phrasal verb *sit down* means "position yourself on a chair." The phrasal verb *stand up* means "get on your feet from a sitting position."

3. Many phrasal verbs have special meanings, for example:

    We **looked up** the words we didn't understand.

    The phrasal verb *look up* means "find information in a dictionary, encyclopedia, etc."

4. Some phrasal verbs do not take objects. We call these intransitive phrasal verbs. Others do take objects. We call these transitive phrasal verbs.

    These two phrasal verbs do not take objects. They are intransitive.

Subject	Phrasal Verb
We	**sat down** at the table.
They	**stood up** to sing the national anthem.

These two phrasal verbs take objects. They are transitive.

Subject	Phrasal Verb	Object
I	**looked up**	**your number.**
The children	**put on**	**their coats.**

17 Practice

Underline the phrasal verbs in these sentences. If the phrasal verb has an object, underline it twice.

1. Please <u>turn on</u> <u>the radio</u>.
2. We told the dog to lie down.
3. I have a cold. I can't get over it.
4. She took off her coat and sat down.
5. What time do you get up in the morning?
6. They picked up their trash before they left the park.
7. Did you turn in your homework?
8. He has been looking for his keys since this morning.
9. The teacher calls on Susan to answer the questions every day.
10. Helen is going to drop by this weekend.

7H Intransitive Phrasal Verbs

Form/Function

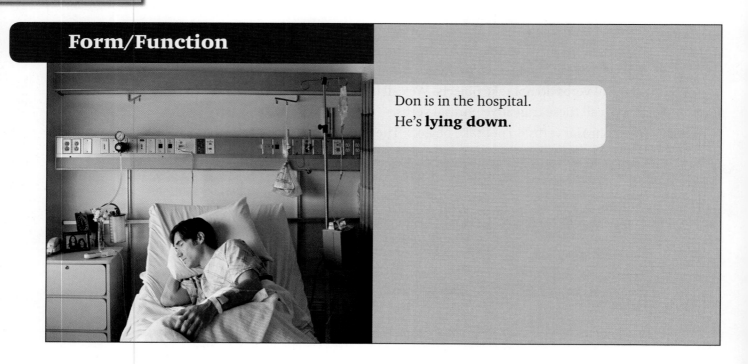

Don is in the hospital.
He's **lying down**.

Here are some common phrasal verbs that are intransitive—they do not take objects.*

Phrasal Verb	Meaning	Example
break down	to stop working (as a machine)	My car has **broken down** three times this month.
get back	to return	They **got back** from Seoul yesterday.
get up	to rise from bed; to rise from a sitting position	We **got up** late this morning.
lie down	to rest in a horizontal position	I have a headache. I'm going to **lie down**.
set out	to leave (on a trip)	The boys **set out** at 6:00 A.M.
sit down	to sit on a chair	You should **sit down** in a job interview.
stand up	to rise from a sitting position	You should **stand up** when you meet someone.
stay up	to keep awake	We **stayed up** late to watch a movie.

* Some of these phrasal verbs can take objects, but the meaning is different. Like other verbs, phrasal verbs can have several meanings.

18 Practice

Complete the conversation with the correct phrasal verb in parentheses.
Use the correct form of the phrasal verb. Then listen to check your answers.

AUDIO
DOWNLOAD

CD2, 14

KAREN: I feel so tired!

JENNY: (stay up/sit down) ___*Sit down*___ for a few minutes. Why are you so tired?
        ₁

KAREN: I (stay up/break down) _____ until midnight last night.
        ₂

JENNY: Why so late?

KAREN: Because I didn't (set out/get back) _____ from the library until 10:00.
        ₃

JENNY: Well, when did you (lie down/get up) _____ this morning?
        ₄

KAREN: At 7:00. Then I had to walk to school.

JENNY: Why?

KAREN: Because my car (break down/set out) _____ two blocks from
        ₅
        my house.

JENNY: Oh no! Maybe you shouldn't sit down. Maybe you should

        (set out/lie down) _____ !
        ₆

19   Read
Read the story. Then write answers to the questions.

NEW SHOES

A man needed a new pair of shoes. Before he went to the market, he drew up a detailed picture of his feet on a piece of paper. He measured his feet and wrote down all the measurements. Then he set off on foot for the shoe store. Later that day, he arrived at the market. However, he found out that he had forgotten to bring the paper with the measurements! He turned around and walked back home to get it. It was sunset by the time he got back to the market, and all the shops were closed. He explained his situation to one of the shopkeepers, who had already packed away all his goods.

"Foolish man!" said the shopkeeper. "Why did you go back home to get your measurements? You should trust your feet next time and try the shoes on in the store!"

1.   What did the man do before he went to the market to get a pair of shoes?

2.   What did he write down?

3.   How did he go to the shoe store?

4.   What happened when he arrived at the market?

5.   What did he do then?

6.   What happened at sunset?

7.   Who did he explain the situation to?

8.   According to the shopkeeper, which should he trust next time, his feet or his measurements?

20 Your Turn

Write about a difficult day that you have had. Use the phrasal verbs below. Be sure to use some phrasal verbs without objects.

Example

As soon as I got up, I knew that it would be a terrible day. I set out for work and discovered that my car had broken down.

drop in	fall behind	point out	run into	wake up
eat out	figure out	put on	take off	work out

7I Transitive Phrasal Verbs: Separable

Form/Function

Susan's **looking up** a fact on the Internet.
She's **looking** it **up**.

Many transitive phrasal verbs—phrasal verbs that have objects—can have their objects in two different positions. We call these *separable* phrasal verbs because the object can separate the verb from the particle. Separable phrasal verbs are very common in English.

1. If a separable phrasal verb has a noun object, the object can come before or after the particle.

Subject	Verb	Particle	Noun Object	Particle
We	**turned**	**on**	the television.	
We	**turned**		the television	**on.**

2. If the object is a pronoun (*me, you, him, her, us, it, them*), the object must come between the verb and the particle.

Subject	Verb	Pronoun Object	Particle
We	**turned**	it	**on.**

CORRECT: We turned **it on**.

INCORRECT: We turned ~~on it~~.

3. Here are common separable phrasal verbs.

Phrasal Verbs	Meaning	Example
call back	to call someone on the phone after he/she has called you	**Call** me **back** when you can.
call off	to cancel something (a meeting, a game, etc.)	They **called** the game **off** because of the storm.
call up	to telephone someone	If you want to go to the movies with Rosa, **call** her **up** and ask her!
fill out	to complete a form or questionnaire	You should **fill** this form **out** for the doctor.
find out	to find information about something	I **found** the answer **out** when I talked to my teacher.
look up	to find information in a dictionary, telephone book, encyclopedia, etc.	I need to **look** his phone number **up**.
pay back	to return money to someone	Thanks for the twenty dollars. I'll **pay** you **back** tomorrow.
pick up	to lift someone/something	Please **pick** the baby **up**.
put back	to return something to its original place	Please **put** the books **back** when you're finished with them.
put down	to put something on a surface like the floor or a table	I **put** your box **down** on the kitchen counter.
put off	to delay something to a later date	We should **put** the party **off** for a week.
put on	to wear something	**Put** your sweater **on** before you go out.
shut off	to stop a machine; turn off	How do you **shut off** this machine?

take back	to return something (usually to a store)	This CD player doesn't work right. I'm going to **take** it **back**.
take off	to remove clothes from the body	It's hot in here. I'm going to **take** my coat **off**.
throw out/away	to put something into the garbage or trash	I accidentally **threw** my homework **out**.
try on	to put on clothing to see if it is the correct size	Be sure to **try** those shoes **on** before you buy them.
turn down	to make the volume softer	The television is too loud. **Turn** it **down**.
turn off	to stop a machine	I can't hear you. **Turn** the radio **off**.
turn on	to start a machine	Please **turn** the oven **on**.
turn up	to make the volume louder	I like that song. **Turn** the radio **up**, please.
wake up	to stop somebody from sleeping	I **woke** the baby **up**.
write down	to write something on a piece of paper	I **wrote** the directions **down**, but now I can't find them.

21 Practice

Complete the sentences with the correct phrasal verb from the list.

call back	pick up	put on	throw out	wake up
look up	put down	take off	turn on	write down

1. My eyes are open at 6:00 every morning, but I __*wake up*__ my husband at 6:30.

2. Then I take shower and _____ my clothes _____ .

3. I _____ the television to listen to the news.

4. When I get to the office, I _____ my coat.

5. I _____ my bag on the floor, next to my desk.

6. Then I _____ the phone.

7. I listen to my calls and _____ important messages _____ on a note pad.

8. When a person says it's urgent and gives me a number, I _____ the person _____ .

9. I read all the mail. I _____ letters that I don't want.

10. I can't remember the numbers, so I _____ phone numbers all the time.

22 Pair Up and Talk

Work with a partner. Ask and answer the questions using separable phrasal verbs and pronouns.

YOU:	What do you do with a form or questionnaire?
YOUR PARTNER:	I fill it out.

1. What do you do with a form or questionnaire?

2. What do you do with old papers or things you do not want anymore?

3. What do you do with junk emails?

4. What do you do with your shoes when you walk in the front door of your house?

5. What do you do with your coat when you go outside?

6. What do you do with the television when you don't want to watch it anymore?

7. What do you do with the lights when you leave the room?

8. What do you do with your MP3 player when you're finished listening to it?

23 Practice

Replace the underlined words with a phrasal verb + an object.
Put the object in the correct place. Remember that sometimes the object can go in two places.

JANET: I'm going to the department store. I want to <u>return a blouse</u>.

1. *take it back*_____

MOTHER: Did you <u>put it on to see if it is the correct size</u> before you bought it?

2. _____

JANET: Yes, I did, but I don't like it now. Can I borrow twenty dollars from you? I'll <u>give the money to you</u> tomorrow.

3. _____

MOTHER: OK. But <u>put the milk in its place</u> before you go.

4. _____

JANET: Sure. Do you want me to <u>turn off the oven</u> as well? I think your cake is done.

5. _____

MOTHER: Yes, please. Thank you.

Form

Amanda **ran into** Jane yesterday.

1. Some transitive phrasal verbs with objects cannot have an object between the verb and the particle. We call these *inseparable* phrasal verbs. The object can only go after the verb and the particle.

   CORRECT: Amanda **ran into** Jane yesterday.
   INCORRECT: Amanda ran ~~Jane into~~ yesterday.

2. There are fewer inseparable phrasal verbs than separable phrasal verbs. Here are some common ones.

Phrasal Verb	Meaning	Example
come across	to find by chance	How did you **come across** that book?
drop off	to fall asleep	He studied until he **dropped off** around midnight.
get around	to travel or find the way	Were you able to **get around** OK in New York?
get into	to enter a car/taxi	We're late! **Get into** the car and let's go!
get off	to leave a bus/train/plane	Where do we **get off** the bus?
get on	to enter a bus/train/plane	Here's the bus. Let's **get on** it.
get on with	to make progress	I'm going to stop watching TV and **get on with** my homework.

get out	leave a car/taxi	We're there. Let's **get out** of the car.
get over	to recover	She has **gotten over** the flu.
go over	to review	Be sure to **go over** phrasal verbs before the test!
look after	to take care of	I have to **look after** the children today.
look forward to	to anticipate with pleasure	I **look forward** to your party on Saturday night.
look into	to investigate	The police are **looking into** the accident.
run into	to meet by chance	I **ran into** an old high school friend yesterday.

24 Practice

Complete the sentences with the correct phrasal verb from the list.
Use the correct form of the phrasal verb.

get into   get on   get over   look into
get off   get out   look after

Last night, Jackie had a problem with her bank account, and she needed to

____look into____ it. She stayed up until 11:30 P.M. This morning, she got up very late! She
          1

quickly _____ a taxi and went to work. When she _____ of the taxi,
                    2   **3**

she felt dizzy. She was trying to _____ a bad cold that she had for a week. She
                                          4

told the people at the office she was going home. She didn't want to go out for a few

days until she was better. She said her husband could _____ her at home. To
                                                              5

_____ and _____ a bus in this cold weather was not going to help her
      6   **7**

get better.

25 Pair Up and Talk
Work with a partner. Ask and answer the questions.

YOU: What are some kinds of transportation you get on and off?

YOUR PARTNER: You get on and off buses and trains.

1. What are some kinds of transportation you get on and off?

2. What are some forms of transportation you get into and out of?

3. What are some things or people you look after?

4. What are some illnesses that you have gotten over?

5. Tell about someone you have run into on the street.

6. What topics have you looked into for your classes?

Listening Puzzle

 AUDIO DOWNLOAD CD2, 15

A Listen and check the correct answer.

❑ A. *Easter Island*

❑ B. *Machu Picchu*

❑ C. *Stonehenge*

B Discuss your answer with your classmates.

 AUDIO DOWNLOAD CD2, 16

C Now listen again and write the sentences you hear.

A Before You Read

Answer the questions.

1. Where can we find rainforests?
2. What kinds of animals live in rainforests?

B Read

WHAT IS HAPPENING TO THE RAINFORESTS IN THE WORLD?

There are huge areas of dense forest in hot, wet parts of the world, or the tropics. The largest forests are around the Amazon River in South America, central
5 Africa, southeastern Asia, and on some Pacific islands. The rainforests cover about 2 percent of Earth's surface, but they contain 40
10 to 50 percent of all living plant and animal species. Scientists believe that over two million species of plants and animals live in the rainforest, and many
15 haven't been studied.

Today, humans are destroying about 50 million acres of rainforest per year, or about the size of a football field per second. At this rate, most of the rainforests will disappear by the
20 next century. Large commercial companies as well as small farmers clear the forests to make land for farming and mining, or for building cities, roads, pipelines, and reservoirs[1].

Why is this bad for the planet? One problem
25 is that scientists who work to make better varieties of plants for food need genes[2] from wild plants. Many of these are **becoming extinct**. More than 40 percent of the drugs we use come from the rainforests. Plants we could
30 use to save our lives are now becoming extinct. Rainforests also take in carbon dioxide from the air and put oxygen back into it. With no more forests, the amount of carbon dioxide in the air will go up. This may change our world climate
35 and have very bad results.

[1.] reservoirs = places where water is kept for future use
[2.] genes = the part of a living cell that controls the qualities
      of a living thing that are passed on from the parent

DID YOU KNOW … ?
At present, 25 percent of Western medicines come from the rainforest, but scientists have tested less than 1 percent of the plants there.

C Notice the Grammar

Underline all separable and inseparable phrasal verbs.

Choose the best answer.

D Look for Main Ideas

1. This reading is mainly about _____ .
   - Ⓐ where rainforests are located on Earth
   - Ⓑ how humans are destroying rainforests
   - Ⓒ how rainforests help us and what's in them
   - Ⓓ plant and animal species in rainforests

2. What is the main idea of paragraph 3?
   - Ⓐ Scientists need rainforest plants.
   - Ⓑ Rainforests can affect world climate.
   - Ⓒ Rainforests provide important things for humankind.
   - Ⓓ Many plants in the rainforests are becoming extinct.

E Look for Details

3. The tropics are _____ areas.
   - Ⓐ cold and dry
   - Ⓑ hot and wet
   - Ⓒ cold and wet
   - Ⓓ hot and dry

4. Why are rainforests important?
   - Ⓐ They have lots of drinking water.
   - Ⓑ They cover 40 percent of Earth's surface.
   - Ⓒ They have almost 50 percent of Earth's plant and animal species.
   - Ⓓ They constantly cause changes in Earth's climate.

5. All of the following are true of rainforests EXCEPT _____ .
   - Ⓐ they take in oxygen and release carbon dioxide into the air
   - Ⓑ there are large rainforests around the Amazon River in South America

READING SKILL:
Outlining

To outline a passage, underline the most important points. Then write them down. This helps you remember what you have read.

   - Ⓒ they provide 40 percent of the drugs we use in medicine
   - Ⓓ they have over two million species of plants and animals

F Make Inferences

6. What can we infer from paragraph 1?
   - Ⓐ There are many plant and animal species that are still unknown.
   - Ⓑ Rainforests occur in most parts of the world.
   - Ⓒ Climate has no effect on rainforests, so they can grow almost anywhere.
   - Ⓓ Scientists haven't spent much time in rainforests.

7. We can infer from the reading that _____ .
   - Ⓐ rainforests are not important to human survival
   - Ⓑ people are being careful not to harm too many rainforests
   - Ⓒ human progress is more important than preserving rainforests
   - Ⓓ the destruction of rainforests is bad for both humans and nature

G Look for Vocabulary

8. The phrase *becoming extinct* in the reading is closest in meaning to _____ .
   - Ⓐ changing greatly
   - Ⓑ moving around
   - Ⓒ becoming greater in number
   - Ⓓ dying off

Writing: Write a Questionnaire

Write questions about games or customs.

STEP **1** Work with a partner. You want to find out what other people know about a topic such as the Olympic Games or a custom in your country. Use the question words and forms you have learned in this unit to write a questionnaire with 20 questions.

Example
What are the Olympic Games?
Which country will host the Olympic Games next time?
When will the Olympic Games be held?
Which Olympic sport is your country good at?

STEP **2** **Evaluate your questionnaire.**

Checklist
_____ Did you write 20 questions?
_____ Are all of your questions about the same general topic?
_____ Do you know the answer to each question?
_____ Are your questions clear?

STEP **3** **Edit your questions. Work with a partner or your teacher to edit the questions. Correct spelling, punctuation, vocabulary, and grammar.**

STEP **4** **Make copies of your questionnaire. Ask people to write their answers. Report the results to the class.**

Self-Test

1. I can't study with the television on. Could you _____ ?

   A. turn off it   Ⓐ Ⓑ Ⓒ Ⓓ
   B. turn on it
   C. turn it off
   D. turn off television

2. If you don't know the meaning of the word, _____ in the dictionary.

   A. look up it   Ⓐ Ⓑ Ⓒ Ⓓ
   B. look it up
   C. look out it
   D. look the word

3. SUE: _____ did you live in Texas?
   TOM: Three years.

   A. When   Ⓐ Ⓑ Ⓒ Ⓓ
   B. How many
   C. What time
   D. How long

4. SUE: _____ didn't you write?
   TOM: Because I didn't have your address.

   A. Why   Ⓐ Ⓑ Ⓒ Ⓓ
   B. What
   C. How
   D. Which

5. He doesn't eat broccoli, _____ ?

   A. doesn't he   Ⓐ Ⓑ Ⓒ Ⓓ
   B. eats he
   C. isn't he
   D. does he

6. TOM: _____ is that bird?
   SUE: It's an eagle.

   A. Which   Ⓐ Ⓑ Ⓒ Ⓓ
   B. What
   C. How
   D. Who

7. You haven't seen my keys, _____ ?

   A. did you   Ⓐ Ⓑ Ⓒ Ⓓ
   B. you have
   C. don't you
   D. have you

8. JOE: _____ wake me up at 7:00?
   ANNE: Yes, I will.

   A. Will you   Ⓐ Ⓑ Ⓒ Ⓓ
   B. Would you
   C. Can you
   D. Could will

9. _____ going?

   A. What are you   Ⓐ Ⓑ Ⓒ Ⓓ
   B. Where you are
   C. Where are you
   D. Where you

10. BILLY: _____ crying?
    SUSIE: No, I'm not.

    A. You are   Ⓐ Ⓑ Ⓒ Ⓓ
    B. Why are you
    C. You
    D. Are you

1. How <u>many</u> does <u>it</u> <u>take</u> <u>to drive</u> to New York
      A   B   C   D
   from here?

   Ⓐ Ⓑ Ⓒ Ⓓ

2. <u>Did</u> they <u>came</u> <u>back</u> from <u>their</u> vacation?
    A   B   C   D

   Ⓐ Ⓑ Ⓒ Ⓓ

3. We <u>don't</u> <u>always</u> <u>have to</u> communicate with
       A   B   C
   words, <u>have</u> we?
            D   Ⓐ Ⓑ Ⓒ Ⓓ

4. We <u>have</u> apple pie <u>and</u> cherry pie. <u>What</u>
       A   B   C
   kind <u>would you</u> like?
          D
                            Ⓐ Ⓑ Ⓒ Ⓓ

5. Here is <u>a form</u>. You <u>have to</u> fill in <u>it</u> and
          A   B   C
   give <u>it</u> to the passport control officer.
        D
                            Ⓐ Ⓑ Ⓒ Ⓓ

6. I can't remember <u>the things</u> I <u>have to</u> do
                    A   B
   every day, so I write down <u>them</u> <u>on</u> a piece
                              C   D
   of paper.
                            Ⓐ Ⓑ Ⓒ Ⓓ

7. They <u>don't</u> have <u>any</u> children, <u>do</u> they <u>have</u>?
         A   B   C   D

   Ⓐ Ⓑ Ⓒ Ⓓ

8. The weather report <u>didn't</u> say <u>anything</u> about
                      A   B
   rain today, <u>did</u> <u>he</u>?
              C   D   Ⓐ Ⓑ Ⓒ Ⓓ

9. You will <u>be</u> <u>back</u> <u>on</u> Monday as usual, <u>will</u> you?
           A   B   C   D

   Ⓐ Ⓑ Ⓒ Ⓓ

10. Brenda <u>was</u> very sick <u>with</u> a bad cold, but now
           A   B
    <u>she's</u> getting it <u>over</u>.   Ⓐ Ⓑ Ⓒ Ⓓ
     C   D

Modal Auxiliaries and Related Forms

Jared plays safely. He **may fall**, so he wears a helmet.

8A | *Can, Could,* and *Be Able To* to Express Ability

Form

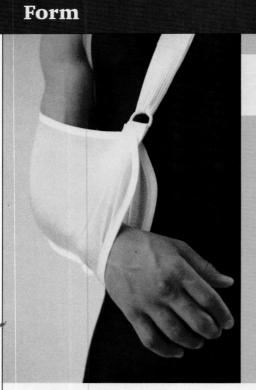

> Fred **could play** football last year, but he **can't play** football now.

1. We use the modal auxiliary *can* + a base verb to express ability in the present or future, and *could* + a base verb to express ability in the past.

   Fred **can scratch** his nose with his left hand.

   Fred **could play** guitar last week.

2. Like all modals, *can* and *could* take the same form for all persons. There is no *-s* ending in the third person singular.

   He **can ride** a bicycle when he is better.

   They **could stay up** all night when they were in high school.

3. We put *not* after *can*, *could*, and other modals to form the negative. Many modals can be contracted in their negative form.

   I **cannot believe** you called him.

   We **couldn't find** their house. We drove around for hours.

Affirmative	Negative Full Form	Negative Contraction
can	cannot	can't
could	could not	couldn't

Note that the full negative form of *can* is written as one word: *cannot*. The full negative form of other modal auxiliaries is written as two words: *could not*; *should not*.

Can: Ability in the Present or Future				Could: Ability in the Past			
Subject	Can Cannot Can't	Base Verb		Subject	Could Could Not Couldn't	Base Verb	
I You He/She/It We They	can cannot can't	play	now. later.	I You He/She/It We They	could could not couldn't	play	then.

4. We put *can*, *could*, and other modals before the subject to form questions.

Questions				Short Answers	
Can	Subject	Base Verb		Yes,	No,
Can	I you he/she/it we they	play	now? later?	you **can**. I/we **can**. he/she/it **can**. you **can**. they **can**.	you **can't**. I/we **can't**. he/she/it **can't**. you **can't**. they **can't**.

5. We can use *be able to* to express ability in the present, past, and future.

Be Able To: Ability in the Present				
Subject	Form of *Be*	*Able To*	Base Verb	
I	am	able to	play	now.
You	are			
He/She/It	is			
We	are			
They				

Be Able To: Ability in the Past				
Subject	Form of *Be*	*Able To*	Base Verb	
I	was	able to	play	yesterday.
You	were			
He/She/It	was			
We	were			
They				

Be Able To: Ability in the Future				
Subject	Form of *Be*	*Able To*	Base Verb	
I				
You				
He/She/It	will be	able to	play	tomorrow.
We				
They				

Function

1. We use *can* + a base verb to express ability in the present or future.

   She **can speak** Japanese.

   He **can play** tennis very well.

   I **can help** you in 15 minutes.

2. We use *could* + a base verb to express ability in the past.

   When I was young, I **could run** 8 kilometers.

   I **couldn't drive** five years ago.

3. *Am/is/are able to* and *was/were able to* have the same general meaning as *can* and *could*. *Can* and *could* are more common in speech.

   I wanted to call you, but I **couldn't remember** your phone number.

   I wanted to call you, but I **wasn't able to remember** your phone number.

4. When we want to suggest that something is frustrating or difficult, we usually use *be able to*.

   I tried very hard, but I **wasn't able to do** all of my math problems.

   After I spoke to my teacher, I **was able to do** them.

5. When we talk about a future ability that we do not have in the present, we use *will be able to*.

   Next year, I'**ll be able to drive**.

6. We must use *be able to*, not *can*, with some grammatical structures, such as with another modal and in the present perfect tense.

   CORRECT: You **should be able to do** this problem.

   INCORRECT: You ~~should can do~~ this problem.

   CORRECT: I **have been able to swim** since I was six.

   INCORRECT: I ~~can have swim~~ since I was six.

1 Practice

Fred has a broken leg and a broken right arm. What can he do? What can't he do? Complete the sentences with *can* or *can't* and one of the verbs from the list.

eat   hold   shake   watch   wear

1. He _can't wear_ his shoes.

2. He _____ his meals by himself.

3. He _____ a glass of water in his hands.

4. He _____ hands with visitors.

5. He _____ television.

2 Practice

Complete the sentences with *could* or *couldn't*.

Tarzan was a human who was born in a jungle. He _____could_____ survive there
                                                        1
because apes took care of him as their own baby. As Tarzan grew, he _____ do
                                                                              2
many things that the apes _____ do. He _____ swing from tree to tree.
                                  3   4
He _____ find nuts and fruit to eat.
        5
    One day, some European men in the jungle saw the strange man. They

_____ understand how he lived there. They tried to speak with him, but he
      6
_____ speak. He _____ only make animal noises. The men took
      7   8
Tarzan back to Europe with them. They taught him many things. After some time, he

_____ speak French. He _____ also walk and eat like other people.
      9   10

3 Pair Up and Talk

Work with a partner. Ask and answer the questions.

1. What other things could Tarzan do in the jungle?

2. What things could he do after he lived in Europe for a while?

4 Pair Up and Talk

Imagine that you are trapped in the jungle. You have been there for two weeks. What can you do? What did you use to do at home? Ask and answer questions with a partner. Use *can, can't, could,* and *couldn't.*

YOU:	I can eat nuts, but I can't eat pizza.
YOUR PARTNER:	Can you drink soda?
YOU:	No. I could drink soda at home, but now I can only drink coconut juice.

5 Practice

Joe likes outdoor activities. Rewrite the sentences using the correct form of *be able to* in place of *can/could* + a verb.

1. It's summer now. Joe and his friends can play baseball outdoors.

    It's summer now. Joe and his friends are able
    to play baseball outdoors.

2. He can go hiking in the mountains.

    _____

    _____

3. He can't go ice skating now, but he could go ice skating last winter.

    _____

    _____

4. Last winter, he couldn't go skiing because he didn't have the money.

    _____

    _____

5. He and I can go mountain climbing now.

    _____

    _____

6. We can't go mountain climbing in the winter because it's too dangerous then.

    _____

    _____

6 Pair Up and Talk

Tom can do some things, but he can't do others. Work with a partner. Use the prompts to ask and answer the questions about what Tom can do now and what he could do as a child.

YOU: Can Tom play tennis?

YOUR PARTNER: Yes, he can.

YOUR PARTNER: Could Tom ice skate as a child?

YOU: No, he couldn't.

Questions	Answers
1. play tennis (now)	yes
2. ice skate/as a child	no
3. run a marathon (now)	no
4. swim/as a child	yes
5. climb a mountain (now)	yes
6. speak Japanese/as a child	yes
7. drive a car/as a child	no
8. skateboard (now)	no

7 Pair Up and Talk

Work with a partner. Ask and answer the questions using *can, can't, could,* and *couldn't.*

YOU: What are three things you can do?

YOUR PARTNER: I can ski, I can speak German, and I can play football.

1. What are three things you can do?

2. What is something you can't do, but want to learn how to do?

3. What is something you couldn't do as a child, but can do now?

4. What is something you can't do now, but could do as a child?

8B

May I, Could I, and Can I to Ask for Permission

Form

RICHARD: **Can I have** another napkin?
ASA: Yes, of course.

Questions				Answers	
Modal	**Subject**	**Base Verb**		**Affirmative**	**Negative**
May				Yes, of course.	
Could	I	use	the phone?	Certainly.	I'm sorry. It's for office use only.
				Sure.*	
Can				No problem.*	
May	I	help	you?	Yes, please.	No, thanks.
Can					

*These expressions are informal English.

Function

1. We use *may I*, *can I*, and *could I* + a base verb to ask for permission to do something. *May I* is the most polite, or formal, of the three. We often use *may I* when speaking to someone who is older, who is in authority over us, or whom we do not know. We also use it often when speaking to someone on the phone when we do not know the person who answers.
2. *Could I* is more polite or formal than *can I*. *Could I* is a good choice for most situations.
3. *Can I* is often used between people who know each other well.

In these sentences, a customer asks for a form from a bank teller.

FORMAL:	**May I take** one of these?	(They do not know each other.)
	Could I take one of these?	(They might or might not know each other.)
INFORMAL:	**Can I take** one of these?	(They have been speaking together or they know each other.)

8 Practice

Complete the conversations with *may I, can I,* or *could I*. In some sentences, there is more than one correct answer.

1. STUDENT: _____May I_____ hand in my homework tomorrow, please?

   TEACHER: No, you may not.

2. STUDENT: _____Can I_____ borrow your grammar book?

   CLASSMATE: Sure.

3. YOU: _____Could I_____ use your computer?

   FRIEND: No problem.

4. YOU: _____Can I_____ have one of your cookies?

   ROOMMATE: Sure.

5. YOU: _____May I_____ speak with Professor Jones, please?

   SECRETARY: She's not here right now. _____May I_____ take a message?

9 Pair Up and Talk

Work with a partner. Ask and answer questions with *may I, can I,* and *could I.*

You are at a friend's house. You want to use the phone.

YOU: Can I use the phone?

YOUR PARTNER: Yes, sure.

1. You are at a friend's house. You want to use the telephone.

2. You want to sit next to a person you don't know in a fast food restaurant.

3. You are in a restaurant. You ask for the check.

4. You are in a shoe store. You want to try on the black shoes in the window in size 10.

5. The teacher is carrying a lot of books. You want to help her carry the books.

6. You are on the phone with a friend. The doorbell rings. You want to call your friend back later.

Form

Could you meet me later for a movie?

	Questions			Answers	
Modal	**Subject**	**Base Verb**		**Affirmative**	**Negative**
Can				Yes, of course.	Sorry, I can't.
Could	**you**	**wait**	a minute, please?	Certainly.	I'd like to, but I don't have time.
Would				Sure.*	
				OK.*	

*These expressions are informal English.

Function

1. We use *would you*, *could you*, and *can you* + a base verb to ask someone to do something. The meaning of these three modals is the same when we use them to make a request.

2. Although they have the same meaning, *would* and *could* are more formal than *can*. We generally use *could* and *would* when we make requests of strangers, older people, or people in authority. We use *would*, *could*, and *can* with friends and family members.

   TO A STRANGER: **Could/Would** you **send** the report, please?

   TO A FRIEND: **Could/Would/Can** you **come** here for a second?

3. We use *please* to make requests more polite. We use *please* especially with *would* or *could*. *Please* usually comes after the subject or at the end of the sentence. When *please* comes at the end of a sentence, we put a comma before it.

   Would you **please** sign this?

   Could you sign this, **please**?

10 Practice

Work with a partner. Make requests with *can you*, *could you*, and *would you*. More than one answer is possible. Then listen to check your answers.

1. You are speaking to your brother.

   YOU: _____Can you_____ hold this for me?

   BROTHER: Sure.

2. You are speaking to a bank teller.

   YOU: _Could you_ give me the balance of my checking account, please?

   BANK TELLER: Certainly. It's $506.25. Is there anything else I can do for you?

3. You are speaking to your boss.

   YOU: _Would you_ look over this report, please?

   BOSS: I can't do it now, but I'll do it as soon as I can.

4. You are speaking to a flight attendant.

   YOU: _____ bring me some water, please?

   FLIGHT ATTENDANT: Certainly.

5. You are speaking to a doctor.

   YOU: _____ give me the same prescription as last time, please?

   DOCTOR: Of course.

11 Pair Up and Talk

Work with a partner. Make requests and answer them with *can*, *could*, and *would*. More than one answer is possible.

YOU: Could you tell me the way to the exit, please?

YOUR PARTNER: Yes, it's over there to the left.

1. Ask a stranger to tell you the way to the exit.
2. Ask your roommate to answer the door.
3. Ask your brother to carry the groceries for you.
4. Ask a server at a restaurant to tell you about today's special.
5. Ask a travel agent to check for the cheapest fare.

Form

Jared skates safely.
He **may fall**, so he wears a helmet.

Subject	Modal (+ *Not*)	Base Verb
I	**may**	
You	**may not***	
He/She/It	**might**	**go.**
We	**might not***	
They	**could****	

* In this meaning, we do not contract *may* and *might* with *not*.
**In this meaning, we do not use *could* in the negative.

Function

1. We use *may*, *might*, or *could* + a base verb to express something that is possible now or in the future. *May*, *might*, and *could* mean "perhaps."

    She **may fall** and **break** something.

    OR She **might fall** and **break** something.

    OR She **could fall** and **break** something.

    OR **Perhaps** she **will fall** and **break** something.

2. Remember, we also use *could* + a base verb to mean past ability, to ask permission, and to make requests. We also use *may* + a base verb to ask for permission.

    I **could run** very fast when I was young.

    Could I **take** one of these?

    Could you **help** me, please?

    May I **take** one of these, please?

3. When expressing possibility, we do not use *may* in *yes/no* questions. *Might* can be used in *yes/no* questions, but it is very formal.

CORRECT:	**Could** that answer be correct?
CORRECT (very formal):	**Might** that answer be correct?
INCORRECT:	~~May~~ that answer be correct?

4. In this meaning, we do not use *could* in the negative.

CORRECT:	Our flight **may not** be late.
CORRECT (very formal):	Our flight **might not** be late.
INCORRECT:	Our flight ~~could not~~ be late. (This sentence means "It is impossible for our flight to be late.")

12 Practice

A Underline the correct verb in parentheses.

ANN: What's for dinner?

BETTY: We (<u>are having</u>/may have) chicken. It's in the oven.
         1

ANN: When will it be ready?

BETTY: I'm not sure. It (will/may) be ready in half an hour.
         2

ANN: What time is John coming?

BETTY: I don't know. It depends on the traffic. He (may/will) be late.
         3

ANN: Is Ted coming at 7:00?

BETTY: Yes. He called. He's on his way. He (will/may) be here at 7:00 for sure.
         4

ANN: Are we having dessert?

BETTY: Yes, we (are/might). It's in the refrigerator.
         5

ANN: It's the doorbell. Who can it be?

BETTY: I don't know. It (is/may be) Ted.
         6

B Listen to check your answers. Now practice the conversation with a partner.

13 Practice

Carla and George are worried about their friend's arrival from the airport. Read their conversation. Underline the correct form in parentheses. In some cases, both forms are possible. Listen to check your answers.

CD2, 19

GEORGE: (<u>Could</u>/May) his flight be late?
                    1

CARLA: Maybe, or he (could/may) be caught in traffic.
                            2

GEORGE: I don't think so. There isn't much traffic at this time.

CARLA: There (might not/mightn't) be a lot of traffic, but perhaps he got lost.
                    3

GEORGE: (May/Could) we call him?
          4

CARLA: I tried. He didn't answer. His cell phone (might not/couldn't) be on.
                                                            5

GEORGE: Let's call the airline. They (may/could not) have some information about
                                        6

the flight.

CARLA: Good idea. Oh! I see lights in the driveway. (Might/Could) that be his car?
                                                                7

14 Pair Up and Talk

Donald worries about everything. Work with a partner. Ask and answer questions about why Donald doesn't do each thing. Use the prompts to answer the questions with *may*, *might*, or *could*.

YOU: Why doesn't Donald fly?
YOUR PARTNER: He doesn't fly because he thinks the plane might crash.

Questions	Answers
1. not/fly	the plane/crash
2. not/go to the beach	he/get sunburned
3. not/go to the zoo	an animal/bite him
4. not/go out when it's raining	he/catch a cold
5. not/drive	he/have an accident
6. not/eat in a restaurant	the food/have bacteria in it
7. not/go downtown at night	a thief/steal his wallet
8. not/want to get married	his wife/divorce him

8E | *Maybe* OR *May Be*

Form/Function

Antonio is thinking about a young woman he saw.
"**Maybe** she's not married," he thinks.

1. *Maybe* (one word) and *may be* (two words) both express possibility.
2. *Maybe* (one word) is an adverb. It comes in front of a subject and a verb. It means "perhaps" or "possibly."
   Maybe she's not married.
3. *May be* (two words) is used as the verb of a sentence.
   She **may be** married.

AUDIO
DOWNLOAD

CD2, 20

15 Practice

Antonio saw an attractive woman on the street yesterday. Her name is Angelica. Listen and complete the sentences with *may be* or *maybe*.

1. Her name is Angelica. ___Maybe___ she's French.

2. He doesn't know what she does. ___maybe___ she's a dancer.

3. Yes, she ___May be___ a ballet dancer.

4. He saw Angelica for the first time yesterday. Why didn't he see her before?
   She ___May be___ from out of town.

5. He said, "Hello," and asked, "What's your name?" She didn't say anything.
   At first Antonio thought, "She ___May be___ from another country." So he said slowly, "My name is Antonio. What is your name?"

6. She looked at him strangely. ___Maybe___ she thought he was impolite.

7. Then she said, "Angelica." ___Maybe___ it wasn't her real name. Then she ran away.

16 **Pair Up and Talk**

Work with a partner. Finish the story about Antonio and Angelica. Use *maybe* and *may be*. When you are finished, share your story with the class.

17 **Your Turn**

Work in pairs or groups. Look at the two photos. Use *may, might,* or *maybe* to make guesses about what you think these objects are.

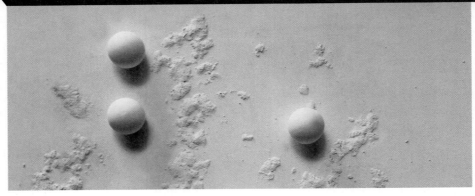

A

1. _____

2. _____

3. _____

4. _____

B

1. _____

2. _____

3. _____

4. _____

Let's and *Why Don't We* to Make Suggestions; *Why Don't You* to Give Advice

Form/Function

> **Why don't we eat** now?

Suggestions

1. We can make suggestions with *let's* and *why don't we* + a base verb. They have the same meaning.
2. *Let's* is a contraction of *let* + *us*. We usually say and write *let's*. *Let us* is very formal. We rarely use it.
3. *Let's* includes you and one or more other people.

Affirmative				
Let's	Base Verb		Ways to Agree	Ways to Disagree
Let's	watch	TV.	Good idea. Sure. OK. Fine with me.	I'd rather not. Let's … instead. Let's not.
	go	dancing.		
	eat	now.		

Negative				
Let's Not	Base Verb		Ways to Agree	Ways to Disagree
Let's not	watch	TV.	I agree. Good idea. Sure. OK.	Oh, I'd really like to. Why not?
	go	dancing.		
	eat	now.		

Why Don't We	Base Verb		Ways to Agree	Ways to Disagree
Why don't we	watch	TV?	Good idea. Sure. OK.	I'd rather not. Let's … instead. Let's not.
	go	dancing?		
	eat	now?		

Advice

4. We use *why don't you* + a base verb to give friendly advice to someone.

Why Don't You	Base Verb		Ways to Agree	Ways to Disagree
Why don't you	rest	a little?	Good idea. OK. I will.	I have no time. I'm OK.
	go	to the doctor?		

18 Practice

Make suggestions with *let's* or *why don't we* and one of the ideas in the list, or use your own ideas.

buy her a gift	go see it	study together in the library
go for a walk	hurry	watch it
go get a pizza	♪ stay home and watch TV	

1. It's a beautiful day.

   Why don't we go for a walk?

2. There's a good movie on at the movie theater here.

   Why don't we watch it

3. It's raining again tonight. I don't want to go out. What should we do?

   _____

4. I'm hungry, but there's nothing to eat here.

   _____

5. There's a good football game on TV now.

   _____

6. It's Carol's birthday next Monday.

   _____

7. We have a test tomorrow.

   _____

8. Class starts in a few minutes.

   _____

19 Practice

A Look at these problems. Give advice to your friend with *why don't you* and one of the ideas from the list, or use your own ideas.

call the store	have a cup of coffee	put on a sweater
go to the dentist	have a piece of fruit	take an aspirin

1. YOUR FRIEND: I can't find my credit card. I think I left it in the department store today.

   YOU: *Why don't you call the store?*

2. YOUR FRIEND: I have a terrible headache.

YOU: _Let's take an aspirin_

3. YOUR FRIEND: I have a toothache.

YOU: _Why don't you go to the dentist_

4. YOUR FRIEND: I'm cold.

YOU: _Let's put on a sweater_

5. YOUR FRIEND: Reviewing for the test is making me sleepy.

YOU: _Why don't you have a cup of coffee_

6. YOUR FRIEND: I'm hungry, but I don't have time to eat lunch right now.

YOU: _Why don't you have a piece of fruit._

B   **Now practice asking and answering the questions with a partner.**

20   Pair Up and Talk

Work with a partner and make suggestions for a class party. Use *let's* or *why don't we*. Give answers. Be sure to talk about the place, date, and time of the party. Discuss food, drinks, and entertainment.

YOU: Why don't we have the party in a hotel?

YOUR PARTNER: No, that's too expensive. Let's have it in the student center.

YOU: Good idea. Let's not have music, though.

YOUR PARTNER: Why not?

21   Pair Up and Talk

Work with a partner or the class. Name some problems that you are having at home or at work. Your partner gives advice.

YOU: My dog is gaining weight.

YOUR PARTNER: Why don't you take him for a walk every day?

YOUR PARTNER: My brother plays loud music when I'm studying.

YOU: Why don't you ask him to turn it down?

8G Should, Ought To, and Had Better to Give Advice

Form

I broke my friend's CD player.
Should I **buy** a new one for him?

Advice

Affirmative Statement			Negative Statement		
Subject	**Modal**	**Base Verb**	**Subject**	**Modal + *Not***	**Base Verb**
You	**should ought to**	**buy** a new one.	You	**should not shouldn't**	**lie** about it.

1. We use *should* and *ought to* + a base verb to say what is the best or right thing to do. *Should* and *ought to* have the same meaning.

2. We usually do not use *ought to* in questions, negative sentences, and short answers. We use *should* instead.

> You **shouldn't stay up** late. You have an exam tomorrow.
> **Should** I **send** a card?
> Yes, you **should**.

Strong Advice or Warning

Affirmative Statements				Negative Statements		
Subject	**Modal**	**Base Verb**		**Subject**	**Modal + *Not***	**Base Verb**
You	**had better 'd better**	**hurry.**		We	**had better not 'd better not**	**wait.**
We		**eat**	now.	She		**leave.**

3. We use *had better* to give a strong recommendation. *Had better* often suggests a warning and is stronger than *should* or *ought to*. The speaker expects the action to happen. The contraction of *had better* is *'d better*.

> It's raining. You **had better take** an umbrella.
> We**'d better not be** late or we'll miss the plane.

4. We rarely use *had better* in questions.

22 Practice

Benny is overweight and is not feeling well. He eats, smokes, and works too much. Use *had better* or *had better not* with the words in parentheses to give him strong advice.

1. (eat less)   You had better eat less.
2. (drink a lot of soft drinks) _____
3. (drink too much coffee)   _____
4. (get more exercise)   _____
5. (use less salt)   _____
6. (eat lots of snacks)   _____
7. (work overtime often)   _____
8. (see a doctor)   _____

23 Practice

Give strong advice in these situations. Write a sentence with *had better* and a sentence with *had better not*.

1. I'm going out, and it's starting to rain.

    You had better take an umbrella.
    You'd better not go out.

2. I think I have a temperature.

    _____

    _____

3. I might miss an important interview. I have to be there in ten minutes.

    _____

    _____

24 Your Turn

Imagine a friend is going out to dinner with his girlfriend's parents. What advice do you have for him? Talk about your answers with a partner. Use *should, shouldn't, ought to, had better,* and *had better not.*

He should go to a nice restaurant. He'd better not be late. He ought to wear a tie.

Prefer …To, Like … Better Than, and *Would Rather* to Express Preference

Form/Function

I **prefer** playing football **to** basketball.

1. We can use *prefer … to* to express preferences. We can use either a noun or a gerund as an object after *prefer*. (A gerund is a verb + *-ing* used as a noun.)

Subject	*Prefer*	Object	*To*	Object
I	prefer	football	to	basketball.
		playing football		playing basketball.

2. We can also use *like* with *better than* or other comparative forms to express preferences. We can use either a noun or a gerund as an object after *like*.

Subject	*Like*	Object	Comparative Form	Object
I	like	football	better than	basketball.
		playing football		playing basketball.

3. We can also use *would rather (not)* to express preferences. We use *than* when we talk about two things.

Subject	*Would Rather (Not)*	Base Verb	Object	*Than*	Object
I	would rather 'd rather	play	football	than	(play) basketball.
	would rather not* 'd rather not*	play	football.		

*We do not use the negative form *wouldn't* in sentences with *would rather* + *than*, except in questions.

CORRECT: **Wouldn't** you **rather play** football **than** basketball?

INCORRECT: Would you rather play football ~~than~~ basketball?

4. In questions with *would rather*, we often use *or*.

Would	Subject	Rather (Not)	Base Verb	Object	Or	Object
Would	you	rather	have	soup	or	salad?
Would	you	rather	see	this movie	or	that one?

5. *Prefer … to, like … better than*, and *would rather* have the same meaning. We use them to say what we prefer to do, or that we like one thing more than another.

Subject	Prefer, Like, or Would Rather + Verb	Object	To or (Better) Than	Object
I	**prefer**	soup	**to**	salad.
I	**like**	soup	**better than**	salad.
I	**'d rather have**	soup	**than**	salad.

25   Practice
Complete the sentences with *(better) than*, *to*, and *or*.

1. I'd rather sit by the window _____*than*_____ sit at the back of the restaurant.
2. I like the table by the window __better than__ the table at the back.
3. I prefer the table by the window _____to_____ the table at the back.
4. I like rice better _____than_____ potatoes.
5. I prefer rice _____to_____ potatoes.
6. I'd rather have rice _____than_____ potatoes.
7. Would you rather have fish _____ meat?
8. I prefer having fish _____ having meat.
9. Do you like having fish __better than__ eating meat?
10. Would you rather pay cash _____than_____ pay with a credit card?
11. I prefer paying with a credit card _____to_____ paying cash.
12. I like paying by credit card _____ paying cash.

Pair Up and Talk
Work with a partner. Use the prompts to ask and answer questions about preferences.

YOU: Let's take the bus.
YOUR PARTNER: I prefer taking a taxi.

Suggestion/Offer	Reply
Student A	**Student B**
1. Let's take the bus.	prefer/take a taxi
2. Would you like to sit down?	prefer/stand
3. Shall we eat at home?	rather/go to a restaurant
4. Do you want to watch TV?	rather/read a book
Student B	**Student A**
5. Shall we drive there?	prefer/go by plane
6. Would you like to write a thank you card?	prefer/call them
7. Do you want to stay a few more minutes?	rather/go now
8. Would you like to eat now?	rather/eat later

27 Pair Up and Talk
Work with a partner. What would you rather do? Use *I'd rather* to talk about what you prefer. Write your answers in the chart. Which ones are the same? Which are different?

I'd rather play soccer than football. Andrei would rather play football than soccer.

	You	Your Partner
1. play football or soccer	_____	_____
2. live in the country or the city	_____	_____
3. be married or single	_____	_____
4. drink tea or coffee	_____	_____
5. do homework or watch TV	_____	_____

Have To, *Have Got To*, and *Must* to Express Necessity

Form

Estela **doesn't have to work** today.

Have To: Present and Future

Affirmative Statements			Negative Statements		
Subject	***Have/Has To***	**Base Verb**	**Subject**	***Not Have To***	**Base Verb**
I	have to*		I	do not have to / don't have to	
You			You		
He/She/It	has to*	work.	He/She/It	does not have to / doesn't have to	work.
We	have to*		We	do not have to / don't have to	
They			They		

*We do not contract *have to* and *has to* with the subject.

CORRECT: I have to work.

INCORRECT: I've to work.

Yes/No Questions				Short Answers	
Do/Does	**Subject**	***Have To***	**Base Verb**	**Yes,**	**No,**
Do	I	have to	work?	you **do**.	you **don't**.
	you			I/we **do**.	I/we **don't**.
Does	he/she/it			he/she/it **does**.	he/she/it **doesn't**.
Do	we			you **do**.	you **don't**.
	they			they **do**.	they **don't**.

Have To: **Past**

Affirmative Statements			Negative Statements		
Subject	*Had To*	**Base Verb**	**Subject**	*Not Have To*	**Base Verb**
I			I		
You			You		
He/She/It	**had to***	**work.**	He/She/It	**did not have to** **didn't have to**	**work.**
We			We		
They			They		

*We do not contract *had to* with the subject.

    CORRECT: I had to work.

    INCORRECT: I'd to work.

Yes/No Questions				Short Answers	
Did	**Subject**	*Have To*	**Base Verb**	**Yes,**	**No,**
	I			you **did.**	you **didn't.**
	you			I/we **did.**	I/we **didn't.**
Did	he/she/it	**have to**	**work?**	he/she/it **did.**	he/she/it **didn't.**
	we			you **did.**	you **didn't.**
	they			they **did.**	they **didn't.**

Have Got To/Must: **Present and Future**

Subject	*Have/Has Got To/Must*	**Base Verb**	
I	**have got to/must** **'ve got to**		
You			
He/She/It	**has got to/must** **'s got to**	**work**	now. later. tomorrow.
We	**have got to/must** **'ve got to**		
They			

Function

1. *Must, have to,* and *have got to* have almost the same meaning. They all mean that it is necessary to do something.

2. *Must* is the strongest form. We use *must* in requirements, rules, and laws. We often use *must* in written instructions.

    You **must take** an entrance exam. (school requirements)

    Drivers **must signal** before they turn right or left. (driver's manual)

3. When *must* expresses necessity, we use it only to refer to the present or the future. To refer to the past, we use *had to*.

    CORRECT: I had to work last Saturday.

    INCORRECT: I ~~must work~~ last Saturday.

4. We usually use *have to* and *have got to* in everyday conversation. *Have to* and *have got to* have the same meaning.

    It's Saturday, but I **have to work**.   OR   It's Saturday, but I**'ve got to work**.

    I **had to work** last Saturday, too.

5. We do not usually use *have got to* in questions and negative statements.

6. We use *have got to* only to refer to present and future necessity. To refer to the past, we use *had to*.

    CORRECT: We had to finish this homework.

    INCORRECT: We ~~had got to~~ finish this homework.

---

28   Practice

Change the written information with *must* to a spoken form with *have to* or *have got to*. More than one answer is possible. Then listen to the answers. Notice that in spoken form, *have to* sounds like "hafta," *has to* sounds like "hasta," and *got to* sounds like "gotta."

AUDIO
DOWNLOAD

CD2, 21

1.   All students must register and pay fees.

    All students have to register and pay fees.

2.   All students must register before taking courses.

    All student had to byore to

3.   Every student must take an English placement exam.

    had got

4.   Every new student must attend orientation during registration week.

5.   Students must present registration forms on the first day of classes.

    Student

29   Your Turn

Write three things you had to do last week and three things you have to/have got to do this week. Share your answers with your partner.

Last week, I had to do my laundry. This week, I've got to write an important essay.

8J Must Not to Forbid and Not Have To to Express Lack of Necessity

Form/Function

Look at the sign!
We **must not swim** here.

1. We use *must not* + a base verb to say that something is not allowed or is forbidden. *Must not* is stronger than *should not*.

Subject	Modal + *Not*	Base Verb
I		
You		
He/She/It	must not	park here.
We/They		

2. We use *not have to* to show that something is not necessary. (See pages 207–208 for the forms of *not have to*.)

Tomorrow is Sunday. You **don't have to** get up early.

I **didn't have to** get up early yesterday.

30 Practice
Look at the following instructions about flights and planes. Then write sentences with *must not* or *don't have to*.

1. It isn't necessary for you to fasten your seatbelt all through a flight, but it's a good idea.

   <u>You don't have to fasten your seatbelt</u>

   <u>all through a flight.</u>

2. It is forbidden to smoke on the aircraft.

   <u>You must not smoke on the aircraft.</u>

3. It isn't necessary for you to carry your medication with you, but it's a good idea.

   <u>You don't have to carry your medication</u>

grill

4. It isn't necessary for you to put labels on your luggage, but it's a good idea in case it gets lost.

    _____

5. It is forbidden to carry knives or sharp objects in your carry-on luggage.

    _____

6. It is forbidden to carry more than two pieces of carry-on luggage.

    _____

31   Practice
Look at these washing labels on clothes. Say what they mean. Use *must*, *must not*, or *don't have to.*

Hand wash or dry clean.
XL

1. You don't have to dry clean this clothing.

Do not bleach.
M

2. _____

Warm iron recommended.
XL

3. You don't have to iron

Dry flat or tumble dry.
S

4. _____

Cold water only.
L

5. _____

Do not dry clean.
M

6. _____

32 Practice

Work with a partner. You are going for a vacation in the sun in the Caribbean. You will be staying at a nice hotel. What must you not forget? What do you not have to take? Write your answers in a list. Do you both agree?

Example

blankets

I don't have to take blankets.

1. blankets
2. a coat
3. gloves
4. a grammar book
5. knives and forks

6. my passport
7. my plane tickets
8. a suit
9. my sunglasses
10. a swimsuit

33 Your Turn

You are going for a weekend at a friend's house. Write three things you must not forget to take with you and three things you don't have to take.

Example

I must not forget my toothbrush.

Things I must not forget

1. _____
2. _____
3. _____

Things I don't have to take

1. _____
2. _____
3. _____

Function

A: Who is that woman? Is she a student?

B: I don't know, but I've seen her go into the teacher's room.

A: Oh. She **must be** a teacher. She **must not be** a student.

1. We use *must* for deductions, or guesses, from facts that we know. *Must* expresses what is logical in the situation.

      FACT: Tony has three houses and four cars.

      DEDUCTION: He **must** be rich.

2. We use *must not* for a negative deduction.

      FACT: Tony has three companies. He works very hard.

      DEDUCTION: He **must not** have a lot of free time.

3. Remember, we also use *must* to express strong necessity, and we use *must not* when we forbid something.

      You **must** do your homework.

      You **must not** drive when the traffic light is red.

34 Pair Up and Talk

Work with a partner to make deductions. Three people are having breakfast in a hotel. Some of their belongings are on their tables. What can you tell about their owners? Complete the sentences with *must*.

A

1. The owner *must be a woman.*
2. The owner
3. The owner

B

1. The owner
2. The owner
3. The owner

C

1. The owner
2. The owner
3. The owner

35   Read

Read the story. Then write answers to the questions.

THE BOASTING TRAVELER

A man returned to his own country after traveling all around the world. He was a boastful[1] man. Naturally, he had to tell others of the many wonderful things he had done in the different places he had visited. Among these, he said, "When I was in Rhodes, I jumped a great distance. No other man could jump so far. There were many people in Rhodes who saw me do it, and I could call them as witnesses."

One of the bystanders interrupted him, saying, "Now my good man, if you can jump so well, we don't have to go to Rhodes to prove it. Let's imagine this is Rhodes for a minute. And now—jump!"

[1.] boastful = showing pride and self-importance

1. What had the man done before he returned to his country?
2. What tells you he was boastful?
3. What did he do in Rhodes?
4. Could any other man do what he did?
5. Who could he call to prove this?
6. Do they have to go to Rhodes to prove this?
7. What is the bystander's suggestion?
8. Do you think he could jump so well?

_____

_____

_____

_____

_____

_____

_____

_____

Form

Turn right at the traffic light.

1. We use the base form of the verb in imperative sentences. The verb is always the same form.
2. We use the imperative to address one or more people. The subject of the sentence, *you*, is understood. It is not stated.

    Open the window.
3. We can use *please* at the beginning or at the end of the sentence. At the end of the sentence, it must follow a comma.

    Please open your books.   OR   Open your books, **please**.
4. For the negative, we use *do not* or *don't* before the base form of the verb.

    Do not be late.   OR   **Don't be** late!

Function

We use the imperative to tell someone to do something. Imperatives are used for these purposes.

Function	Example
1. Commands	**Wash** your hands.
2. Requests	Please **turn off** the lights.
3. Directions	**Turn** right at the traffic light.
4. Instructions	**Cook** for 15 minutes.
5. Warnings	**Be** careful.
6. Advice	**Get** some sleep.

36 Practice

Complete the teacher's instructions with the verbs in the list. Use *don't* where necessary.

be	chew	close	do	sit	stop	talk	work

1. _____Close_____ your books.
2. _____ on your cell phone.
3. _don't chew_ gum in class.
4. _____work_____ with your partner.
5. _____Do_____ homework in class.
6. _____Be_____ quiet!
7. _____ down.
8. _____ that noise!

Listening Puzzle

  CD2, 22

A   Listen and check the correct answer.

❑ A. *penguin*

❑ B. *sea lion*

❑ C. *walrus*

B   Discuss your answer with your classmates.

CD2, 23

C   Now listen again and write the sentences you hear.

Reading Challenge

A Before You Read
Answer the questions.
1. How was the mail delivered in your country in past times? How is it delivered today?
2. Was it difficult to travel across your country in the past? How did people travel?

B Read

THE PONY EXPRESS

The Pony Express was a postal service that **linked** the east of the United States with the far west. It began in 1860 when there was no railway that went farther west than the

5 Mississippi and Missouri rivers. All the mail had to travel by stagecoach on a long, slow route that took about one month.

10 The Pony Express went from the state of Missouri to Sacramento, California. There were 180 stations along the route, about 10 to 15 miles (16 to 24 kilometers) apart. There were 80 15 riders and 400 horses. The riders went as fast as 25 miles (40 kilometers) an hour from one station to the next. At each station, a new horse was ready for them. Each rider had to go 75 miles (120 kilometers) before passing the mail 20 to the next rider. In this way, the Pony Express could deliver the mail in about nine days.

The Pony Express riders faced many dangers. They had to cross deserts, mountains, and rivers. They had to travel in all kinds of 25 weather. Bandits or Native Americans could attack them. The riders were not big and strong, either. They were thin teenagers because adult riders weighed too much. Yet only one rider died, and the mail was lost only once.

30 The Pony Express lasted only 18 months. It ended in 1861 when a telegraph line was built across the country. What the riders could do in nine days, the telegraph could do in a few minutes.

C Notice the Grammar
Underline all forms of modals.

Choose the best answer.

D Look for Main Ideas

1. Paragraph 2 is mostly about _____ .
   - A why people needed the Pony Express
   - B the number of horses and riders the Pony Express needed
   - C how the Pony Express delivered the mail
   - D what distance each Pony Express rider had to cover

2. What is the main idea of paragraph 3?
   - A Sometimes Pony Express riders had to face bad weather.
   - B The land between Missouri and California was hard for riders to cross.
   - C Only one young Pony Express rider lost his life.
   - D There were many dangers along the Pony Express route.

E Look for Details

3. What was at every Pony Express station?
   - A new riders
   - B a fresh horse
   - C more mail
   - D bandits

4. In which paragraph does the author talk about the start of the telegraph?
   - A paragraph 1
   - B paragraph 2
   - C paragraph 3
   - D paragraph 4

5. Which of the following is NOT true of the Pony Express?
   - A It delivered mail in about nine days.
   - B It linked the northern and southern parts of the U.S.
   - C Each rider rode 75 miles.
   - D The stations were 10 to 15 miles apart.

F Make Inferences

6. What can we infer about the Pony Express riders?
   - A They were courageous horsemen.
   - B They were experienced fighters.
   - C They wanted fame and fortune.
   - D They couldn't endure much hardship.

7. We can infer from the reading that the Pony Express _____ .
   - A wasn't very important in its day
   - B needed to have older and stronger riders
   - C was a failure in the end
   - D provided a brief but vital service to the country

G Look for Vocabulary

8. The word *linked* in the reading is closest in meaning to _____ .
   - A crossed
   - B passed by
   - C connected
   - D went around

Writing: Write a Friendly Letter

Write a letter to a friend about changes in your life.

STEP 1   **Read the situation.**

You have been accepted at a famous university to study for your Bachelor of Arts degree. The university is famous, but it is not in your city. You have to leave home and move far away. You are writing a letter to a friend explaining the changes in your life.

STEP 2   **Think about these facts and write sentences using modals.**

1. move to a new city or country
2. make new friends
3. live in the school dorm or find a cheap apartment
4. leave everything behind
5. not come home for long periods

STEP 3   **Rewrite the sentences as a paragraph as in the model letter below.**

> Dear Paul,   May 1, 20XX
>   I'm writing to tell you that I got accepted at the University of
> _____ . It's a famous university, but it is not in my city, so I have to
> go live there. I'm going next month. I have to do many things.
> Your friend,

STEP 4   **Evaluate your paragraph.**

Checklist

_____ Did you write the letter in correct letter form (date, greeting, body, closing, and signature)?

_____ Did you indent your paragraph?

_____ Did you use some modal auxiliaries in your sentences?

STEP 5   **Work with a partner or your teacher to edit your sentences. Check spelling, punctuation, and grammar.**

STEP 6   **Write a final copy of your paragraph.**

Self-Test

1. You _____ put that blouse in the washing machine. It says dry clean only.

   A. must   Ⓐ Ⓑ Ⓒ Ⓓ
   B. mustn't
   C. don't have to
   D. have to

2. I _____ read until I was six.

   A. can't   Ⓐ Ⓑ Ⓒ Ⓓ
   B. shouldn't
   C. couldn't
   D. mustn't

3. _____ I borrow your pen, please?

   A. May   Ⓐ Ⓑ Ⓒ Ⓓ
   B. Would
   C. Should
   D. Will

4. I _____ go to the market. I need some eggs for this cake.

   A. might   Ⓐ Ⓑ Ⓒ Ⓓ
   B. could
   C. must
   D. mustn't

5. We _____ leave now. It's getting late.

   A. could   Ⓐ Ⓑ Ⓒ Ⓓ
   B. should
   C. might
   D. are able to

6. PAM: What should we have for lunch?
   NATE: _____ pizza?

   A. Why don't we have   Ⓐ Ⓑ Ⓒ Ⓓ
   B. I'd rather have
   C. We'd better have
   D. We have to have

7. _____ you open the door for me, please?

   A. May   Ⓐ Ⓑ Ⓒ Ⓓ
   B. Could
   C. Should
   D. Might

8. I'm sorry, I _____ to play football with you next week. I'm going out of town.

   A. can't   Ⓐ Ⓑ Ⓒ Ⓓ
   B. don't have
   C. won't be able
   D. must not

9. I don't know her. She _____ a student.

   A. maybe   Ⓐ Ⓑ Ⓒ Ⓓ
   B. may be
   C. 'd rather be
   D. should

10. _____ You are going to fall.

    A. You may be careful.   Ⓐ Ⓑ Ⓒ Ⓓ
    B. You could be careful.
    C. You are careful!
    D. Be careful!

1. You <u>don't</u> <u>have be</u> <u>a</u> citizen <u>to get</u> a
        A   **B**   **C**   **D**
   driver's license.
                        Ⓐ   Ⓑ   Ⓒ   Ⓓ

2. <u>You</u> must <u>to drive</u> with a seatbelt <u>in</u>
    A   **B** **C**   **D**
   this country.
                        Ⓐ   Ⓑ   Ⓒ   Ⓓ

3. In most <u>movie theaters</u>, senior citizens
             A
   <u>can't</u> <u>have to</u> pay full price for <u>a movie</u>.
    B   **C**   **D**
                  Ⓐ   Ⓑ   Ⓒ   Ⓓ

4. The store <u>maybe</u> very <u>crowded</u> tomorrow
            A   **B**
   because <u>there is</u> <u>a</u> big sale.
           C   **D**
                  Ⓐ   Ⓑ   Ⓒ   Ⓓ

5. You <u>could</u> not <u>sign</u> <u>anything</u> before reading
         A   **B**   **C**
   <u>it</u> carefully.
   D   Ⓐ   Ⓑ   Ⓒ   Ⓓ

6. <u>Would</u> you <u>rather see</u> a movie <u>to</u> stay at home
     A   **B**   **C**
   and <u>watch</u> a video?
       D
                  Ⓐ   Ⓑ   Ⓒ   Ⓓ

7. <u>You better</u> <u>study</u> more, or you <u>might</u> not <u>pass</u>
    A   **B**   **C**   **D**
   the class.
                  Ⓐ   Ⓑ   Ⓒ   Ⓓ

8. Karen <u>was</u> able <u>change</u> <u>the</u> flat tire
        A   **B**   **C**
   <u>by herself</u> yesterday.
     D
                  Ⓐ   Ⓑ   Ⓒ   Ⓓ

9. You <u>mightn't</u> try <u>to take</u> the entrance exam
         A   **B**
   without <u>preparing</u> for <u>it</u> first.
           C   **D**
                  Ⓐ   Ⓑ   Ⓒ   Ⓓ

10. We <u>must</u> to work overtime last week <u>in order to</u>
       A   **B**
    <u>finish</u> <u>the project</u> by the deadline.
     C   **D**
                   Ⓐ   Ⓑ   Ⓒ   Ⓓ

Unit 9
Gerunds and Infinitives

Climbing mountains is dangerous. Melanie loves **climbing** mountains.

9A Gerund as Subject and Object
(**Climbing mountains is dangerous.**
I love climbing rocks.)

9B Verb + Gerund (**enjoy skiing, go dancing**)

9C Verb + Infinitive (**Try to call her.**)

9D Verb + Gerund or Infinitive
(**Pete loves golfing. He loves to golf on vacation.**)

9E Preposition + Gerund (**I apologize for being late.**)

9F Infinitive of Purpose
(**I went out to buy some groceries.**)

9G Adjective + Infinitive (**I'm pleased to see you.**)

9H *Enough* and *Too* with Adjectives and Adverbs; *Enough*
and *Too* with Infinitives; *Enough* with Nouns
(**I'm not old enough to drive. I have enough money.**
I'm too tired to study.)

9I *Be Used To* + Gerund and *Be Accustomed To* + Gerund
(**I'm used to eating dinner late.**)

9J *Be Supposed* + Infinitive (**You were supposed to call.**)

✦ Listening Puzzle: Traveling Homes

✦ Reading Challenge: The Tomato

✦ Writing: Describe Personal Qualities

✦ Self-Test

Form/Function

> **Climbing** mountains is dangerous.
> Melanie loves **climbing** mountains.

1. To form a gerund, we add *-ing* to the base form of the verb. See page 9 for spelling rules for adding *-ing* to the base form of verbs.

Base Verb	Gerund
climb	climbing
go	going
run	running
watch	watching

2. We can use a gerund like a noun. It can be the subject or the object of a sentence.

Subject	Verb	Object
Climbing rocks	takes	a lot of energy.

Subject	Verb	Object
Melanie	loves	**climbing** rocks.

3. We can use a gerund as the subject of a question.
   Is **climbing** rocks dangerous?

1 Practice

Complete the sentences with the gerund form of the verbs in the list.
You may use a verb more than one time. Then write S for *subject*
and O for *object*.

drive	fly	sleep	watch
fish	play	wash	

1. ___Flying___ in an airplane is not really dangerous. ___S___
2. John doesn't like ___flying___ in airplanes. He travels by car. ___O___
3. He loves his car and enjoys ___driving___ it. ___O___
4. On Sundays, he likes ___driving___ his car on the highway. _____
5. ___Playing___ football is too tiring for John. ___S___
6. He prefers ___watching___ football on television. ___O___
7. On vacation, he likes ___fishing___ in a river. ___O___
8. ___fishing___ in a river is relaxing for John. _____
9. He likes ___washing___ his dirty clothes in the washing machine. ___O___
10. John also likes ___sleeping___ late on Sundays. ___O___

2 Pair Up and Talk

Work with a partner. Say four things that you like or that you think are fun.
Use the prompts or your own ideas. Fill out the chart with your answers.

YOU: Dancing is fun.
YOUR PARTNER: I love listening to music.

cook	read	sing	swim	write letters
dance	ride a horse	skate	water-ski	
learn English	run	ski	windsurf	

Things I like	Things we both like	Things my partner likes
I like cook	We like singing	He love dancing
	We like swimming	
	We like learning	
	We like reading	

9B | Verb + Gerund

> I enjoy **skiing** in the mountains.
> The kids came with me this year.

1. We can use a gerund as the object of certain verbs. Here are some of the verbs.

consider	finish	keep on	quit
discuss	give up	(do) not mind	start
dislike	imagine	postpone	stop
enjoy	keep	put off	think about

2. We use a gerund after the verb *go* for some activities.

go **bowling**	go **fishing**	go **jogging**	go **sightseeing**
go **camping**	go **golfing**	go **running**	go **skating**
go **climbing**	go **hiking**	go **sailing**	go **swimming**
go **dancing**	go **hunting**	go **shopping**	go **walking**

3 Practice
Listen and complete the sentences.

AUDIO DOWNLOAD

CD2, 24

I would like to discuss ___*moving*___ to a new city by the ocean. I can imagine
___living___ in a place where we could go ___sailing___ on the weekends. I know
that you dislike go ___swimming___, but wouldn't it be fun to go ___walking___ on the beach
in the mornings? You might also like to go ___fishing___ or ___golfing___ while I
___shopping___ in the tourist shops nearby. When friends come to visit us, we could
___sightseeing___ up the coast. Will you think about ___living___ this cold, depressing
city? I don't want to keep on ___paying___ these awful heating bills.

4 Pair Up and Talk

Write two things you enjoy doing, dislike doing, and don't mind doing. Then ask two classmates about themselves and complete the chart.

I enjoy going to the movies. I dislike cleaning the house, but I don't mind cooking.

Student	Enjoy Doing	Dislike Doing	Don't Mind Doing
1. _Me_	_____	_____	_____
2. _____	_____	_____	_____
3. _____	_____	_____	_____

9C Verb + Infinitive

Form/Function

She **tried to give** him his medicine, but he refused to open his mouth.

We use an infinitive (*to* + the base form of a verb) after certain verbs when we need to use a verb. Here are some of the verbs.

agree	can't wait	forget	learn	need	pretend	try	would love
appear	decide	hope	manage	offer	promise	want	would prefer
can't afford	expect	intend	mean	plan	refuse	would like	

5 Practice

Complete the sentences with the infinitive form of the verbs in the list.

A be   catch   get in   get into   steal

A thief tried _____*to get in*_____ to my office last week. He planned
1

_____*to steal*_____ some of my files. He managed _____*to get into*_____ the
2   3

building. He passed by the security guard. He pretended _____*to be*_____ an
4

electrician. When the security guard tried _____*to catch*_____ him, he ran away.
5

B ask   go   take   visit

I have an old friend in Montreal, Canada. I promised _____*to visit*_____ her.
1

I'm planning _____*to go*_____ in November. I wanted _____*to ask*_____ you
2   3

about the weather. Do I need _____*to take*_____ a heavy coat with me?
4

6 Practice

Complete the sentences with the infinitive form or the simple present
or simple past of the verbs in the list.

buy   do   drive   fix   give   pay   want

I can't wait _____*to drive*_____ my new car on the highway. I can't afford
1

_____*to pay*_____ a mechanic to repair it, so I will learn how _____*to fix*_____
2   3

it myself. My parents _____*bought*_____ a new car last month. They might
4

_____*give*_____ it to me in five years. I don't expect them _____*to do*_____
5   6

it, but they say they _____*want*_____ to.
7

PUTTING A BELL ON THE CAT

The mice wanted to have a meeting. At the meeting, they wanted to decide on a plan to free themselves of their enemy—the *CAT*. At least, they wanted to find a way of knowing when she was coming so they could run away. They couldn't afford to wait any more. They were tired of staying in their holes day and night for fear of the cat.

They discussed many plans, but none was good enough. At last, a very young mouse got up and said, "I have a plan. It's very simple. We have to hang a bell around the cat's neck. When the bell starts ringing, we know the cat is coming."

Why didn't they think of this before? The mice were really excited about finally having a good plan. But then an old mouse got up and said, "The plan of the young mouse is very good. But let me ask one question: Who will put the bell on the cat?"

1. What did the mice want to have?
2. Why did they want to do this?
3. What did they at least have to do?
4. Why couldn't they afford to wait?
5. What was the young mouse's plan?
6. How would they know the cat was coming?
7. What were the mice excited about?
8. What was the old mouse's question?

Gerunds and Infinitives   **229**

Function

Meg loves **water-skiing**.
She loves **to water-ski** in Hawaii.

We can use a gerund or an infinitive after certain verbs. The meaning is the same. Here are some examples.

begin	continue	like	start
can't stand	hate	love	try

8 Practice
Complete the sentences with a gerund and an infinitive of each of the verbs given.

1. do
   A: Does Ted hate ___*doing*___ his homework?

   B: Yes, Ted hates ___*to do*___ his homework.

2. sit
   A: Does he like ___to___ in front of the television?

   B: Yes, on weekends he likes ___sitting___ in front of the television.

3. argue
   A: He and his girlfriend seem happy. Does he like ___to argue___ ?

   B: No, he doesn't like ___arguing___.

4. go out
   A: I think she loves ___to go out___ with her friends on weekends. Does Ted?

   B: No. He loves ___going out___ with his friends on weeknights.

9 Pair Up and Talk

Work with a partner. Say four things about yourself using the phrases below with an infinitive or gerund. Say three true things and one false thing. See if your partner can guess which one is false.

YOU: I love going to the movies. I can't stand to be late. I don't like talking on the phone. I like reading.

YOUR PARTNER: You love talking on the phone!

YOU: Right!

can't stand   hate   like   love

10   Practice

Complete the sentences with the gerund or the infinitive of the verbs in parentheses. Sometimes two answers are possible.

A

Gary is learning (play) ___*to play*___ the guitar. He wants (write) ___to write___
                      1   **2**

his own music, and he hopes (become) ___to become___ a famous guitarist one day. He
                                          3

would like (make) ___to make___ a lot of money and travel around the world.
                           4

B

Janet would like (be) ___to be___ an artist because she loves
                            1

(draw) ___drawing___ . She has decided (go) ___to go___ to art school next year.
         2   **3**

A famous art school in New York agreed (give) ___to give___ her a scholarship.
                                             4

Without it, she could not afford (go) ___to go___ .
                                 5

C

Tony doesn't like (study) ___studying___ . He loves (repair) ___to repair___
                             1   **2**

all kinds of things, but he prefers (repair) ___repairing___ cars. He wants
                                        3

(be) ___to be___ a mechanic. He hopes (have) ___to have___ his own garage
          4   **5**

one day.

CD2, 25

11   Practice

Listen and underline the correct words. Underline *a* if the verb takes an infinitive, or underline *b* if the verb takes a gerund. If both sentences are correct, underline *c*.

1. a. <u>to go</u>   b. going   c. both are correct
2. a. to wait   b. waiting   c. both are correct
3. a. to visit   b. visiting   c. both are correct
4. a. to listen   b. listening   c. both are correct
5. a. to go   b. going   c. both are correct
6. a. to fall   b. falling   c. both are correct
7. a. to dance   b. dancing   c. both are correct
8. a. to call   b. calling   c. both are correct

12   Pair Up and Talk

Write 10 sentences about a friend or family member. Use the verbs from List 1 followed by a gerund or an infinitive. You can use the ideas in List 2, or you can use your own ideas. Then take turns interviewing a partner.

YOU:	My sister likes sewing.
YOUR PARTNER:	What does she dislike doing?
YOU:	She dislikes watching soap operas.

List 1

| dislike | hate | keep on | love | not mind | try |
| enjoy | hope | like | need | prefer | want |

List 2

cook	listen to rock music	ride motorcycles
dance	play chess	sew
eat healthy food	play sports	stay out late with friends
exercise	read about philosophy	watch soap operas

Form/Function

Josh is good **at surfing**.

1. We can use a gerund after a preposition. The gerund is the object of the preposition.
   I apologize **for being** late.
2. Prepositions can follow certain verbs and adjectives.

Prepositions Following Verbs		Prepositions Following Adjectives	
apologize **for**	insist **on**	capable **of**	interested **in**
approve **of**	succeed **in**	excited **about**	pleased **about**
believe **in**	think **about**	fond **of**	tired **of**
care **about**	worry **about**	good **at**	sad **about**

I am **thinking about** leaving early today. (verb + preposition)
He is **good at** surfing. (adjective + preposition)

13 Practice
Complete the conversation with the gerund form of the verbs in parentheses.

JOSH: I'm tired of (do) _____*doing*_____ the same thing every day.
1

TONY: Well, what are you good at?

JOSH: I'm good at (skateboard) __skateboarding__ and (surf) __surfing__ . I dream
about (go) __going__ to Hawaii one day.
2   3

TONY: Can't you think of (do) __doing__ anything else?
5

JOSH: I have always been interested in (write) __writing__ for a newspaper. I have
often thought of (be) __being__ a journalist. I'm not afraid of
6   7
(go) __going__ to dangerous places.
8

TONY: But it's hard work!

JOSH: I don't care about (work) __working__ hard as long as I enjoy it. I don't even
9
care if I don't get paid for (do) __doing__ it.
10

14   Pair Up and Talk

Jeff and Jon are twins. They are in high school. They look the same, but
they are very different. Work with a partner. Use the prompts to ask and
answer questions about Jeff and Jon.

YOUR PARTNER: What does Jeff succeed in?
YOU: Jeff succeeds in playing soccer.

Questions	Jeff	Jon
1. what/does/succeed in	play soccer	pass tests
2. what/is/fond of	use his new mp3 player	use his new calculator
3. what/does/think about	drive cars	do difficult math problems
4. what/is/excited about	play in a soccer game	go to college
5. what/does/worry about	look cool	fail tests
6. what/is/interested in	listen to music	read books

15   Pair Up and Talk

Tell a partner about yourself, using the prompts below.

I'm good at swimming.

believe in	don't look forward to	interested in	not interested in
don't believe in	good at	look forward to	not very good at

9F | Infinitive of Purpose

Function

We hold our nose **to show** that something smells bad.

We put a finger to our mouth **to ask** for quiet.

We cross our middle and index fingers **to wish** good luck.

1. We use an infinitive to talk about the reason or purpose for doing something (why someone does something).

    I went to the cafeteria **to have** some lunch.

    He's going to the supermarket **to buy** groceries.

2. In more formal English, we use *in order to*.

    She left early **in order to avoid** the heavy traffic.

    We're saving money **in order to buy** a new car.

3. We can also use *for* to show purpose. We use a noun after *for*.

    I went to the cafeteria **for** lunch.

    He's going to the supermarket **for** milk and bread.

16 Practice

Listen and underline the correct object for each verb. Then listen again and write the verbs.

AUDIO
DOWNLOAD

CD2, 26

1. a. English   b. <u>some clothes</u>   _____buy_____

2. a. a check   b. breakfast   _____

3. a. lunch   b. a credit card   _____

4. a. a computer   b. Spanish   _____

5. a. some letters   b. a truck   _____

6. a. a hat   b. a car   _____

7. a. a pizza   b. a flight   _____

8. a. an email   b. a seat   _____

17 Pair Up and Talk

Work with a partner. Use the phrases in Practice 16 to talk about why you went to the following places.

YOU: Why did you go to the post office?
YOUR PARTNER: I went to the post office to mail some letters.

1. the post office   4. the travel agency   7. night school

2. the department store   5. a fast food restaurant

3. the bank   6. a car rental agency

18 Practice

Complete the sentences with *to* or *for*.

1. I go to school _____*to*_____ learn English.

2. Some people need English _____ get a better job.

3. We need a grammar book _____ learn the rules.

4. We need a dictionary _____ vocabulary.

5. We use the Internet _____ research.

6. Our teacher sometimes uses videos _____ discussion.

9G Adjective + Infinitive

Form/Function

We were **amazed to see** the astronauts walking in space.

1. We can use an infinitive after certain adjectives. Here are some of the adjectives.

afraid	easy	glad	right	sorry
difficult	foolish	happy	sad	surprised
disappointed	frightened	pleased	safe	wrong

I am **pleased to see** you.

She was **surprised to get** a letter.

2. We can also use adjectives with infinitives after *it*.

It is **difficult to speak** English.

It is **important to finish** on time.

19 Practice
Complete the sentences with the infinitive of the verbs in the list.

fasten find fly get on have travel

1. People say it's dangerous ___*to fly*___ on a plane.

2. I wasn't afraid ___to travel___ by plane.

3. I was the first ___to get___ the plane.

4. It was necessary ___to fasten___ the seat belt for takeoff and landing.

5. I was happy ___to have___ my feet on the ground again.

6. I was pleased ___to find___ my friends waiting for me.

1. Learning to use the computer is easy.

    It is easy to learn to use a computer.

2. Being polite to customers is important.

    _____

3. Making mistakes when you speak English is normal.

    _____

4. Traveling to new countries is interesting.

    _____

5. Living in Tokyo is expensive.

    _____

6. Waiting for more than 10 minutes is unusual here.

    _____

9H   *Enough* and *Too* with Adjectives and Adverbs; *Enough* and *Too* with Infinitives; *Enough* with Nouns

Form/Function

He is not **big enough** to wear the clothes. The clothes are **too big** for him to wear.

1. We use *enough* after adjectives and adverbs but before nouns. *Enough* means that there is the right amount of something—not too much and not too little.

Adjective/Adverb + *Enough*			
Subject	Verb	Adjective/Adverb + *Enough*	Infinitive
She	isn't	old **enough**	to drive.
It	is	warm **enough**	to swim.

Enough + Noun			
Subject	Verb	*Enough* + Noun	Infinitive
I	have	**enough** eggs	to make an omelet.
He	has	**enough** money	to buy a CD.

2. We use *too* before adjectives and adverbs. *Too* means "more than enough." It has a negative meaning.

Subject	Verb	*Too* + Adjective/Adverb	Infinitive
I	am	**too** tired	to go out.
He	writes	**too** well	to fail the test.

21   Pair Up and Talk

Can you do these things? Ask and answer each question with *too* or *enough*. You may use the adjectives in the list in your answers. Write the answers in the chart.

brave	fast	poor	serious	slow
dangerous	funny	rich	short	tall

Questions	My answers	My partner's answers
1. Can you touch the ceiling?	No, I can't. I'm not tall enough to touch the ceiling.	No, she can't. She's too short to touch the ceiling.
2. Can you make people laugh?		
3. Can you jump from an airplane?		
4. Can you run a mile (1.6 kilometers) in one minute?		

22 Practice
Complete the sentences with *too much* or *too many*.

Bob and I decided that we had ___too many___ things in our garage. We considered
                                   1
having a yard sale, but that would be _____ trouble. _____ people
                                            2   3
would come to our house. We thought of hiring someone to take it all away. That would
cost _____ money. So, we gave everything to the Good Times Charity Shop. We
           4
will never collect _____ stuff in our garage again.
                          5

9I *Be Used To* + Gerund and *Be Accustomed To* + Gerund

Form/Function

I'm **not used to eating** this kind
of food. I'm also **not accustomed
to eating** with chopsticks. I'm
used to eating with a knife and
fork because I grew up in the U.S.

1. We use *be used to* + gerund or *be accustomed to* + gerund to talk about something that we are
    familiar with because we have done it often. *Be used to* and *be accustomed to* have the
    same meaning.
    I **am used to eating** with chopsticks because I live in Japan.
    I **am accustomed to eating** with chopsticks because I live in Japan.
2. Do not confuse *be used to* + gerund with *used to* + a base verb. We use *used to* + a base verb to
    talk about something that happened or was true in the past, but it is different or not true now.
    I **used to eat** with chopsticks when I lived in Japan. (Now I don't.)
3. We form questions with *be used to* and *be accustomed to* to ask about someone else's familiarity
    with something.
    Are you **used to eating** with chopsticks?
    Aren't you **accustomed to eating** with chopsticks?

1. I (write) _____ used to write _____ on a typewriter many years ago. Now I write on
    a computer. At first it was hard, but now I (write) _ *am used to writing* _ on my
    computer and can't live without it.

2. My brother (live) _____ in London, but now he lives in New York.
    It was strange for him at first, but now he (live) _____ in New
    York, and he loves the lifestyle.

3. I have to be at work at 7:00 every morning, so I (go) _____ to bed
    early. I (not/go) _____ to bed late.

4. Lisa is getting up at 6:00 tomorrow morning to go to the airport. She (not/get up)
    _____ before 8:00.

5. Suzy found Japan strange at first. For example, she (not/take off)
    _____ her shoes before going into a house.

6. For six months after I bought the car, I (not/drive) _____ it much,
    but now I (drive) _____ it, and I love it.

24   **Pair Up and Talk**
Work with a partner. Ask and answer questions with *be used to*.

YOU: What time are you used to getting up?
YOUR PARTNER: I'm used to getting up at 6:30 in the morning.

1. What time are you used to …

    a. getting up?

    b. going to bed?

    c. eating lunch?

    d. eating dinner?

2. What language are you used to speaking at home?

3. What are you used to drinking in the morning with breakfast?

4. What are you used to eating for breakfast?

9J Be Supposed + Infinitive

Form/Function

Son, you're **supposed to tell** us where you are going!

Subject	Be (Not) Supposed	Infinitive	
He	was supposed	to write	to me.
You	are supposed	to help	your mother at home.
We	aren't supposed	to go	into that building.

We use *be supposed* + infinitive to talk about something that is expected of someone or something.

It **is supposed to rain** tomorrow. (That is what the weather bureau predicted.)

Kevin **is supposed to be** home by ten. (His parents have told him to do this.)

25 Practice

Kevin is supposed to follow his parents' rules. Which of the things from the list is he supposed to do or not supposed to do? Write sentences.

be on time for meals

play loud music until three in the morning

stay out all night on weekends

talk back to his parents

tell his parents where he is going

wear dirty shoes inside the house

1. *He is supposed to be on time for meals.*

2. He isn't supposed to play loud music until three in the morning

3. _____

4. _____

5. _____

6. _____

26 Your Turn

Imagine you have a daughter who is 15 years old. She doesn't like school, doesn't do her homework, and barely passes her classes. She is only interested in clothes, make up, and going out with her friends. She always asks you for more and more spending money every week. She doesn't work. Work with a partner. Make sentences about what you think she is supposed to do and what you, her parents, are supposed to do. Write them into a chart.

Things our daughter is supposed to do	Things we are supposed to do as parents
She is supposed to do her homework.	We are supposed to teach her to be careful with money.

Listening Puzzle

CD2, 27

A Listen and check the correct answer.

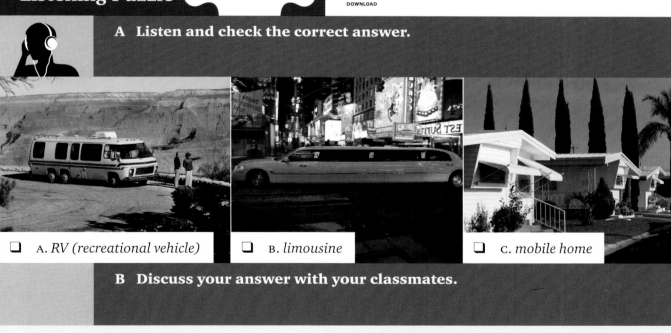

❑ A. *RV (recreational vehicle)* ❑ B. *limousine* ❑ C. *mobile home*

B Discuss your answer with your classmates.

AUDIO DOWNLOAD
CD2, 28

C Now listen again and write the sentences you hear.

A Before You Read

Answer the questions.

1. Do people in your country eat tomatoes? How do they usually eat them?
2. What are some foods made with tomatoes?

B Read

THE TOMATO

Tomatoes originally grew in South America in what is today Peru, Ecuador, Colombia, and Chile. These tomatoes were very small, like cherries. From there, tomatoes spread to ₅ Mexico. The Aztec Indians grew larger tomatoes that were yellow. After the Spanish conquered Mexico in 1521, they brought some ₁₀ tomatoes back to Spain. They called the tomato the "golden apple." The Spanish didn't eat tomatoes raw. They cut them up, ₁₅ **seasoned** them, and then fried them.

People started to grow tomatoes in other parts of Europe but only used them for decorations. Some rich people started to eat them but preferred to serve them on silver ₂₀ plates. The acid of the tomato took out the lead in the silver, and the rich began to die of lead poisoning. Doctors thought they were poisonous. However, poor people continued to eat tomatoes on wooden plates and never had a ₂₅ problem.

In the late 1800s, immigrants from Italy came to the U.S. and brought the tomato with them. Around 1880, the pizza was invented. A chef in Naples offered to prepare a special dish ₃₀ in honor of Queen Margaret's visit. He made a pizza from three ingredients that represented the Italian flag: tomatoes for red, basil for green, and mozzarella cheese for white. The pizza is named Margarita pizza, after the queen. Pizza ₃₅ is now the number one favorite of young people in the U.S.

C Notice the Grammar

Underline all forms of infinitives.

Choose the best answer.

D Look for Main Ideas

1. What is the main topic of paragraph 1?
   - Ⓐ The Spanish cooked tomatoes.
   - Ⓑ The Aztecs changed the size and color of the tomato.
   - Ⓒ The Spanish conquerors brought the tomato to Spain.
   - Ⓓ The tomato had its beginnings in South America and Mexico.

2. Paragraph 3 is mainly about _____ .
   - Ⓐ the invention of the pizza
   - Ⓑ immigrants to the U.S.
   - Ⓒ Queen Margaret's visit to Naples
   - Ⓓ the popularity of the pizza in the U.S.

3. Which of the following is NOT true about tomatoes in other parts of Europe?
   - Ⓐ People used them as decorations.
   - Ⓑ Some rich people who ate them died.
   - Ⓒ Some people served them on silver plates.
   - Ⓓ Doctors thought they were healthy.

E Look for Details

4. The Aztec Indians grew tomatoes that were _____ .
   - Ⓐ large and yellow
   - Ⓑ small and red
   - Ⓒ green like apples
   - Ⓓ without acid

5. A chef in Naples made a pizza for Queen Margaret that had _____ .
   - Ⓐ all the foods she liked the best
   - Ⓑ special seasonings
   - Ⓒ the colors of the Italian flag
   - Ⓓ fried tomatoes

READING SKILL:
Using Prior Knowledge

Using prior knowledge means using what you already know to help you understand the topic of a passage. Things you already know about the topic can help you read more efficiently.

F Make Inferences

6. What can we infer about people in the 1800s?
   - Ⓐ The poor knew better than to eat on silver plates.
   - Ⓑ People didn't know the real cause of their poisoning.
   - Ⓒ The rich led more dangerous lives than the poor.
   - Ⓓ Doctors had advanced scientific knowledge.

7. We can infer from the reading that _____ .
   - Ⓐ eating foods from other cultures is dangerous
   - Ⓑ chefs don't like to share their recipes
   - Ⓒ contact among cultures changes people's eating habits
   - Ⓓ Americans don't like to eat food from other cultures

G Look for Vocabulary

8. The word *seasoned* in the reading is closest in meaning to _____ .
   - Ⓐ served on a plate
   - Ⓑ cut into small pieces
   - Ⓒ put herbs and spices on
   - Ⓓ cooked thoroughly

Writing: Describe Personal Qualities

Write a paragraph about your personal qualities.

STEP 1   **Choose one of these topics:**

1. You want a pen pal in another country.
2. You want to find a future husband/wife.
3. You want to find a roommate to share your apartment.

STEP 2   **Answer these questions about yourself. Write down your answers. You can add other questions if you wish. Use gerunds and infinitives in some of your answers.**

1. What do you like/not like doing?
2. What do you hate/love?
3. What are you interested in?
4. What do you enjoy doing?

5. What are you good at doing?
6. What are you used to doing?
7. What do you need to do for the future?

STEP 3   **Write your information in the form of a paragraph.**

STEP 4   **Evaluate your paragraph.**

Checklist

_____ Did you indent your paragraph?

_____ Did you give information about yourself?

_____ Did you give information that would help you reach your goal
(finding a pen pal, a husband or wife, or a roommate)?

STEP 5   **Edit your paragraph. Work with a partner or your teacher to check your spelling, punctuation, vocabulary, and grammar.**

STEP 6   **Write your final copy.**

Self-Test

A **Choose the best answer, A, B, C, or D, to complete the sentence. Darken the oval with the same letter.**

1. It is important _____ on time.

   A. to be   Ⓐ Ⓑ Ⓒ Ⓓ
   B. being
   C. to being
   D. be

2. I went to the bank _____ some traveler's checks.

   A. for get   Ⓐ Ⓑ Ⓒ Ⓓ
   B. for getting
   C. getting
   D. to get

3. She was happy _____ .

   A. see me   Ⓐ Ⓑ Ⓒ Ⓓ
   B. me seeing
   C. to see me
   D. to seeing me

4. This coffee is _____ for me.

   A. to sweet   Ⓐ Ⓑ Ⓒ Ⓓ
   B. too sweet
   C. enough sweet
   D. two sweet

5. It wasn't _____ to the beach.

   A. too warm go   Ⓐ Ⓑ Ⓒ Ⓓ
   B. enough warm to go
   C. warm enough to go
   D. too warm to going

6. He loves _____ on the pond in the winter.

   A. skate   Ⓐ Ⓑ Ⓒ Ⓓ
   B. go skating
   C. to go skating
   D. going skate

7. _____ an easy form of exercise for most people.

   A. Run is   Ⓐ Ⓑ Ⓒ Ⓓ
   B. To run
   C. Running is
   D. Running

8. He left without _____ goodbye.

   A. to say   Ⓐ Ⓑ Ⓒ Ⓓ
   B. saying
   C. say
   D. to saying

9. Thank you _____ me with my homework.

   A. to help   Ⓐ Ⓑ Ⓒ Ⓓ
   B. helping
   C. for helping
   D. for to help

10. We aren't _____ this cold weather.

   A. used to   Ⓐ Ⓑ Ⓒ Ⓓ
   B. use
   C. use to
   D. used

B Find the underlined word or phrase, A, B, C, or D, that is incorrect. Darken the oval with the same letter.

1. <u>Watch</u> sports on television <u>is</u> <u>a lot of</u> <u>fun</u>.
     A   B   C   D

   Ⓐ Ⓑ Ⓒ Ⓓ

2. <u>It is</u> dangerous for anybody <u>to going</u>
     A   B
   <u>jogging</u> in this park <u>at night</u>.
     C   D

   Ⓐ Ⓑ Ⓒ Ⓓ

3. Some people <u>are</u> <u>good at</u> and <u>have</u>
                 A   B   C
   a talent for <u>learn</u> languages.
              D

   Ⓐ Ⓑ Ⓒ Ⓓ

4. We <u>were</u> considering <u>to go</u> on vacation
       A   B
   in June, but we <u>postponed</u> <u>it</u> for
                   C   D
   another month.

   Ⓐ Ⓑ Ⓒ Ⓓ

5. Some students <u>go</u> to the library <u>to studying</u>
                 A   B
   because <u>it</u> is <u>quiet</u>.
          C   D

   Ⓐ Ⓑ Ⓒ Ⓓ

6. The summers <u>are</u> usually <u>warm</u> in this part
              A   B
   of the country, but this year <u>it is</u> supposed to
                           C
   <u>being</u> cool.
     D

   Ⓐ Ⓑ Ⓒ Ⓓ

7. I <u>wasn't</u> <u>accustomed</u> to <u>eat</u> with chopsticks
      A   B   C
   until I <u>went</u> to Japan.
          D

   Ⓐ Ⓑ Ⓒ Ⓓ

8. Many students <u>use</u> the Internet <u>for</u> do
              A   B
   <u>their</u> <u>research</u>.
    C   D

   Ⓐ Ⓑ Ⓒ Ⓓ

9. In some countries, <u>it is necessary</u> <u>to pass</u> an
                     A   B
   entrance exam before <u>enter</u> <u>a</u> university.
                 C D

   Ⓐ Ⓑ Ⓒ Ⓓ

10. <u>Traveling</u> to new <u>countries</u> <u>are</u> interesting <u>for</u>
       A   B   C   D
    most people.

   Ⓐ Ⓑ Ⓒ Ⓓ

Unit 10

Comparative and Superlative Forms

Buildings are getting **taller and taller.**

10A | Adjectives and Adverbs

Form

Basketball players are **tall**.
They throw the ball **quickly** and **accurately** into the net.

1. We can make adverbs by adding *-ly* to many adjectives. Sometimes the spelling of the adjective changes before *-ly* is added.

Spelling Rule	Adjective	Adverb
To form most adverbs, add *-ly* to the adjective.	quick	quick**ly**
	accurate	accurate**ly**
If the adjective ends in *l*, add *-ly*.	wonderful	wonderful**ly**
If the adjective ends in *le*, drop the *e* and add *-y*.	gentle	gent**ly**
If the adjective ends in a consonant + *y*, drop the *y* and add *-ily*.	easy	eas**ily**

2. Some adverbs are irregular. Some have the same form as the adjective or a completely different form.

Adjective	Adverb	Adjective	Adverb
good	well*	early	early
fast	fast	late	late
hard	hard		

* *Well* is also an adjective meaning "not ill; in good health."
   How are you? I'm very well, thank you.

3. Adjectives can go before nouns.
   He is a **tall** man.
   Adjectives can also go after verbs such as *appear, be, become, feel, get, look,* and *seem.*
   He is **tall**. He looks **good**.

4. Most adverbs go after verbs and objects, but adverbs of frequency usually go before all verbs except *be*. An adverb of frequency tells how often something happens. (See page 6 for more information on adverbs of frequency.)

Subject	Adverb of Frequency	Verb	Object
He	**always**	eats	breakfast.

Subject	Verb	Object	Other Adverb
She	drives	the car	**dangerously.**

5. Adverbs can also go before adjectives, other adverbs, and past participles.
   He was **surprisingly** polite.

Function

1. Adjectives describe nouns. They have the same form in the singular and plural.
   He is a **tall** player. They are **tall** men. (The adjective *tall* describes the nouns *player* and *men*.)
2. Adverbs tell you how something happens or how somebody does something. Adverbs describe verbs, adjectives, or other adverbs.
   He plays **well**. (*Well* describes the verb *plays*.)
   He is **incredibly** fast. (*Incredibly* describes the adjective *fast*.)
   He plays **amazingly** well. (*Amazingly* describes the adverb *well*.)

1 Practice
Underline the correct word. Draw an arrow from the adverb or adjective to the word it describes.

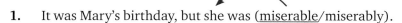

1. It was Mary's birthday, but she was (<u>miserable</u>/miserably).

2. She was waiting (impatient/impatiently) to get a phone call.

3. No one called to wish her a (happy/happily) birthday.

4. Mary felt (sad/sadly).

5. Then her friend called (unexpected/unexpectedly).

6. Mary's friend told her to come to her house (immediate/immediately).

7. She arrived at her friend's house and knocked on the door (soft/softly).

8. All her family and friends were there. They all sang "Happy Birthday" (loud/loudly).

10B | Participles as Adjectives

Form

Melissa was **irritated** by Daniel. He was late again, and they missed an **exciting** part of the movie.

1. We can often use present participles and past participles of verbs as adjectives.
2. We form present participles with the base verb + -ing. We form regular past participles with the base verb + -ed. See the spelling rules for -ing and -ed forms on pages 9 and 29.

Base Form	Present Participle	Past Participle
amuse	amus**ing**	amus**ed**
bore	bor**ing**	bor**ed**
excite	excit**ing**	excit**ed**
frighten	frighten**ing**	frighten**ed**
interest	interest**ing**	interest**ed**
relax	relax**ing**	relax**ed**
surprise	surpris**ing**	surpris**ed**

Function

1. Past participles used as adjectives describe someone's feelings.

   The boys were **excited** during the game.

   To show what caused the feeling, we can use a prepositional phrase. Most past participles take the preposition *by*. Others take other prepositions. For example, *interested* takes *in*.

   We were amused **by the children's behavior**.

   He was frightened **by the loud noise**.

   They are interested **in astronomy**.

2. Present participles used as adjectives describe the person or thing that produces the feeling.

   She was having a **relaxing** vacation.

   The boys were watching an **exciting** football game.

1. This was a very (<u>fascinating</u>/fascinated) book.
2. At first I thought it was (boring/bored), but it wasn't.
3. I was very (interested/interesting) in the people in this book.
4. I was (surprised/surprising) by the ending of the story.
5. I was (shocked/shocking) to know it was based on a true story.

ALAN: I was (<u>surprised</u>/surprising) at how good the weather was.
             1
BRENDA: Yes, it was really sunny. It was (surprising/surprised).
             2
ALAN: And, I was (interesting/interested) in so many things there.
             3
BRENDA: I was (fascinating/fascinated) by the king's furniture.
             4
ALAN: Yes, the furniture was (fascinating/fascinated).
             5
BRENDA: But I was (tiring/tired) after the museum.
             6
ALAN: Yes, it was (tired/tiring).
             7
BRENDA: Now I am (exhausted/exhausting).
             8
ALAN: Vacations are always (exhausted/exhausting).
             9

bored   boring   interested   interesting

1. *I think that history is interesting.*
2. _____
3. _____
4. _____

5 Read

Read the story. Then write answers to the questions.

THE LION AND THE GNAT

An annoying gnat was buzzing around a lion's head. "Go away, you terrible insect," said the irritated lion. But the gnat wasn't bothered.

"Do you think," said the gnat, "I am afraid of you because they call you king?"

The next moment, he flew at the lion and stung him on the nose. The lion was now more irritated and struck the gnat as hard as he could. But he only hurt himself with his claws. Again and again the gnat stung the lion. The lion was exhausted and covered with wounds made by his claws. Finally, he gave out the loudest roar and gave up the fight.

The gnat flew away and was going to tell the rest of the world about his most amazing victory. As he flew away, he went straight into a spider's web. Now the gnat, which had defeated the strongest of all animals, was the meal of a little spider.

1. What kind of a gnat was buzzing around the lion?

2. How did the lion feel? _____

3. How did the gnat feel? _____

4. How did the lion feel after the gnat stung him? _____

5. What was the lion covered with? _____

6. What did the lion do when he gave up the fight? _____

7. What was the gnat going to do when it flew away? _____

8. Where did the gnat fly? _____

Form/Function

> The coffee **smells good**.

1. We can use adjectives after verbs of existence, such as *be, get*, become,* and *seem*.

   He **seems nice**.

   Be quiet!

   I'm **getting hungry**.

2. We can also use adjectives after verbs of the senses like *look, feel, sound, taste,* and *smell*.

   You **look tired**.

   The coffee **smells good**.

   This soup **tastes strange**.

* In this meaning, *get* usually means "become."

6 Practice

Guests are coming to Ann's house this evening, but things have gone wrong.
Listen and underline the correct word to finish each sentence.

AUDIO
DOWNLOAD

CD3, 2

1.	a. tell	b. <u>miserable</u>
2.	a. tired	b. excited
3.	a. clean	b. burned
4.	a. wet	b. warm
5.	a. clean	b. dirty
6.	a. sweet	b. cold
7.	a. small	b. dry
8.	a. jealous	b. happy

1. Tony was getting (<u>hungry</u>/hungrily).
2. Dinner was (<u>ready</u>/readily).
3. The soup smelled (<u>good</u>/well).
4. It tasted (<u>good</u>/well).
5. Tony finished the soup (quick/<u>quickly</u>).
6. His grandmother had cooked (good/<u>well</u>).
7. She cooked some (specially/<u>special</u>) pasta for him.
8. It looked (<u>delicious</u>/deliciously).
9. He looked at the dish (hungry/<u>hungrily</u>).
10. He ate it (<u>quickly</u>/quick) because it was so good.

10D *As* + Adjective + *As*; *As* + Adverb + *As*

Form

May and June are twins.
May is **as tall as** June.

1. We can use *as … as* with adjectives and adverbs.

Adjectives					
Subject	**Verb (+ *Not*)**	***As***	**Adjective**	***As***	
May	is/isn't	as	tall old	as	June.
I	am/'m am not/'m not		good		
You/We/They	are/'re are not/aren't/'re not		funny		

Adverbs					
Subject	**Verb (+ *Not*)**	***As***	**Adverb**	***As***	
I/You/We/They	learn don't learn	as	quickly	as	June.
May	learns doesn't learn				
	runs doesn't run		fast		
	studies doesn't study		hard		
	laughs doesn't laugh		loudly		

2. We can add an auxiliary verb or repeat the first verb at the end of the sentence.

> May is as funny as June.
> May is as funny as June **is**.
> May plays as beautifully as June.
> May plays as beautifully as June **does**.
> May plays as beautifully as June **plays**.

Function

1. We use *as … as* to show that two people or two things are the same or equal.
> May is **as old as** June. (May and June are the same age.)
2. We use *not as … as* for the negative form.
> May is **not as funny as** June.
3. When we use *not as … as* instead of the comparative, it sometimes sounds more polite.
> Ben is **shorter than** Jim.
> Ben is **not as tall as** Jim.

8 Practice
Use the prompts to write sentences with *as ... as* or *not as ... as*.

1. autumn/cold/winter

   Autumn is not as cold as winter.

2. the month of September/long/the month of June

   _____

3. in the winter months, California/cold/New York

   _____

4. September/popular/July for vacations in North America

   _____

5. in the fall, plants/grow/fast/in spring

   _____

6. days in summer/short/days in winter

   _____

9 Practice
Many languages have sayings that include a phrase similar to *as ... as*. Listen and underline the correct word to finish each saying. Notice that *as* often sounds like "uz." Then work with a partner to explain how the sayings are different in another language that you know.

CD3, 3

1. a. <u>a feather</u>   b. a car
2. a. soup   b. sugar
3. a. a mouse   b. a lion
4. a. gold   b. a tomato

5. a. water   b. ink
6. a. grass   b. the sky
7. a. a house   b. a bird
8. a. a dog   b. a child

10 Pair Up and Talk
Compare yourself today with the way you were five years ago. Use *as ... as* or *not as ... as*. Talk about your answers with a partner.

Today, I study as hard as I did five years ago.

be happy   be healthy   be poor   sleep late   study hard

10E Comparative Forms of Adjectives and Adverbs

Form

Fifty years ago, office machines were **simpler than** office machines today.

1. Adjectives and adverbs form their comparatives in the same ways.

Short Adjectives and Adverbs					
Adjective + -er + Than			**Adverb + -er + Than**		
A typewriter is	slow**er than**	a computer.	She can type	fast**er than**	I can.

Long Adjectives and Adverbs					
More/Less + Adjective + Than			**More/Less + Adverb + Than**		
A computer is	**more** useful **than**	a typewriter.	She types	**less** accurately **than**	I do.

2. We use these rules for spelling the comparative forms of short (one-syllable) adjectives and adverbs and for two-syllable adjectives ending in -y.

Spelling Rule	Adjective	Comparative Adjective	Adverb	Comparative Adverb
Add -er to most one-syllable adjectives and adverbs.	cheap	cheap**er than**	fast	fast**er than**
If a one-syllable adjective or adverb ends in e, or a two-syllable adjective ends in le, add -r.	wide	wid**er than**	late	lat**er than**
	simple	simpl**er than**		
If a one-syllable adjective ends in a single vowel plus a consonant, double the consonant and add -er.	hot	hott**er than**		
If a two-syllable adjective ends in a consonant plus y, change the y to i and add -er.	noisy	nois**ier than**		

3. Some adjectives and adverbs have irregular comparative forms.

Adjective	Adverb	Comparative Form for Both
good	well	**better than**
bad	badly	**worse than**
far	far	**farther/further than**

4. We use these rules for using the -er form or the *more* form of the comparative.

Rules for Using -er or *More*	Adjectives	Adverbs
Use -er with one-syllable adjectives and adverbs.	small**er than**	fast**er than**
Use -er with two-syllable adjectives that end in a consonant + *y*.	pretti**er than**	
Use *more* + adjective/adverb + *than* with most adjectives and adverbs of two syllables or more.	**more** crowded **than**	**more** seriously **than**
Some two-syllable adjectives use -er or *more*.	angri**er/more** angry **than**	
	simpl**er/more** simple **than**	
	friendli**er/more** friendly **than**	
	gentl**er/more** gentle **than**	
	narrow**er/more** narrow **than**	
	quiet**er/more** quiet **than**	
	polit**er/ more** polite **than**	

5. We can use a noun after *than*. We can also use a subject pronoun or a possessive noun or pronoun + a verb after *than*. We can omit the verb.

      I am taller than **my mother (is).**   I am taller than **she (is).**

      My hair is darker than **my mother's (is).**   My hair is darker than **hers (is).**

      I study harder than she **(does).**   I study harder than she **(studies).**

6. We can use *less* before an adjective or adverb with two or more syllables.

      He is **less serious** than she is.

      She speaks **less fluently** than he does.

We do not usually use *less* with one-syllable adjectives or adverbs. Instead, we use *not as* (adjective/adverb) *as*.

CORRECT:	This CD is**n't as good as** the other one.
INCORRECT:	This CD is less good than the other one.
CORRECT:	She is**n't** singing **as well as** she usually does.
INCORRECT:	She is singing less well than she usually does.

Function

1. We use comparative forms of adjectives and adverbs to show the difference between two things.

   Watching television is **more relaxing than** ironing.

2. We use *less* to show a lower degree.

   This test was **less difficult than** the last test.

3. If we use a pronoun after *than*, and if we omit the verb, we can use either a subject pronoun or an object pronoun. In formal English, we use a subject pronoun, but in informal English, we use an object pronoun.

   FORMAL: She is taller than **I**.

   INFORMAL: She is taller than **me**.

   If we include the verb, we must use a subject pronoun.

   She is taller than **I am**.

4. We use *very* to describe adjectives and adverbs; however, we use *much* with comparative forms of adjectives and adverbs.

   It's **very** cold today.

   It's **much** colder today than yesterday.

---

11   Practice

Complete the sentences with the comparative form of the words in parentheses.

1. A bicycle is (quiet) ___*quieter than*___ a car.

2. A bicycle is (cheap) __cheaper than__ a car.

3. A bicycle is (easy to park) __easier to park than__ a car.

4. A car goes (fast) __faster than__ a bicycle.

5. A car is (expensive) __more expensive__ a bicycle.

6. A car is (comfortable) __more comfortable__ a bicycle.

7. In China, a bicycle is (popular) __popular than__ a car.

8. A bicycle runs (economically) __more economically than__ a car.

9. A bicycle is (light) __lighter than__ a car.

10. A car is (difficult to use) __more difficult to use than__ a bicycle.

12 Practice

Complete the sentences with the comparative form of the words
in parentheses. Then listen to check your answers.

CD3, 4

JANE: I want to fly to Los Angeles tomorrow morning. Are there any flights

that are (early) __*earlier*__ __*than*__ the one at 10:00?
　　　　　　　　　　　 1　　　　　　 2

TRAVEL AGENT: Yes, there are. Flight 1620 is at 5:30. And flight 1535 is

(late) __*later*__ __*than*__ flight 1620. It leaves at 7:00.
　　　　 3　　　　　 4

JANE: Are there a lot of people on the 5:30 flight?

TRAVEL AGENT: No. The 7:00 flight is usually much (crowded) __*more crowded*__
　　　　　　　　　　　　　　　　　　　　　　　　　　　　　　　　5

__*crowded*__ __*than*__ the 5:30 flight.
　　 6　　　　　 7

JANE: I think the 5:30 flight will work (well) __*better*__ __*than*__
　　　　　　　　　　　　　　　　　　　　　　　　 8　　　　　 9

the 7:00 flight. Will it be (cheap) __*cheaper*__ __*than*__
　　　　　　　　　　　　　　　　　 10　　　　　 11

the 7:00?

TRAVEL AGENT: No. In fact, it's $10 (expensive) __*more*__ __*expensive*__
　　　　　　　　　　　　　　　　　　　　 12　　　　　 13

__*than*__ the other flights.
　 14

13 Pair Up and Talk

Work with a partner. Give your opinion about each pair of nouns.
Use the adjectives.

I think dogs are friendlier than cats.

1. cats/dogs—friendly

2. fish/lizards—beautiful

3. spiders/snakes—dangerous

4. little boys/little girls—noisy

5. Los Angeles/Chicago—interesting

6. summers in the Sahara Desert/summers in Iceland—hot

14 Practice
Complete the sentences using a comparative form of an adverb and your own additional information. You can use the adverbs from the list or your own.

cautiously   comfortably   dangerously   fast   high   slowly

1. The bullet trains in Japan go ___*faster than the trains in the United States*.___
2. A space shuttle flies _____
3. City buses go _____
4. Passengers in a large car usually travel _____
5. In fast traffic, you should drive _____
6. Race car drivers live _____

15 Practice
Complete the sentences with *much* or *very*.

1. Learning another language is ____*very*____ difficult.

2. Learning another language is _____ more difficult than learning geography.

3. English books are _____ expensive these days.

4. Dictionaries are _____ more expensive than books.

5. Chinese is _____ harder than English as a language.

6. English spelling rules are _____ unreliable.

16 Your Turn
Write sentences comparing people in your family. Use adjectives or adverbs.

Example
My father is older than my mother.

1. _____

2. _____

3. _____

4. _____

Comparative and Superlative Forms   263

Form

My wedding day was **the happiest** day of my life.

1. Adjectives and adverbs form their superlative forms in the same ways.

Short Adjectives and Adverbs					
The + Adjective + -est			*The + Adverb + -est*		
Mt. Everest is	**the** high**est**	mountain.	She runs	**the** fast**est**	of us all.
Long Adjectives and Adverbs					
The Most/Least + Adjective			*The Most/Least + Adverb*		
Which is	**the most** dangerous **the least** dangerous	city?	He speaks	**the most** loudly **the least** loudly	of us all.

2. We use the definite article *the* before superlative adjectives and adverbs.

   The Crown is **the** best hotel in town.

   It has **the** most expensive restaurant.

3. The spelling rules for short comparative adjectives and adverbs on page 259 also apply to short superlative forms.

Adjective or Adverb	Comparative	Superlative
late	la**ter than**	the late**st**
hot	hot**ter than**	the hot**test**
noisy	nois**ier than**	the nois**iest**

4. Some adjectives and adverbs are irregular.

Adjective	Adverb	Comparative Form (Both)	Superlative Form (Both)
good	well	**better**	**best**
bad	badly	**worse**	**worst**
far	far	**farther/further**	**farthest/furthest**

Function

1. We use superlative forms of adjectives and adverbs to compare three or more things.
2. We use -*est* and *most* in superlatives to show the highest degree.

    Antarctica is **the** cold**est** place in the world.

    Tokyo is **the most** crowded city in the world.

3. We use *the least* to show the lowest degree.

    Antarctica is **the least** populated place in the world.

4. We often use the preposition *in* after superlatives. We use *in* with nouns of locations such as *the world,* countries, and cities; and with group nouns such as *the class, my family,* and *the group.*

    Ted is the best student **in the class.**

    The elephant is the biggest land animal **in the world.**

    Sarte is the most expensive restaurant **in New York City.**

5. We often use the preposition *of* with expressions of time and quantity, and with plural nouns.

    I know three very good restaurants, but this one is the best **of all.**

    Yesterday was the longest day **of the year.**

    He is the youngest **of the students.**

6. We do not use *least* with one-syllable adjectives.

    CORRECT: John is the shortest of my three brothers.

    INCORRECT: John is ~~the least tall of~~ my three brothers.

---

17   Practice
Complete the sentences with the superlative form of the words in parentheses.

1. Our teacher is Ms. Flint. She gives (clear) _the clearest_ explanations of all the teachers.

2. We think Peter speaks English (fluently) _the most_ in our class.

3. All the teachers give us homework, but Ms. Flint gives (difficult) _the most_ homework.

4. Terry is always the first person to arrive in the class. He comes to class (early) _the earliest_

5. Kate takes the class seriously. She's (responsible) _the most_ student in the class.

6. Tony works (hard) _the hardest_ of all the students.

7. He is also (good) _the best_ student in the class.

8. He answers the teacher's questions (easily) _the most easily_ of us all.

1.   The blue whale is _____*the*_____ biggest _____*of*_____ all the animals.

2.   The giraffe is _____ tallest animal _____ the world.

3.   The elephant is _____ biggest _____ all the animals on land.

4.   People think the lion is _____ strongest _____ the animals.

5.   The ostrich is _____ biggest bird _____ the world.

6.   The snail is _____ slowest animal _____ all.

7.   Lions sleep for _____ greatest part _____of_____ the day.

8.   Antarctica has _____ least number of land animals _____ the world.

19   Pair Up and Talk
Imagine there is a fire in your house. You can only take five things away.
Which of the five things from the list will you take with you? Think about
which is the least expensive, the most expensive, etc. Then discuss your
decisions with your partner and the rest of the class. Use superlative
forms with the words and phrases in the list or use your own ideas.

My old photographs are the most important of all, so I will take them.
My radio is the easiest to replace, so I won't take it.

beautiful   hard/easy to replace   useful
cheap   important   valuable

1.   your passport

2.   your favorite book

3.   old photographs

4.   your computer

5.   an antique vase

6.   your sunglasses

7.   your jewelry

8.   your cell phone

9.   your music files

10.   your radio

Comparative and Superlative Forms of Nouns

Form

Cookies have a lot of calories.
Cake has **more calories** than cookies.
Ice cream has the **most calories** of all my favorite desserts.

Comparative Nouns

1. We use *more* to compare both count and noncount nouns.

    Those classes have a lot of students, but this class has **more students** than that one does.

    Our teacher gives us **more homework** than your teacher does.

2. We use *fewer* with count nouns. We use *less* with noncount nouns.

    This class has **fewer students** than that one does.

    Our teacher gives us **less homework** than your teacher does.

Superlative Nouns

3. We use *the most* with superlative count and noncount nouns.

    Those classes have a lot of students, but this class has **the most students**.

    Your teacher gives you more homework than Ryan's teacher, but our teacher gives us **the most homework**.

4. We use *the fewest* with count nouns. We use *the least* with noncount nouns.

    This class has **the fewest students** out of all the classes in school.

    Of all the math teachers in school, our teacher gives us **the least homework**.

As ... As **with Nouns**

5. We can use *as ... as* with count and noncount nouns. We use *many* with count nouns and *much* with noncount nouns.

Count Noun	She has	as	many	DVDs	as	I do.
Noncount Noun			much	money		

Function

1. We use the comparative forms of nouns with *more*, *fewer*, and *less* to compare the different quantities of two nouns.

   I have **more** homework than my friend.
   My friend has **less** homework than I do.
   Your class has **fewer** tests than our class does.

2. We use the superlative forms of nouns with *the most*, *the fewest*, and *the least* to show the largest and smallest quantity in a group of two or more.

   Out of all the English classes in school, Tony's class gets **the most** homework.
   Rachel's class only has one test a week. Jake's has fewer. Your class has **the fewest** tests.

3. We use *as ... as* to show that things or people are the same in two situations.

   I have 100 DVDs. Amy has 100 DVDs. I have **as many DVDs** as Amy (has).

20   Practice

A   Listen and write the missing numbers in the chart.

CD3, 5

Food (per 100 gm)	Protein	Carbohydrate	Fat	Calories (kcal)
Bread	7.3	40	2.4	200
Pasta	2.0	14	0.4	60
Pizza	15.0	37	10	280
Rice	6.0	52	0.4	225
Ice Cream	4.0	21	10	190

2. less
3. as much
4. fewer
5. the most
6. fewer
    less

in Part A to complete the sentences. Use *more/the most*,
est, and *as ... as*.

_____ *more* _____ protein than pasta.

_____ protein than rice.

_____ fat as ice cream.

_____ calories than pizza.

_____ calories.

_____ calories than rice.

10H | The Double Comparative

Form/Function

Buildings are getting **taller and taller**.

1. We use "comparative *and* comparative" to show that something increases or decreases all the time.

   The weather is getting **colder and colder**.

   Things are getting **more and more expensive**.

2. We can use these sentence structures to show that two things change together or that one thing depends on another thing. The second part of the comparative is often the result of the first part.

The + Comparative Clause	*The* + Comparative Clause
The more you study,	the more you learn.
The sooner we leave,	the sooner we'll get there.
***The* + Comparative**	***The* + Comparative Clause**
The harder the test,	the more you learn.
The more people in the room,	the hotter it will get.

21   Practice
Rewrite the sentences about the world today using "comparative *and* comparative" with the underlined adjectives.

1. The world's population is getting <u>big</u>.

   The world's population is getting bigger and bigger.

2. The air is becoming <u>polluted</u>.

_____

3. Medicine is getting <u>good</u>.

   _____

4. People's lives are getting <u>long</u>.

   _____

5. Forests are becoming <u>small</u>.

   _____

6. The problem of feeding the world's people is getting <u>bad</u>.

   _____

22 Practice

Complete the sentences with "*the* + comparative clause, *the* + comparative clause" or with "*the* + comparative, *the* + comparative clause."

1. If the hotel is famous, it is expensive.

   The more famous the hotel, *the more expensive* it is.

2. The hotel is near the beach. It is crowded.

   _____ the hotel is to the beach, _____ it is.

3. The room is big. The price is high.

   _____ the room, _____ the price is.

4. If you reserve early, the room is good.

   _____ you reserve, _____ room you get.

5. The hotel is far from downtown. It is cheap.

   _____ the hotel is from downtown, _____ it is.

6. You pay more. The service is good.

   _____ you pay, _____ service you get.

23 Pair Up and Talk

Work with a partner. Write two sentences about your class or school. Use "comparative *and* comparative." Then talk about how you learn. Use "*the*+comparative, *the*+comparative clause."

We have more and more tests every year.

YOU: The harder the test, the more I study.

1. _____

2. _____

10I | *The Same As, Similar To, Different From, Like, and Alike*

Form/Function

The twins dress **alike**.

1. We use *the same* and *the same … as* to say that things are the same.

    John has a black 2002 Toyota. Jane has a black 2002 Toyota.

    John's car is **the same** color **as** Jane's.

    John's car is **the same** year **as** Jane's car.

    Their cars are **the same**.

2. We use *like* and *alike* to say that things are the same or almost the same. *Like* and *alike* are used in different structures.

Noun	Be + Like	Noun
John's car	**is like**	Jane's car.

Noun	Noun	Verb + Alike
John's car	and Jane's car	**are alike.**
Betty	and Cathy	**look alike.**

   We can also use *alike* with a plural noun or pronoun.

   The twins dress **alike**.

   They talk **alike**.

   They think **alike**.

3. We use *similar* and *similar to* to say that things are different in small ways.

    John has a black Toyota. Paul has a black Mazda. Both cars are small.

    John's car is **similar to** Paul's car.

    John and Paul's cars are **similar**.

4. We use *different* and *different from* to say that things are quite different. We usually use *from* after the adjective *different*. The grammatically correct word is *different from* although some people use *different than* in everyday conversation.

    John has a black Toyota. Mike has a red Volkswagen.

    John's car **is different from** Mike's car.

    John and Mike's cars are **different**.

24 Practice
Underline the correct form.

1. Mike and Jane live in the town of Homa. Mike lives in (the same town/<u>the same town as</u>) Jane.

2. They both live in (the same/the same as) town.

3. Mike and Jane were born in Homa and have lived there all their lives. Mike talks (like/alike) Jane.

4. Mike and Jane talk (like/alike).

5. Ted is Mike's brother. He lives in the town of Chester. Ted lives in a (different/different from) town.

6. Mike and Ted live in (different/different from) towns.

7. Ted looks (like/alike) Mike.

8. Ted and Mike look (like/alike).

9. Mike's truck is (similar/similar to) Ted's truck.

10. Mike and Ted's trucks are (similar/similar to).

11. Ted is a mechanic. Mike is an engineer. Mike's job is (different/different from) Ted's job.

12. Mike and Ted's jobs are (different/different from).

25 Pair Up and Talk
Work with a partner or a group. Compare the four houses.

The first house and the fourth house are alike.

| House 1 | House 2 | House 3 | House 4 |

Listening Puzzle

A Listen and check the correct answer.

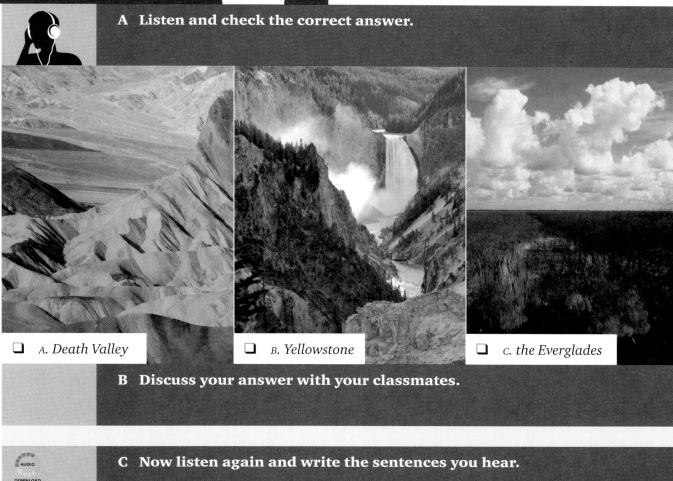

☐ A. Death Valley ☐ B. Yellowstone ☐ C. the Everglades

B Discuss your answer with your classmates.

C Now listen again and write the sentences you hear.

CD3, 7

Comparative and Superlative Forms **273**

Reading Challenge

A Before You Read

Answer the questions.

1. What land animal do you think lives the longest?
2. Do you think animals in captivity live longer lives or shorter lives? Why?

B Read

ANIMALS THAT LIVE THE LONGEST

Albatross

Tortoise

Killer Whale

Tiny animals, in general, have the shortest lives. For example, a mayfly after it gets its wings lives for only one day. On the other hand, another small insect, the jewel beetle from
5 tropical South America, lives for 30 years and is the insect that lives the longest.

Except for humans, Asian elephants live the longest of all land mammals. They live for more than 60 years. At around
10 60, the elephant's teeth wear out. Since it cannot chew anymore, it eventually dies of hunger.

Precise information on
15 the life span of birds is difficult to collect. The larger the bird, the longer it lives. The albatross is probably the longest living bird. It lives to over 70 years. However, birds **in captivity** seem to live longer than birds in the wild.

20 Reptiles that live the longest are tuataras and tortoises. They live longer than any other land animals. Tuataras live on small islands near New Zealand. When the weather is cold, a tuatara breathes about one time in an hour.
25 Because their lives are so slow, these creatures can live for 120 years or more. There are several kinds of tortoises that live for more than 100 years. Records state that one giant tortoise found in 1766 in Mauritius lived 152 years.

30 In the water, the killer whale lives the longest of all mammals. In the wild, male killer whales live up to 50 years and females up to 80. As for fish, the lake sturgeon lives the longest. It lives 80 years.

> **DID YOU KNOW … ?**
> The life of an average house spider is four days.

C Notice the Grammar

Underline all forms of the comparative and superlative.

Choose the best answer.

D Look for Main Ideas

1. What is the main topic of this reading?
    - (A) Life in captivity increases the life span of animals.
    - (B) Tiny animals have the shortest lives.
    - (C) Life spans differ among animals.
    - (D) Reptiles live longer than mammals.

2. Paragraph 4 is mostly about _____ .
    - (A) the long life span of tuataras
    - (B) a giant tortoise that lived 152 years
    - (C) the lives of tuataras and tortoises
    - (D) how cold weather affects reptiles

E Look for Details

3. Asian elephants die when they _____ .
    - (A) can no longer eat
    - (B) reach 80 years old
    - (C) are put in captivity
    - (D) can only move very slowly

4. How long does a jewel beetle live?
    - (A) only one day
    - (B) 30 years
    - (C) 80 years
    - (D) 60 years

5. All of the following are true EXCEPT _____ .
    - (A) tuataras can breathe slowly
    - (B) tiny animals generally have short lives
    - (C) the longest living land mammals are Asian elephants
    - (D) birds live longer than fish

READING SKILL: Paraphrasing

Paraphrasing is making a new sentence with the same meaning as the old one. Paraphrasing helps you understand sentences. It is also a good way to explain something. Try it yourself. Write a paraphrase of a sentence from the reading.

F Make Inferences

6. We can infer from the reading that _____ .
    - (A) a bear would probably have a shorter life span than a rat
    - (B) a parrot in a zoo wouldn't live as long as one living in a tropical forest
    - (C) an eagle would probably live longer than a hummingbird
    - (D) mammals that live in the water have longer lives than land mammals

7. What can we infer from paragraph 4?
    - (A) Living on small islands can help animals live longer.
    - (B) Cold weather endangers the lives of reptiles.
    - (C) An animal's level of activity can affect its life span.
    - (D) For animals, it's safer to live on land than in the sea.

G Look for Vocabulary

8. The phrase *in captivity* in the reading is closest in meaning to _____ .
    - (A) free to come and go
    - (B) raised with others of their kind
    - (C) living on an island
    - (D) kept in a protected place

Writing: Write a Comparative Paragraph

Write a paragraph that compares two schools you have attended.

STEP **1**   Think about two schools you have attended. Make notes in the chart.

	School 1	School 2
1. Classes attended		
2. Teachers		
3. Homework		
4. Friends		
5. Free time		

STEP **2**   Write sentences about the two schools. In general, which school was better and which was worse?

STEP **3**   Choose some of your sentences and write them in a paragraph. Give reasons why one school was better or worse. Write a title to your paragraph, for example, "The Best School."

The Best School

    Fifteen years ago, I attended high school. When I was a child, I attended kindergarten. In kindergarten, I had more free time. In high school, I had harder classes, and ...

STEP **4**   Evaluate your paragraph.

Checklist

_____ Did you write a title and put it in the right place?

_____ Did you indent the first line of your paragraph?

_____ Did you say which school was better or worse?

STEP **5**   Edit your work. Work with a partner or your teacher to edit your paragraph. Correct spelling, punctuation, vocabulary, and grammar.

STEP **6**   Write your final copy.

Self-Test

1. Mary is _____ Tina.

   A. as much tall as   Ⓐ Ⓑ Ⓒ Ⓓ
   B. as tall than
   C. as tall as
   D. as taller as

2. As we walked, it got darker and _____ .

   A. darker   Ⓐ Ⓑ Ⓒ Ⓓ
   B. more dark
   C. the darker
   D. the darkest

3. This question is _____ than the others.

   A. less difficult   Ⓐ Ⓑ Ⓒ Ⓓ
   B. the oldest
   C. least difficult
   D. less difficulter

4. This is _____ building in the city.

   A. the most oldest   Ⓐ Ⓑ Ⓒ Ⓓ
   B. the oldest
   C. oldest
   D. most oldest

5. The more you study, _____ .

   A. the more you learn   Ⓐ Ⓑ Ⓒ Ⓓ
   B. the more than you learn
   C. you learn more
   D. more you learn

6. It's _____ here in the country than in the city.

   A. more peacefully   Ⓐ Ⓑ Ⓒ Ⓓ
   B. more peaceful
   C. peacefuller
   D. the more peaceful

7. The Bellevue is _____ of the five hotels in this area.

   A. the very expensive   Ⓐ Ⓑ Ⓒ Ⓓ
   B. least expensive
   C. the less expensive
   D. the least expensive

8. Ted is a _____ his brother.

   A. better student from   Ⓐ Ⓑ Ⓒ Ⓓ
   B. better student than
   C. gooder student than
   D. best student

9. Carol drives _____ than her sister.

   A. more careful   Ⓐ Ⓑ Ⓒ Ⓓ
   B. more carefully
   C. carefullier
   D. the more carefully

10. The older she gets, the _____ she becomes.

   A. quieter   Ⓐ Ⓑ Ⓒ Ⓓ
   B. more quieter
   C. quiet
   D. quietlier

1. This year computers <u>are</u> <u>more cheap</u> <u>than</u>
        A B   C
   <u>last year</u>.
    D   Ⓐ Ⓑ Ⓒ Ⓓ

2. Our neighbors bought a television set that <u>is</u>
                A
   twice <u>so</u> <u>expensive</u> as <u>ours</u>.
     B C   D
          Ⓐ Ⓑ Ⓒ Ⓓ

3. This is the <u>most funniest</u> movie I <u>have</u>
     A   B
   <u>ever</u> <u>seen</u>.
    C D Ⓐ Ⓑ Ⓒ Ⓓ

4. <u>The more</u> time I spend with my
    A
   grandmother, <u>the</u> more <u>than</u> she
        B   C
   appreciates <u>it</u>.
      D   Ⓐ Ⓑ Ⓒ Ⓓ

5. It is <u>getting</u> <u>the</u> warmer and <u>warmer</u> as
      A B   C
   spring <u>approaches</u>.
      D   Ⓐ Ⓑ Ⓒ Ⓓ

6. My mother and <u>I</u> <u>are</u> <u>like</u> in <u>character</u> and
        A B C   D
   alike
   physical appearance.
         Ⓐ Ⓑ Ⓒ Ⓓ

7. My English teacher <u>is</u> <u>different</u> <u>to</u> my history
          A B C
   teacher <u>in many ways</u>.
      D   Ⓐ Ⓑ Ⓒ Ⓓ

8. I am <u>very</u> <u>interesting</u> <u>to see</u> the new exhibit at
      A   B   C
   <u>the Science Museum</u>.
      D   Ⓐ Ⓑ Ⓒ Ⓓ

9. There are many <u>interested</u> <u>sights</u> <u>to see</u>
         A   B C
   <u>in New York City</u>.
    D   Ⓐ Ⓑ Ⓒ Ⓓ

10. My job and Tony's job <u>are</u> <u>similar</u> each <u>other</u>
             A B   C
    to
    <u>in many ways</u>.
     D   Ⓐ Ⓑ Ⓒ Ⓓ

Unit 11

The Passive Voice

The Eiffel Tower **was built** in 1889.

11A Active and Passive Voice Verbs: Simple Present, Simple Past, Present Perfect, Past Perfect, and Future

Form

The Eiffel Tower **was built** in 1889.
It **was designed** by Gustave Eiffel.
It **is made** of iron, and it **has been repaired** many times.
It **is visited** by millions of tourists every year.

1. A sentence with an active voice has a subject, a verb, and an object.

Subject	Active Verb	Object
Gustave Eiffel	designed	the Eiffel Tower.

2. A sentence with a passive voice has a subject, a verb, and sometimes an agent.

Subject	Passive Verb	Agent
The Eiffel Tower	was designed	(by Gustave Eiffel).

3. We form the passive voice with *be* + a past participle. The verb *be* can be in any form: *am/is/are*, *was/were, has been/have been/had been, be*, and so on. We put the past participle after the form of *be*.

4. For regular verbs, the past participle ends in *-ed*. The past participle of irregular verbs is usually different.

Type of Verb	Base Form	Past Participle
Regular	visit	visited
Irregular	write	written

Verb Form	Active Voice	Passive Voice
Simple Present	Mr. Stone teaches me.	I **am taught** by Mr. Stone.
	Mr. Stone teaches Joe.	Joe **is taught** by Mr. Stone.
	Mr. Stone teaches us.	We **are taught** by Mr. Stone.
Simple Past	Mr. Stone taught me.	I **was taught** by Mr. Stone.
	Mr. Stone taught us.	We **were taught** by Mr. Stone.
Present Perfect	Mr. Stone has taught me.	I **have been taught** by Mr. Stone.
	Mr. Stone has taught him.	He **has been taught** by Mr. Stone.
Past Perfect	Mr. Stone had taught me.	I **had been taught** by Mr. Stone.
	Mr. Stone had taught us.	We **had been taught** by Mr. Stone.
Future	Mr. Stone is going to teach us.	We **are going to be taught** by Mr. Stone.
	Mr. Stone will teach me.	I **will be taught** by Mr. Stone.
	Mr. Stone will teach us.	We **will be taught** by Mr. Stone.
Modals	Mr. Stone can teach us.	We **can be taught** by Mr. Stone.
	Mr. Stone should teach us.	We **should be taught** by Mr. Stone.

5. If we change an active voice sentence to a passive voice sentence, the object of the active voice sentence becomes the subject of the passive voice sentence.

In a passive sentence, we can express the subject of the active voice sentence as an agent. We state the agent with a prepositional phrase with *by*.

	Subject	Verb	Object
ACTIVE:	Mr. Stone	teaches	me.
PASSIVE:	I	am taught	(by Mr. Stone).
	Subject	**Verb**	**Agent**

6. We can form the passive voice only with transitive verbs—verbs that have an object.

Subject	Verb	Object
Paolo	wrote	the essay.

The verb *wrote* has an object, so it is transitive, and we can make the sentence passive.

The essay **was written** (by Paolo).

We cannot use the passive form if the verb is intransitive. An intransitive verb does not have an object.

Subject	Intransitive Verb
The book	fell.
The plane	will arrive.

INCORRECT: The book ~~was fallen~~.
INCORRECT: The plane ~~will be arrived~~.

Function

Millions of hamburgers **are eaten** every day in the United States.

We use the passive when we do not know who does an action or if it is not important or necessary to say who does something.

A van Gogh painting **was stolen** from the National Gallery. (We do not know who stole it.)

1 Practice
Change these sentences from the active voice to the passive voice.

1. Helen invites me.   *I am invited by Helen.*
2. Helen invites Ted.   _____
3. Helen invited us.   _____
4. Helen has invited you.   _____
5. Helen had invited them. _____
6. Helen will invite Tony. _____

2 Practice
Complete the sentences with the simple past passive form of the verbs in parentheses.

1. The world's biggest explosion (cause) __was caused__ by a volcano on the island of Krakatoa in Indonesia in 1883.

2. The explosion (hear) _____ in India and Australia.

3. A very big wave, about 115 feet (35 meters) high, (create) _____ by the explosion.

4. Thousands of people (drown) _____ by the wave.

5. Dust from the explosion (carry) _____ to many parts of the world.

6. The weather around the world (affect) _____ for many years.

3 Practice
What happens when you go to the doctor? Work with a partner. Use the prompts to write sentences in the simple present passive.

1. The nurse weighs you. — _You are weighed (by the nurse)._

2. The nurse takes your temperature. — Your temperature is taken by the nurse.

3. The doctor takes your blood pressure. — You blood pressure is taken by doctor

4. The doctor looks at your throat. — Your throat is looked at by doctor

5. The doctor checks your lungs. — Your lungs is check by doctor

6. The doctor sends you to a technician. — You are sent to technician

7. The technician takes blood samples. — blood samples are sent by technician

8. The doctor writes you a prescription. — _____

4 Practice

Jim and Berta saw an old house for sale one year ago, but they did not want to buy it because it needed too much work. They are looking at the house again, and they are noticing some changes. Complete the sentences with the subjects and verbs given. Use the present perfect passive.

1. the outside walls/paint   *The outside walls have been painted.*
2. the front door/change   The front door has been changed
3. the big trees/cut down   The big tree has been changed
4. a lot of flowers/plant   _____
5. a new garage/build   _____
6. the windows/repair   _____

5 Practice

AUDIO DOWNLOAD

CD3, 8

A Listen and write the missing words.

German immigrants __introduced__ the hamburger to the United States. The word
                              1
hamburger _____ from the German city of Hamburg. In 1904, at the St. Louis Fair,
                    2
they _____ hamburgers on buns. McDonald's® _____ hamburgers a
            3   **4**
popular American food.

The McDonald brothers opened the first McDonald's® restaurant in California in 1949.

The restaurant _____ only three things: hamburgers, French fries, and milkshakes.
                          5
People _____ outside the restaurant to eat. The business became too big for the
            6
McDonald brothers. The brothers _____ McDonald's®. Ray Kroc _____
                                              7   **8**
the restaurant. Since then, the company _____ opened over 25,000 McDonald's®
                                                      9
restaurants around the world. People _____ more than 40 million hamburgers
                                                  10
every day. Ray Kroc became a millionaire.

B Use the sentences from Part A to talk about McDonald's in the passive voice where possible. Use the correct tense. Not all sentences can be passive.

The hamburger was introduced to the United States by German immigrants.

284   Unit 11

Function

The telephone was invented **by Alexander Graham Bell**.

We use a prepositional phrase with *by* in a passive sentence to express the agent when it is important to know who does the action.

The telephone was invented **by Alexander Graham Bell**. (The person who invented it is important to the writer's meaning.)

Hamlet was written **by Shakespeare**. (The person who wrote it is important to the writer's meaning.)

6 Practice

Rewrite the sentences in the passive voice. Use the *by* phrase only when necessary. Use the correct verb form.

1. Someone built this store in 1920.

    This store was built in 1920.

2. An artist painted the ceiling by hand.

    _____

3. The famous architect George Emery designed the building.

    _____

4. Today, they sell beauty products in the store.

    _____

5. They make their creams from plants.

    _____

Rewrite the sentences in the passive voice. Use the *by* phrase only when necessary. Use the correct verb form.

1. People sell billions of bottles of Coca-Cola® every year.

   Billions of bottles of Coca-Cola® are sold every year.

2. People drink Coca-Cola® all over the world.

   Cocacola is drunk all over the world.

3. Dr. John Pemberton invented Coca-Cola® in 1886, in Atlanta, Georgia.

   _____

4. He sold it as medicine.

   It was sold as medicine

5. A man named Asa Candler bought the business from Pemberton.

   _____

6. He opened the first factory in Texas in 1895.

   The first factory was opened

7. World War I made Coca-Cola® popular outside the U.S. because they sent it to soldiers.

   Coca-cola popular

8. They use many advertisements to make Coca-Cola® popular.

   Many advertisements are used to make Cocacola Popular

8 Practice

Complete the sentences with the correct form of the verb in parentheses. Use the active and passive voice when necessary. Some verbs are intransitive and cannot be passive.

The Olympic Games

A

The first Olympic Games (hold) ___*were held*___ in the town of Olympia in ancient

Greece. They (hold) _____ in 776 B.C. The games (continue) _____

until about A.D. 393. Then the games (ban) _____ by a Roman emperor.

B

A winner of a race in ancient Greece (receive) _____ a wreath. The wreath
                                                        1
(made) _was made_ of the branches of a special olive tree. Only the winner of a race
        2
(recognize) _____ . A runner in second or third place
            3
(not, be) _____ .
          4

C

In 1875, parts of the Olympic stadium (discover) _was discovered_ and people
                                                  1
(become) _became_ interested in the Olympic Games again. The French educator
         2
Pierre de Coubertin (renew) _renewed_ the Olympic Games in the 1890s. The first
                            3
modern Olympic Games (hold) _were held_ in Athens in 1896. After more than 1,500
                            4
years, Athens (choose) _was chosen_ by the organizers to be the place for the first
                       5
modern Olympics. As in ancient times, the athletes were men. Women
                                                                    allowed
(admit) _admitted_ in 1900. Even in 1932, women (not, allow) _weren't_ to
        6   **7**
participate in more than three events. Since 1896, summer and winter Olympic Games
(hold) _were held_ every four years.
       8
       (have been held.)

D

The Olympic flag (use) _____ for the first time in 1920. The first Olympic
                       1
village (build) _____ in 1932. Today, before the games, the Olympic torch
                2
(light) _____ at the Temple of Hera, in Olympia, Greece. Then it (carry)
        3
_____ by runners to the city where the games (hold) _____ .
4   **5**
Sometimes, the torch (carry) _____ halfway around the world. Every four years,
                             6
the summer and winter games (be) _____ in a different country. Do you know
                                 7
where the next Olympic Games (hold) _____ ?
                                    8

THE THIEF AND HIS MOTHER

A boy stole a lesson book from one of his school friends and took it home to his mother. The boy was not scolded, but he was encouraged by his mother. The next time, he stole a coat and brought it to her. Again he was commended. The young man became an adult and continued to steal things of greater and greater value. One day, he was caught in the act! His hands were bound behind him, and he was led to the place of public execution. His mother followed in the crowd and beat her breast in sorrow. The young man said, "I wish to say something to my mother in her ear." She came close, and when she put her ear near him, he nearly bit it off. The people around were horrified, and the mother blamed him as an unnatural child. He replied, "Ah! If I was beaten by you when I first stole and brought to you that lesson book, I would not have come to this, nor have been led to a disgraceful death."

1. What did the boy steal? _____

2. How was he treated by his mother? _____

3. How was he treated by his mother the second time? _____

4. What happened one day? _____

5. Where was he taken? _____

6. Why did the young man want his mother? _____

7. What did the young man do to his mother's ear? _____

8. What should have happened to him when he first brought his mother the lesson book? _____

Form/Function

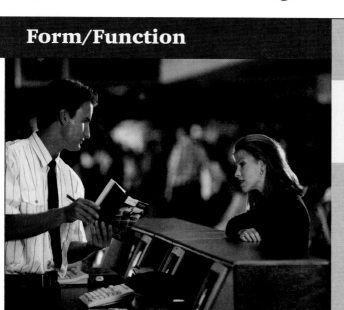

At the airport, tickets **are being checked**. Questions **are being asked**.

	Subject	Am/Is/Are	(Not) Being	Past Participle
Present Progressive Passive	I	am	(not) being	**asked** questions.
	He/She/It	is		**understood**.
	We/You/They	are		**cheated**.
Past Progressive Passive	I/He/She/It	was	(not) being	**asked** questions.
	We/You/They	were		**understood**.

1. The present progressive passive shows that something is taking place right now.

    ACTIVE: Someone **is asking** him questions.

    PASSIVE: He **is being asked** questions.

2. The past progressive passive shows that something was taking place at a specific time in the past.

    ACTIVE: Someone **was asking** him questions.

    PASSIVE: He **was being asked** questions.

3. We can use the *by* phrase if we want to say who or what did the action.

    He was being asked questions **by the airline clerk**.

10   Your Turn

What is happening at the airport? Complete the sentences with the present progressive passive of the verbs in parentheses. Then talk with a partner about what other things are happening.

1.   Arriving and departing flights (show) _are being shown_ on television screens.

2.   Departing flights (announce) _____ .

3.   One flight (cancel) _____ .

4.   Passports (check) _____ .

5.   Luggage (taken) _____ away on a conveyor belt.

11   Practice

At four o'clock yesterday, many preparations were being made at the Grand Hotel for the big reception for the president. Complete the sentences with the past progressive passive of the verbs in the list.

bring   cook   decorate   make   practice   rehearse   set   tell

1.   A cake _____ _was being made_ _____ .

2.   Food _____ .

3.   Tables _____ .

4.   More tables _____ because there weren't enough.

5.   The reception hall _____ with flowers.

6.   Security guards _____ what to do.

7.   Music _____ by the band.

8.   Speeches _____ .

12   Pair Up and Talk

What other things do you think were being done? Work with a partner. Give five more examples.

Flowers were being arranged.

11D | The Passive Forms of Modals

Form

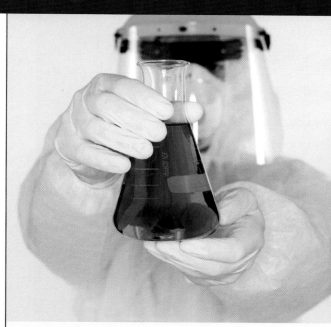

Toxic gases **must not be put** into the air. Dangerous chemicals **must be removed** from the water.

We form the passive of modals with modal + *be* + past participle. We form the passive of modal negatives with modal + *not* + *be* + past participle.

Active Voice Modal			Passive Voice Modal	
Subject	**Active Modal**	**Object**	**Subject**	**Passive Voice Modal**
We	will clean	the air.	The air	will be cleaned.
	can clean			can be cleaned.
	should clean			should be cleaned.
	ought to clean			ought to be cleaned.
	must clean			must be cleaned.
	have to clean			has to be cleaned.
	may clean			may be cleaned.
	might clean			might be cleaned.
	must not pollute			must not be polluted.
	don't have to pollute			doesn't have to be polluted.

13 Practice

People are talking about the environment. Rewrite the sentences in the passive voice.

1. We should not cut down the forests.

   Forests should not be cut down.

2. We should protect animals in danger.

   _____

3. We must not spray food plants with chemicals.

   _____

4. We could use electric cars.

   _____

5. We can use other kinds of natural energy.

   _____

6. The government ought to ban leaded gasoline.

   _____

7. We will destroy our planet.

   _____

8. We must take action now.

   _____

14 Your Turn

Write five other things we can do to help our environment. Then talk about your ideas with a partner.

1. _____

2. _____

3. _____

4. _____

5. _____

11E | *Have* Something Done

Form/Function

Bobby **is having his hair cut**.

1. We use *have* + object + past participle to say somebody does a job for us. We do not do it ourselves.

Verb Form	Subject	Form of *Have*	Object	Past Participle
Simple Present		have/have/has		
Present Progressive		am/are/is having		
Simple Past		had	my hair	
Past Progressive		was/were/was having	your hair	
Simple Future	I	will have	our hair	
	You/We/They	am/are/is going to have	their hair	cut.
Future Progressive	He/She/It	will be having	his hair	
Present Perfect		have/have/has had	her hair	
Present Perfect Progressive		have/have/has been having	its hair	
Past Perfect		had had		
Past Perfect Progressive		had been having		

2. We can use a *by* phrase to say who performed the action.
   He had his hair cut **by a very good barber**.

Karen O'Shea is a famous movie star. She is very rich and has everything done for her. Read the questions and write Karen O'Shea's answers. Use a *by* phrase to say who performed the action.

1. Do you style your hair yourself? (Lorenzo)
    No, I have it styled by Lorenzo.

2. Do you drive your car yourself? (my chauffeur)
    _____

3. Will you design your next dress yourself? (Alfani)
    _____

4. Do you cook your food yourself? (my chef)
    _____

5. Do you make your appointments yourself? (my assistant)
    _____

6. Did you plant these flowers yourself? (my gardener)
    _____

7. Do you fly your plane yourself? (my pilot)
    _____

8. Do you buy your groceries yourself? (my housekeeper)
    _____

16   Pair Up and Talk

This is a busy week for Helen. Talk about her schedule. Use *have* something done and the correct verb form.

Yesterday, she had her checks deposited to her bank account.

Yesterday	Right Now	Tomorrow
her checks/deposit to her bank account	her oil/change	her washing machine/fix
her eyes/test for new glasses	her suit/dry clean	her teeth/clean
some photos/take for a passport	a tree/cut down in the backyard	some new business cards/make

A   Listen and check the correct answer.

❏   A. *corn*   ❏   B. *wheat*   ❏   C. *rice*

B   Discuss your answer with your classmates.

AUDIO DOWNLOAD
CD3, 10

C   Now listen again and write the sentences you hear.

A Before You Read

Answer the questions.

1. Why did the Egyptians build pyramids?

2. How do you think they were built?

B Read

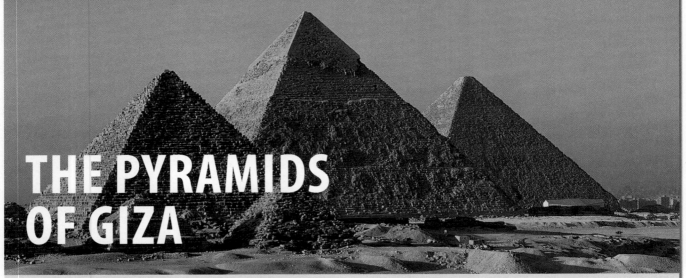

THE PYRAMIDS OF GIZA

DID YOU KNOW ... ?
Egypt has more than 80 pyramids still standing.

The pyramids of Giza in Egypt were built about 5,000 years ago. The pyramids are huge stone tombs that were built for the pharaohs, or rulers, of Egypt. When a pharaoh died, the ⁵ body was mummified[1] and then hidden inside a pyramid with the pharaoh's treasures. There are three pyramids ¹⁰ at Giza. The Great Pyramid, the largest, is taller than a 40-story building. It is one of the largest man-made structures in the world.

The pyramids were built by **teams** of workers. There were architects, engineers, and ¹⁵ mathematicians. They were helped by farm workers who were not able to work in the fields because of the Nile River floods[2]. The farm workers lived in villages around the pyramids. They were paid in food and lodging. The wheel ²⁰ was not invented in Egypt at that time, so huge blocks of stones were pulled. Millions of blocks were needed to build one pyramid. The Great Pyramid took 23 years to build. It is built so perfectly that a razor blade cannot even be put ²⁵ between the stones.

The builders were afraid that the mummies and treasures might be stolen by robbers. Secret tunnels and passageways were made inside the pyramids. However, thieves still got in and stole ³⁰ all the treasures.

[1.] *mummified = preserved by a special treatment*

[2.] *floods = when dry land is covered with water*

C Notice the Grammar

Underline all forms of the passive voice.

Choose the best answer.

D Look for Main Ideas

1. What is the main topic of paragraph 1?
   - (A) Giza has three pyramids.
   - (B) The Great Pyramid is one of the world's largest man-made structures.
   - (C) The pyramids were tombs built for the pharaohs.
   - (D) The pyramids were built 5,000 years ago.

2. Paragraph 2 is mainly about _____ .
   - (A) the perfect way in which the pyramids were built
   - (B) the materials used to build the pyramids
   - (C) the workers who built the pyramids
   - (D) the time it took to build the pyramids

E Look for Details

3. Egyptians had all of the following in their pyramids EXCEPT _____ .
   - (A) treasures belonging to the pharaoh
   - (B) the bodies of workers
   - (C) secret tunnels
   - (D) mummies of kings and queens

4. What were the pyramids made out of?
   - (A) huge bricks
   - (B) large stone blocks
   - (C) dried mud and straw
   - (D) cement and steel

5. The workers made passageways inside the pyramids to _____ .
   - (A) protect treasures from robbers
   - (B) hide from their enemies
   - (C) hide from their pharaohs
   - (D) live in while they worked

READING SKILL: Reading Faster

Reading quickly is a valuable skill. Time your reading to see how many words per minute you read. To increase your speed, skim passages for main ideas. Try to guess the meanings of words that you don't know. Scan passages for the answers to questions.

F Make Inferences

6. What can we infer about the Egyptians?
   - (A) They were afraid of their rulers.
   - (B) They didn't know how to farm.
   - (C) They had many slaves.
   - (D) They were great engineers.

7. We can infer from the reading that

   _____ .
   - (A) the architects were paid the most
   - (B) the pharaohs were not respected by their people
   - (C) the Egyptians knew how to control the Nile River
   - (D) the building of a pyramid was an enormous task

G Look for Vocabulary

8. The word *teams* in the reading is closest in meaning to _____ .
   - (A) groups of people who work together
   - (B) crowds of people who gather together
   - (C) several individuals who each work alone
   - (D) pairs of people who act alike

Writing: Describe a Place

Write a paragraph about a city or town.

STEP 1   **Work with a partner. Think of a town or city (maybe your hometown or a city you know). Ask and answer questions using the passive voice as much as possible. These prompts may help you.**

1. Where is it located?
2. When was it founded?
3. Who/What was it named after?
4. What is/was it famous for?
5. What are some famous places in the city? Who are they visited by? Why?
6. How has your city changed?

STEP 2   **Write answers to the questions in Step 1.**

STEP 3   **Rewrite your answers in paragraph form.**

STEP 4   **Evaluate your paragraph.**

Checklist
_____ Did you write a title (the name of the city or town)?
_____ Did you write the title with a capital letter for each word?
_____ Did you indent the first line of your paragraph?
_____ Did you write any sentences in the passive voice?

STEP 5   **Edit your work. Work with a partner or your teacher to edit your sentences. Correct spelling, punctuation, vocabulary, and grammar.**

STEP 6   **Write your final copy.**

Self-Test

1. The house _____ recently.

   A. has been painted   Ⓐ Ⓑ Ⓒ Ⓓ
   B. has painted
   C. been painted
   D. was been painted

2. My car radio _____ .

   A. was stole   Ⓐ Ⓑ Ⓒ Ⓓ
   B. stolen by someone
   C. was stolen
   D. is stolen by a person

3. _____ in the United States?

   A. People grow rice   Ⓐ Ⓑ Ⓒ Ⓓ
   B. They grow rice
   C. Is rice grown
   D. Is rice grow

4. When _____ ?

   A. did someone   Ⓐ Ⓑ Ⓒ Ⓓ
      invent paper
   B. was paper invented by someone
   C. someone invented paper
   D. was paper invented

5. Lillian is at the beauty salon. She _____ .

   A. is having her   Ⓐ Ⓑ Ⓒ Ⓓ
      hair cut
   B. is cut her hair
   C. is cutting her hair by someone
   D. has her hair cut

6. Paul's jacket is dirty. He _____ at the dry cleaners.

   A. is cleaning it   Ⓐ Ⓑ Ⓒ Ⓓ
   B. was cleaned it
   C. is having it cleaned
   D. clean it

7. This machine _____ after 6:00 P.M.

   A. must not use   Ⓐ Ⓑ Ⓒ Ⓓ
   B. must not be used
   C. must not be use
   D. not be use

8. The mural was painted _____ Diego Rivera.

   A. in   Ⓐ Ⓑ Ⓒ Ⓓ
   B. by
   C. when
   D. was

9. The vegetables _____ before you eat them.

   A. should be washing
   B. should washed   Ⓐ Ⓑ Ⓒ Ⓓ
   C. should wash
   D. should be washed

10. Vicky is at the opthalmologist. She is _____ by the doctor.

    A. testing her eyes
    B. tested her eyes   Ⓐ Ⓑ Ⓒ Ⓓ
    C. her eyes tested
    D. having her eyes tested

B   Find the underlined word or phrase, A, B, C, or D, that is incorrect. Darken the oval with the same letter.

1. An island <u>named</u> Easter Island <u>by</u> the Dutch
            A   **B**

   navigator Jacob Roggeveen in 1772 when

   he <u>reached</u> <u>it</u> on a Sunday.
        C   **D**

   Ⓐ Ⓑ Ⓒ Ⓓ

2. Many blind people can <u>use</u> <u>their</u> fingertips
                     A   **B**

   <u>to read</u> what <u>was written</u> on a page.
     C   **D**

   Ⓐ Ⓑ Ⓒ Ⓓ

3. The nurse Florence Nightingale <u>was call</u> the
                              A

   Lady of the Lamp <u>because</u> she <u>walked</u> from
                 B   **C**

   bed to bed in the middle of the night <u>with</u>
                                 D

   her lamp.
             Ⓐ Ⓑ Ⓒ Ⓓ

4. The Royal Flying Doctor Service <u>in</u> Australia
                              A

   <u>is started</u> <u>by</u> John Flynn <u>in</u> 1928.
    B   **C**   **D**

   Ⓐ Ⓑ Ⓒ Ⓓ

5. Workers <u>was gathered</u> from all over Russia
             A

   <u>to build</u> <u>the</u> city <u>of</u> St. Petersburg.
     B   **C**   **D**

   Ⓐ Ⓑ Ⓒ Ⓓ

6. <u>When</u> Marco Polo <u>returned</u> from China, he
    A   **B**

   <u>was written</u> a book about <u>his travels</u>.
      C   **D**

   Ⓐ Ⓑ Ⓒ Ⓓ

7. The Taj Mahal <u>is consider</u> to be one of the
                A

   <u>most beautiful</u> <u>buildings</u> <u>in the world</u>.
       B   **C**   **D**

   Ⓐ Ⓑ Ⓒ Ⓓ

8. Special diets <u>is</u> <u>needed</u> <u>by people</u> who suffer
             A   **B**   **C**

   from <u>certain diseases</u>.
         D   Ⓐ Ⓑ Ⓒ Ⓓ

9. Moby Dick was <u>a great white</u> whale <u>whose</u>
                A   **B**

   story <u>was wrote</u> <u>by the American novelist</u>
         C   **D**

   Herman Melville.
            Ⓐ Ⓑ Ⓒ Ⓓ

10. Frozen foods, such as frozen <u>fish</u> and
                          A

    vegetables, <u>introduced</u> in the 1920s when
            B

    people <u>began</u> to buy freezers for <u>their homes</u>.
         C   **D**

    Ⓐ Ⓑ Ⓒ Ⓓ

Unit 12

Conjunctions and Noun Clauses

It started to rain, **so** Adam opened his umbrella.

12A The Conjunctions *And*, *But*, and *Or*
(Doctors and nurses work in hospitals. You can visit the museum or the church.)

12B The Conjunction *So*
(It started to rain, so he opened his umbrella.)

12C *Too*, *So*, *Either*, and *Neither*
(I do, too. So do I.)

12D Noun Clauses Beginning with *Wh-* Words
(I know what the answer is.)

12E Noun Clauses Beginning with *If* or *Whether*
(I wonder if I locked the door.)

12F Noun Clauses Beginning with *That*
(I realized that I had made a mistake.)

12G Expressions that Introduce Noun Clauses with *That*
(I'm sorry that I couldn't come.)

✦ Listening Puzzle: Planets

✦ Reading Challenge: The Bermuda Triangle

✦ Writing: Describe an Event

✦ Self-Test

The Conjunction *So*

Form/Function

It started to rain, **so** Adam opened his umbrella.

So is a conjunction that connects two sentences. *So* gives us the result. We use a comma before *so*.

	Cause	Result
Two Sentences	It started to rain.	Adam opened his umbrella.
One Sentence	It started to rain,	**so** Adam opened his umbrella.

3 Practice
Complete the sentences with *and*, *but*, *or*, or *so*. Put commas where necessary.

Thomas Edison was a great inventor. He went to school _____*but*_____ didn't enjoy
                                                              1
it. He didn't do his schoolwork _____ the principal of the school told him not to
                                        2
come back. He only went to school for three _____ four months _____
                                                    3   4
he never stopped learning. His mother gave him science books. He stayed at home

_____ read the books. Edison needed money to buy more books _____
        5   6
he started to work on a train. He loved to do experiments. One day he blew up the

office where he worked _____ he lost his job. Edison always worked long hours
                              7
_____ slept for only five _____ six hours a day. Edison invented over
        8   9
1,000 items and processes. His most important are sound recording _____ the
                                                                            10
lightbulb.

Form

Linda has curly hair. **So does** Nancy.
Linda has curly hair. Nancy **does**, **too**.
Linda doesn't have straight hair. **Neither does** Nancy.

Affirmative Statement	Agreement with *Too*			Agreement with *So*		
	Subject + Verb	*Too*		*So*	Auxiliary Verb	Subject
I like Ken.	I **do**, I **like** him,				do	I.
I am a student.	I **am**, * I'**m** a student,				am	I.
We are studying.	They **are**, * They'**re** studying,	**too.**		**So**	are	they.
Bob went to Seoul last year.	Karen **did**, Karen **went** there,				did	Karen.
Tina can drive.	Tom **can**, Tom **can drive**,				can	Tom.

* If no information is repeated from the affirmative statement, we do not contract auxiliary verbs with their subjects when expressing agreement with *too*.

CORRECT:	I am, too.	She is, too.	They are, too.
INCORRECT:	I'm, too.	She's, too.	They're, too.

Negative Statement	Agreement with *Either*		*Either*	*Neither*	Agreement with *Neither*	
	Subject + Verb + *Not*	*Either*			**Auxiliary Verb**	**Subject**
I'm not hungry.	I'm not, I'm not hungry,				am	I.
I don't like football.	Paul doesn't, Paul doesn't like it,				does	Paul.
I didn't enjoy the movie.	They didn't, They didn't enjoy it,	either.	**Neither**		did	they.
They won't go.	We won't, We won't go,				will	we.
I can't do that.	I can't, I can't do it,				can	I.

1. When the main verb is a form of *be* (*am, is, are, was,* or *were*), we use the main verb in the agreement.

   A: I **am** not hungry.   B: Neither **am** I.

2. When the main verb is any other verb in the simple present or simple past, we use the auxiliary verbs *do, does,* or *did* in the agreement.

   A: Casey **liked** the movie.   B: So **did** I.

3. When the verb is an auxiliary verb + another form of a verb, we use the auxiliary verb in the agreement.

   A: I **am studying**.   B: We **are**, too.

4. When we use *so* or *neither*, we put the auxiliary verb before the subject.

   A: Susan **wasn't** in class.   B: Neither **was** I.

5. When we use *too* or *either*, we can also use the entire verb and other information from the original statement.

   A: I **don't like** football.   B: I **don't like it**, either.

Function

1. We use *too* and *so* to agree with or add information to affirmative ideas.

   A: I'm tired.   B: I'm tired, **too**.   OR **So** am I.

   A: Ken is strong.   B: Ben is, **too**.   OR **So** is Ben.

2. We use *either* and *neither* to agree with or add information to negative ideas.

   A: Ken doesn't have a mustache.

   B: Ben does**n't** have a mustache, **either**.   OR **Neither** does Ben.

3. In informal conversation, we often use *me too* and *me neither*.

   A: I like Ken.   B: **Me too**.

   A: I'm not hungry.   B: **Me neither**.

4 Practice

Ken met Monica at a party. They are finding out that they have a lot in common. Write sentences showing agreement using *so* and *neither*. Listen to check your answers. Then practice the conversation with a partner.

AUDIO
DOWNLOAD

CD3, 11

1. MONICA: I love this kind of music.

   KEN: *So do I.* _____

2. MONICA: I haven't been to a party for a long time.

   KEN: _____

3. MONICA: I am very shy.

   KEN: _____

4. MONICA: I am not good at making conversation.

   KEN: _____

5. MONICA: I love to read.

   KEN: _____

6. MONICA: I live alone.

   KEN: _____

7. MONICA: I came to this city a few years ago.

   KEN: _____

8. MONICA: I don't have many friends.

   KEN: _____

5 Practice

Fill in the blanks with the names of students in your class and the correct auxiliary.

1. _____*Berta*_____ wears eyeglasses, and so _____*does Kim.*_____

2. _____ is wearing black shoes, and so _____

3. _____ always sits near the door, and so _____

4. _____ wasn't late to class, and neither _____

5. _____ is absent from class today, and so _____

6. _____ wants to learn English, and so _____

6 Practice

Judy and Laura went to a new restaurant. They always agree. Complete the sentences. Listen to check your answers. Then practice the conversation with a partner.

CD3, 12

1. JUDY: I haven't been here before.

    LAURA: And I ___*haven't*___ , either.

2. JUDY: I like the décor and atmosphere.

    LAURA: And I _____ , too.

3. JUDY: I don't like this dish.

    LAURA: And I _____ , either.

4. JUDY: My food isn't fresh.

    LAURA: And neither _____ .

5. JUDY: My meal is cold.

    LAURA: And _____ , too.

6. JUDY: I don't have a napkin.

    LAURA: And neither _____ .

7. JUDY: I am disappointed.

    LAURA: And so _____ .

8. JUDY: I won't come here again.

    LAURA: And _____ , either.

7 Pair Up and Talk

Work with a partner. Give your opinions about television, holidays, and music. Your partner will agree or disagree. Use *so*, *neither*, *too*, and *not ... either*.

YOU: I like game shows.

YOUR PARTNER: So do I, but I don't like police shows.

YOU: Neither do I.

Form

Mr. Shin, I know **what the answer is**.

Introduction to Noun Clauses

1. A noun clause is a dependent clause. It cannot stand on its own. It is connected to a main clause. A noun clause has a subject and a verb.

Main Clause	Noun Clause
I know	what the answer is.

2. There are three kinds of noun clauses.

Type of Clause	Main Clause	Noun Clause
Wh- Clauses (see below)	The students know	what the answer is.
If Clauses (see section 12E)	I don't know	if it's cold outside or not.
That Clauses (see section 12F)	She explained	that she had to leave.

3. We often use a noun clause after expressions like these:

I know	I believe
I don't know	I wonder
Do you know	Can/Could you tell me

Noun Clauses Beginning with *Wh-* Words

Main Clause		Wh- Noun Clause		
Subject	**Verb**	**Wh- Word**	**Subject**	**Verb**
I	don't know	where	she	is.
		when		arrives.
		how		knew.
We	wondered	where	he	was.
		what		was doing.
		why		called.

1. The word order in a *wh-* noun clause is the same as in a statement: subject + verb.

   CORRECT: I don't know where **he is** going.

   INCORRECT: I don't know where ~~is he~~ going.

2. We use a period at the end of a sentence if the main clause is a statement. We use a question mark at the end of a sentence if the main clause is a question.

   CORRECT: I wonder where she is going. ("I wonder" is a statement.)

   INCORRECT: I wonder where she is going ~~?~~

   CORRECT: Can you tell me what time it is? ("Can you tell me" is a question.)

   INCORRECT: Can you tell me what time it is~~.~~

Function

1. We often use *wh-* noun clauses after verbs such as *know, understand, remember, wonder,* and *believe.* Most of these verbs express thinking, uncertainty, or curiosity.

   Peter left for work this morning. I don't know **when he left**.

2. We use sentences with *wh-* noun clauses in place of direct questions because they can make a question more indirect, and therefore more polite.

   DIRECT QUESTION: What time is it?

   WH- CLAUSE: Can you tell me what time it is?

8 Practice

A police officer is asking you questions about an accident. You can't remember much and are not sure. Complete the sentences with noun clauses. Listen to check your answers. Then practice the conversation with a partner.

CD3, 13

1. POLICE OFFICER: What color was the car?

   YOU: I can't remember _____ *what color it was.* _____

2. POLICE OFFICER: How many people were there in the car?

   YOU: I don't know _____

3. POLICE OFFICER: How fast was the car going?

   YOU: I don't know _____

4. POLICE OFFICER: What was the license plate number?

   YOU: I don't know _____

5. POLICE OFFICER: Where were you standing?

   YOU: I can't remember _____

6. POLICE OFFICER: How many other witnesses were there?

   YOU: I don't know _____

7. POLICE OFFICER: When did the accident happen?

   YOU: I am not certain _____

8. POLICE OFFICER: Where was the pedestrian*?

   YOU: I'm not sure _____

   * A pedestrian is a person travelling on foot.

9 Pair Up and Talk

Work with a partner to ask and answer polite questions for these situations.

YOU: Excuse me. Can you tell me where the dressing room is?

YOUR PARTNER: I'm sorry. I don't know where it is.

1. You are in a department store. You are looking for the dressing room.

2. You are in a train station. You are looking for platform 15.

3. You are at the airport. You are looking for the baggage claim area.

4. You are in a supermarket. You are looking for the eggs.

Form

I wonder **if I locked the door**.

Main Clause		Noun Clause with *If* or *Whether*		
Subject	**Verb**	***If/Whether***	**Subject**	**Verb**
I	don't know	**if**	I	**locked the door (or not).**
	can't remember	**whether**		

1. *If/whether* clauses have a subject and a verb. There is no comma between the *if/whether* clause and the main clause.
2. When we change a *yes/no* question to a noun clause, we use *if* or *whether* to introduce the clause. *If/whether* clauses are like *yes/no* questions, but the word order is like a statement (subject + verb).

Yes/No Question	**Did** I **lock** the door?
Noun Clause	I don't know **if** I **locked** the door.

3. The phrase *or not* often comes at the end of the *if/whether* clause.

   I don't know **if** I locked the door **or not**.

   I wonder **whether** the flight has arrived **or not**.

   We can put *or not* immediately after *whether*, but not immediately after *if*.

CORRECT:	I wonder **whether or not** the flight has arrived.
INCORRECT:	I wonder if ~~or not~~ the flight has arrived.

Function

1. *If* and *whether* have the same meaning when they begin noun clauses.
2. As with *wh-* clauses, we often use *if/whether* clauses after verbs that express mental activity such as thinking, uncertainly, or curiosity.

   I **can't remember** if I locked the door.

   I **don't know** whether he is coming or not.

10 Practice

Brenda was in a hurry this morning. She can't remember certain things she did or didn't do. Rewrite the questions as noun clauses with *if* or *whether*.

1. Did I lock the door? I wonder *if I locked the door.*
2. Did I turn off the gas? I'm not sure _____
3. Is the TV still on? I don't know _____
4. Did I mail my bills? I'm not sure _____
5. Did I take my medicine? I can't remember _____
6. Did I feed the cat? I can't remember _____

11 Practice

You have met someone you like, but you are worrying about it. Complete the questions with noun clauses with *wh-* words or with *if/whether*.

1. What kind of job does he/she have?

   I wonder *what kind of job she has.*

2. Where does he/she live?

   I wonder _____

3. How old is he/she?

   I wonder _____

4. Is he/she at home right now?

   I wonder _____

5. Is he/she thinking about me?

   I wonder _____

6. Should I call him/her?

   I don't know _____

7. Did he/she say he/she would call me?

   I can't remember _____

8. Does he/she want me to call?

   I wonder _____

12 Practice

You are meeting some people at the airport. Rewrite the questions using noun clauses starting with *wh-* words or with *if/whether.*

1. Where can I park my car?

   Can you tell me *where I can park my car?* _____

2. What time does the flight arrive?

   Do you know _____

3. Do the passengers come out here?

   Can you tell me _____

4. Why aren't they there?

   I don't know _____

5. Is the flight delayed?

   I wonder _____

12F Noun Clauses Beginning with *That*

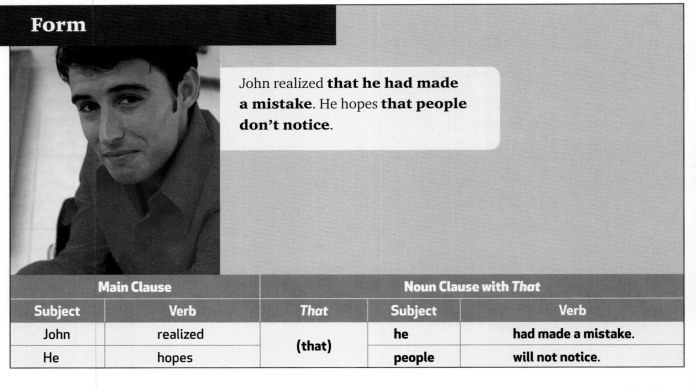

Form

John realized **that he had made a mistake**. He hopes **that people don't notice**.

Main Clause		Noun Clause with *That*		
Subject	Verb	*That*	Subject	Verb
John	realized	(that)	he	had made a mistake.
He	hopes		people	will not notice.

A noun clause can begin with *that*. Like other clauses, *that* clauses have a subject and a verb. We can usually omit *that*.

Function

1. We use *that* clauses after certain verbs that express feelings, thoughts, and opinions. Here are some of these verbs.

agree	doubt	figure out	imagine	predict	realize	suppose
assume	dream	find	know	presume	recognize	suspect
believe	expect	forget	learn	pretend	regret	teach
decide	fear	guess	notice	prove	remember	think
discover	feel	hope	observe	read	show	understand

2. We often omit *that*, especially when we speak. The meaning of the sentence does not change.

    MARY: I know (that) she is coming soon.

    JOHN: I hope (that) she does.

3. When the introductory verb is in the present, the verb in the noun clause can be in the present, past, or future. It depends on the meaning of the sentence.

    I know she **is** here.

    I know she **will be** here.

    I know she **was** here a few hours ago.

4. To avoid repeating information in giving answers to questions, we can use *so* after verbs like *think, believe, hope, be afraid,* and *guess*.

    MARY: Is Nancy here today?

    JOHN: I **think so**. (*So* = "that Nancy is here today")

Negative answers can be formed with *so* or with *not*, depending on the verb.

Question	Affirmative Answer	Negative Answer
Is Nancy here today?	I think **so**.	I don't think **so**. I think **not**. *
Did the rain stop?	I believe **so**.	I don't believe **so**.
Are we having dinner soon?	I hope **so**.	I hope **not**.
Is Tony going with us?	I guess **so**.	I guess **not**.
Did you get your grade on the test?	I'm afraid **so**.	I'm afraid **not**.
* *I think not* is formal.		

13　Your Turn

Work with a partner or a group. Write sentences that give your own opinion about each statement. Then write two more sentences about any subject. Start your sentences with *I believe/think that* or *I don't believe/think that.*

1.　People can live without light.

　　I don't believe that people can live without light.

2.　There are too many talk shows on television.

　　_____

3.　People will drive cars with atomic power in our lifetime.

　　_____

4.　Computers will have emotions.

　　_____

5.　_____

6.　_____

14　Practice

Complete the sentences with the verbs in parentheses and *so* or *not.*

1.　KEN:　Do we have class today?

　　SUE:　(think) __I think so__ . There is no change that I know of.

2.　KEN:　Can you lend me your book until tomorrow?

　　SUE:　(be afraid) _____ . I need it tonight.

3.　KEN:　Are we going to have a test today?

　　SUE:　(believe) _____ . The teacher just told me to be ready for it.

4.　KEN:　Is it going to be an essay?

　　SUE:　(guess) _____ . The other tests have been essays.

5.　KEN:　Are you ready for it?

　　SUE:　(hope) _____ . I studied all night.

6.　KEN:　Can we use a dictionary during the test?

　　SUE:　(afraid) _____ . Our teacher never lets us do that.

15 Read

Read the story. Then write questions for the answers.

A BIG QUIET HOUSE

There was once a man who wished his small, noisy house was larger and quieter, so he went to a wise old woman and explained his problem. She said, "I know the answer to your problem. Just do as I say."

The man agreed. "If you have a chicken, some sheep, a horse, and a cow," she said, "bring them into the house with you."

"I wonder if this will work," thought the man. So he did it. Now his house was already small, and with all those animals in it, there was no room at all. He returned to the wise old woman and said, "I need more room! The animals are so noisy I can't think!"

"Now take all the animals out of your house," she answered.

The man took out all the animals and went into his house again. He was amazed that the house looked much bigger! It was also quiet, too!

1. _____ ? He explained his problem to a wise old woman.
2. _____ ? She said, "I know the answer to your problem."
3. _____ ? The woman told him to bring a chicken, some sheep, a horse, and a cow into the house.
4. _____ ? He wondered if this would work.
5. _____ ? Yes, he put the animals in his house.
6. _____ ? She told him to take all the animals out of his house.
7. _____ ? No, he didn't know what would happen at this point.
8. _____ ? The man noticed that the house looked much bigger.

Expressions That Introduce Noun Clauses with *That*

Form/Function

> **It is true** that a cat is not able to taste sweet things.

1. We can use *that* clauses after expressions with *be* + an adjective, or with *be* + a past participle. These expressions show feeling. We can omit the word *that*.

Main Clause	That Clause
I am sorry	(that) you couldn't come.
I am disappointed	(that) I failed the test.

2. Here is a list of some of the adjectives and past participles that can introduce *that* clauses.

be afraid	be delighted	be happy	be proud	be terrified
be amazed	be disappointed	be horrified	be sad	be thrilled
be angry	be fortunate	be impressed	be shocked	be worried
be aware	be furious	be lucky	be sure	it is a fact
be convinced	be glad	be pleased	be surprised	it is true

16   Practice

Look at the following facts and write your opinion about each one. Use a *that* clause and one of the expressions from the list.

I am (not) aware that   I am (not) surprised that
It is (not) a fact that   It is (not) true that

1.   There is a town called "Chicken" in Alaska.

   I am surprised that there is a town
   called "Chicken" in Alaska.

2. There are 15,000 different kinds of rice.

_____

3. Clouds are higher during the day than during the night.

_____

4. Men laugh longer, more loudly, and more often than women.

_____

5. The elephant is the largest animal on land.

_____

Listening Puzzle

 AUDIO DOWNLOAD   CD3, 14

A Listen and check the correct answer.

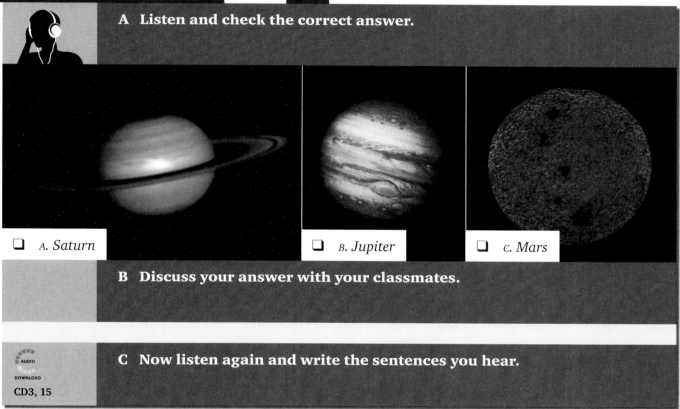

❑ A. *Saturn*   ❑ B. *Jupiter*   ❑ C. *Mars*

B Discuss your answer with your classmates.

AUDIO DOWNLOAD
CD3, 15

C Now listen again and write the sentences you hear.

A Before You Read

Answer the questions.

1. What is an area of the world that is considered mysterious? Why is there mystery surrounding it?

2. Do you believe things happen that cannot be explained?

B Read

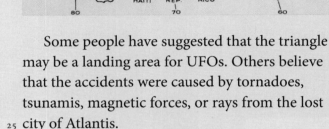

THE BERMUDA TRIANGLE

DID YOU KNOW ... ?

Japan has a similar mysterious area called Dragon's Triangle. Ships and planes have disappeared there as well. On the globe, Dragon's Triangle lies at the exact polar opposite of the Bermuda Triangle.

The Bermuda Triangle, also known as the Devil's Triangle, is an imaginary area. It is part of the North Atlantic Ocean, roughly between ⁵ Florida, Bermuda, and San Juan, Puerto Rico— making it into the shape of a triangle. The area has become noted because a ¹⁰ large number of ships and planes have disappeared mysteriously in this region.

According to ¹⁵ some people, more than 200 mysterious disappearances have occurred in the Bermuda Triangle. The most famous disappearances are of the U.S. Navy ship USS *Cyclops* in 1918 and ²⁰ the aircraft of Flight 19 in December 1945.

Some people have suggested that the triangle may be a landing area for UFOs. Others believe that the accidents were caused by tornadoes, tsunamis, magnetic forces, or rays from the lost ²⁵ city of Atlantis.

Scientists have studied the evidence and do not agree. They say that the Bermuda Triangle has had no more accidents than anywhere else. They say that the disappearances were due to ³⁰ bad weather conditions or mechanical failure. The U.S. Navy does not believe the Bermuda Triangle exists. The U.S. Board of Geographic Names does not recognize the Bermuda Triangle as an official name. It is also a fact that ³⁵ Lloyd's of London, the world's leading insurance specialist, does not charge more money for **vessels** going through this area.

C Notice the Grammar

Underline all noun clauses.

Choose the best answer.

D   Look for Main Ideas

1. What is the main topic of this reading?
    A There is mystery and controversy surrounding the Bermuda Triangle.
    B Many mysterious disappearances have occurred in the area.
    C Scientists cannot find evidence of the existence of the Bermuda Triangle.
    D Some people believe that UFOs land in the Bermuda Triangle.

2. Paragraph 3 is mostly about _____ .
    A why vessels may have disappeared there
    B the fact that the Bermuda Triangle is not an officially named place
    C the number of accidents that occur there
    D those who don't recognize the existence of the Bermuda Triangle

E   Look for Details

3. Why is the Bermuda Triangle mysterious?
    A It has strange weather patterns.
    B Its borders are shaped like a triangle.
    C It is a secret landing area for aircraft.
    D Ships and planes have disappeared there.

4. What do scientists say about the Bermuda Triangle?
    A There is evidence that it really exists.
    B The area causes unexplained events to occur.
    C Vessels don't have more accidents there.
    D The weather is worse there than any place else in the world.

5. Disappearances in the Bermuda Triangle are NOT explained by _____ .
    A magnetic forces
    B tornadoes
    C extremely deep water
    D UFOs

F   Make Inferences

6. We can infer from the reading that _____ .
    A there are strong disagreements about the existence of the Bermuda Triangle
    B it was never really a mystery
    C scientists have solved the mystery
    D the U.S. Navy wants to protect its ships from the Bermuda Triangle

7. We can infer from the last sentence that Lloyd's of London _____ .
    A wants ships to go there
    B believes it's not a dangerous area
    C loses money by insuring ships
    D knows that ships will avoid it

G   Look for Vocabulary

8. The word *vessels* in the reading is closest in meaning to _____ .
    A large boats or ships
    B containers that hold water
    C any means of transportation
    D airplanes

Writing: Describe an Event

Write a personal letter that describes something that happened to you in your life.

STEP 1   **Write sentences about an event that happened to you recently that made you feel sad, happy, upset, etc. Use conjunctions and noun clauses in your answers.**

1. When did it happen?
2. Where did it happen?
3. What happened?

4. What was the result?
5. How did you feel about it?

STEP 2   **Write a letter to a friend or a family member about this experience. Use the sentences from Step 1 and the following model as a guide.**

> Dear Meg,   January 3, 20XX
>
>   Happy New Year! We had a good holiday season here. I feel especially happy because of a great thing that happened to me last week.
>
>   You know that I have been seeing Joe for about a year. Well, on Tuesday, he came over to our house and _____
> You can imagine how I felt. Please write back and let me know what you think.
> Your friend,
> Cathy

STEP 3   **Evaluate your letter.**

Checklist

_____ Did you put the date at the top of your letter?

_____ Did you start your letter with "Dear" and the person's name?

_____ Did you write an introductory paragraph?

_____ Did you describe the event that happened to you?

_____ Did you write a concluding paragraph?

_____ Did you end your letter with a phrase such as "Yours truly," or "Love," and your name?

STEP 4   **Edit your work. Work with a partner or your teacher to edit your paragraph. Check spelling, vocabulary, and grammar.**

STEP 5   **Write your final copy.**

Self-Test

1. TOM: I hate fish.
   JACK: I _____ . I don't like the smell.

   A. too   Ⓐ Ⓑ Ⓒ Ⓓ
   B. either
   C. neither
   D. do, too

2. Lee was born in Hong Kong. So _____ his sister.

   A. didn't   Ⓐ Ⓑ Ⓒ Ⓓ
   B. did
   C. was
   D. wasn't

3. I wonder _____ the movie.

   A. if liked she   Ⓐ Ⓑ Ⓒ Ⓓ
   B. if did she like
   C. if she liked
   D. if or not she liked

4. I don't know _____ .

   A. what job she does   Ⓐ Ⓑ Ⓒ Ⓓ
   B. if job she does
   C. what does she job
   D. what job does she

5. It is a fact _____ everybody dreams.

   A. that   Ⓐ Ⓑ Ⓒ Ⓓ
   B. if
   C. what
   D. whether

6. He had a rash, a headache, _____ a temperature from the bad cold.

   A. but   Ⓐ Ⓑ Ⓒ Ⓓ
   B. so
   C. and
   D. or

7. I have a computer, _____ I read the news on the Internet.

   A. so   Ⓐ Ⓑ Ⓒ Ⓓ
   B. that
   C. or
   D. but

8. BILL: Are we having a test today?
   LISA: _____ .

   A. I hope not   Ⓐ Ⓑ Ⓒ Ⓓ
   B. I don't hope so
   C. I don't guess so
   D. I don't think

9. CHRIS: Is the teacher here today?
   PAT: _____ .

   A. I think   Ⓐ Ⓑ Ⓒ Ⓓ
   B. I don't hope
   C. I guess so
   D. I believe

10. Stan doesn't have a car and _____ .

    A. neither does not John   Ⓐ Ⓑ Ⓒ Ⓓ
    B. neither does John
    C. neither John does
    D. John doesn't neither

B **Find the underlined word or phrase, A, B, C, or D, that is incorrect. Darken the oval with the same letter.**

1. It is a fact what about two-thirds of your
   <u>A</u>   <u>B</u>

   body is water.   Ⓐ Ⓑ Ⓒ Ⓓ
   <u>C</u> <u>D</u>

2. Chimpanzees are very intelligent creatures
   <u>A</u>   <u>B</u>

   and too are dolphins.
   <u>C</u> <u>D</u>

   Ⓐ Ⓑ Ⓒ Ⓓ

3. I asked that salt water freezes at a lower
   <u>A</u>   <u>B</u>   <u>C</u>

   temperature than fresh water.
   <u>D</u>

   Ⓐ Ⓑ Ⓒ Ⓓ

4. Most vegetarians eat dairy products, such
   <u>A</u>

   as cheese and milk, and vegans avoid all
   <u>B</u>   <u>C</u>

   animal products.   Ⓐ Ⓑ Ⓒ Ⓓ
   <u>D</u>

5. Many island people in Indonesia and the
   <u>A</u>

   Philippines live on boats but in houses
   <u>B</u>   <u>C</u>

   made of wood over the water.
   <u>D</u>

   Ⓐ Ⓑ Ⓒ Ⓓ

6. I think if the most popular sport in Japan
   <u>A</u>   <u>B</u>   <u>C</u>

   is baseball.
   <u>D</u>   Ⓐ Ⓑ Ⓒ Ⓓ

7. I don't know if makes the sky blue, do you?
   <u>A</u> <u>B</u>   <u>C</u>   <u>D</u>

   Ⓐ Ⓑ Ⓒ Ⓓ

8. I wonder if or not a person can grow after the
   <u>A</u>   <u>B</u>   <u>C</u>   <u>D</u>

   age of eighteen.   Ⓐ Ⓑ Ⓒ Ⓓ

9. Picasso was a painter who painted in several
   <u>A</u>   <u>B</u>

   different styles, but greatly influenced
   <u>C</u>

   other painters of his time.   Ⓐ Ⓑ Ⓒ Ⓓ
   <u>D</u>

10. Can you tell me how far is it from here to the
    <u>A</u> <u>B</u> <u>C</u>   <u>D</u>

    train station?   Ⓐ Ⓑ Ⓒ Ⓓ

Unit 13

Adjective and Adverb Clauses

Although Matthew has a car, he uses a bicycle in the city.

13A | Adjective Clauses with *Who*, *Whom*, and *That* Referring to People

Form/Function

A pilot is a person **that flies airplanes**.
I know a man **who is a pilot**.

1. An adjective clause is used with a main clause. An adjective clause describes or gives information about a noun in the main clause.

Main Clause	Adjective Clause
A pilot is a person	**that flies airplanes**.
I know a man	**who is a pilot**.

2. *Who* and *that* are relative pronouns. Relative pronouns begin adjective clauses.
3. We use *who* or *that* to refer to people.* *Who* and *that* can be the subject of an adjective clause.

* Although *who* and *that* are both correct, *who* is preferred for people.

Main Clause	Adjective Clause		
	Subject	**Verb**	
There is the woman	**who**	flew	the plane.
There's the flight attendant	**that**	helped	us.

4. *Whom* also refers to people. In an adjective clause, *whom* is always an object.

Main Clause	Adjective Clause		
	Object	**Subject**	**Verb**
That's the pilot	**whom**	I	know.

Whom is very formal English. When writing, we use *whom* only in formal situations such as writing for school. When speaking, we use *whom* only in formal situations such as giving a speech. We use *that* or *who*, not *whom*, as an object relative pronoun in ordinary speech or writing.

5. An adjective clause comes after the noun it describes. Sometimes the main clause comes in two parts.

> The pilot whom I know is young.

Main Clause:	The pilot is young
Adjective Clause:	whom I know
CORRECT:	The **pilot whom** I know is young.
INCORRECT:	The pilot is young ~~whom I know~~.

1 Practice

Complete the definitions with an adjective clause using *who* or *that*. Use the phrases from the list. Then listen to check your answers.

cuts men's hair	serves people in a restaurant
fixes cars	trains athletes
fixes teeth	works in a bank
helps sick people	writes for a newspaper

1. A mechanic *is a person who fixes cars.* _____
2. A barber _____
3. A doctor _____
4. A coach _____
5. A waiter _____
6. A journalist _____
7. A dentist _____
8. A teller _____

2 Practice

Read the first two sentences. Then complete the third sentence with an adjective clause. Use *who* if the relative pronoun is the subject. Use *whom* if it is the object.

1. That's the woman. I dated her a few times last year.

   That's the woman *whom I dated a few times last year.* _____

2. She's the one. She had a lot of money.

   She's the one _____

3. She had an assistant. The assistant did everything for her.

She had an assistant _____

4. She had a driver. She paid him to take care of her three cars.

She had a driver _____

5. Unfortunately, she wasn't the woman. I wanted to marry her.

Unfortunately, she wasn't the woman _____

6. I found another woman. She works as a librarian.

I found another woman _____

7. She says I'm the man. She wants to marry me.

She says I'm the man _____

8. She's the woman. She will be my wife.

She's the woman _____

9. We'll be two people. We won't have much money.

We'll be two people _____

10. But we'll be two people. We will be happy.

But we'll be two people _____

3 Pair Up and Talk

Work with a partner. Use the statements to ask and answer questions. Combine two sentences into one sentence. Use *who* if the relative pronoun is a subject. Use *whom* if it is an object.

YOU: Who was Grace Kelly?

YOUR PARTNER: Grace Kelly was an actress who married the prince of Monaco in 1956.

1. Grace Kelly was an actress. This actress married the prince of Monaco in 1956.

2. The Beatles were four young men. These young men became famous all over the world.

3. Brad Pitt is an actor. This actor stars in a lot of popular movies.

4. The man was a movie director. We saw him in the restaurant.

5. James Dean was an actor. This actor died young.

6. Louis Armstrong was a famous jazz musician. This musician played the trumpet.

7. Celine Dion is a singer. I'm sure you have heard her.

8. Sophia Loren is a famous movie star. Everybody knows her.

13B | Adjective Clauses with *That* and *Which* Referring to Things

Form/Function

An orange is a kind of fruit **that** has a lot of vitamin C.

1. We use *who* (*whom*)/*that* to refer to people. We use *that/which* to refer to things.
    Casimir Funk was the man **who/that** invented the word *vitamin*.
    An orange is a fruit **that/which** has a lot of vitamin C.
2. *That* and *which* can be subject relative pronouns or object relative pronouns.
    You must get the vitamins **that/which** are important to your health.
    (*That/which* is the subject of the verb *are*.)
    The vitamins **that/which** I take are expensive.
    (*That/which* is the object of the verb *take*.)
3. When an adjective clause has a subject relative pronoun, its verb agrees with the word that the relative pronoun refers to.

    A fruit that **is** healthy is the orange.

    A person who **plays** sports needs a lot of energy.

    It is important to eat vegetables that **are** good for you.

    People who **play** sports need a lot of energy.

4 Practice

Complete the sentences with *who* or *which*. Then check whether you think the sentences are true or false. Compare your answers with a partner.

1. A person _____who_____ drinks a lot of water is healthy.   T ____ F ____

2. Food _____ is fresh is good for you.   T ____ F ____

3. Carrots are vegetables _____ make your hair red.   T ____ F ____

4. People _____ drink a lot of coffee sleep a lot.   T ____ F ____

5. Foods _____ have a lot of sugar and fat can make you fat.   T ____ F ____

6. Spinach is a food _____ is good for you.   T ____ F ____

5 Practice

Underline the correct verb in parentheses.

1. Kangaroos are animals that (<u>live</u>/lives) in Australia.

2. A kangaroo is an animal that (carry/carries) its baby in a pouch.

3. The ostrich is also a bird that (live/lives) in Australia.

4. An ostrich is a bird that (doesn't/don't) fly.

5. Some animals that (live/lives) in New Zealand are special, too.

6. A kiwi is a bird that (have/has) very small wings and cannot fly.

13C Omission of *Who*, *That*, and *Which*

Form/Function

He's the funny tourist we met yesterday.

1. When the relative pronoun *who (whom)*, *which*, or *that* is the object of an adjective clause, we can leave it out.

    He's the funny tourist **that** we met yesterday.

    OR He's the funny tourist we met yesterday. (*That* is left out.)

2. We cannot leave out *who, which,* and *that* when they are the subject of the sentence.

    CORRECT: The man who talked to us yesterday is funny.

    INCORRECT: ~~The man talked to us yesterday is funny.~~ (*Who* cannot be left out.)

6 Practice

**Complete the sentences with the relative pronouns *who, that,* or *which*.
If the relative pronoun can be left out, write *X*.**

1. Albert Einstein is a name ___X___ everybody knows.

2. Albert Einstein was a genius __who__ started to speak when he was three years old.

3. Albert was a boy _____ hated school, but he loved to read at home.

4. Science was the subject _____ he loved the most.

5. He had a violin _____ he played often.

6. After his graduation from college, Einstein got a government office job _____ he didn't like very much.

7. He was a man _____ people didn't understand.

8. Einstein was a man _____ wanted to find answers to many difficult questions.

9. Einstein had many ideas _____ changed the world.

10. Einstein was a man _____ often forgot things.

11. He wore a coat _____ was old.

12. Clothes were things _____ were not important to him.

13. Princeton, New Jersey, was the town in the United States _____ became Einstein's home.

14. In 1922, he received a prize _____ made him famous. It was the Nobel Prize.

15. When Einstein died at the age of 76 in New Jersey, scientists _____ admired his work were sad.

16. Because of Einstein, scientists have important knowledge _____ they can use to help us understand the universe.

A: What's a mermaid?

B: A mermaid is a woman **whose** body is like a fish from the waist down.

1. We use the relative pronoun *whose* to show possession. We use *whose* instead of possessive adjectives like *my*, *your*, and *his* with people, animals, and things.

   A mermaid is a woman. **Her** body is like a fish from the waist down.

   A mermaid is a woman **whose** body is like a fish from the waist down.

   I know the man. **His** house is by the river.

   I know the man **whose** house is by the river.

2. We use *whose* to refer to people. In informal English, we also use *whose* to refer to things.

   New York is a city **whose** restaurants are very good.

3. Do not confuse *whose* with *who's*. They sound the same, but their meanings are different.

	Form	Example
Who's	A contraction of *who is*	A: **Who's** that? B: It's Jack.
Whose	A relative pronoun	That's the man **whose** car was stolen.

7 Practice

Complete the questions with *who* for people, *that* for things, and *whose* to show possession. Then underline the answer that you think is correct. Listen to check your answers.

AUDIO
DOWNLOAD

CD3, 17

1. Who was the person _____*who*_____ invented the lightbulb?

   a. George Washington   b. <u>Thomas Edison</u>   c. Vincent van Gogh

2. What is the name of the long river _____ is in Africa?

   a. the Nile   b. the Mississippi   c. the Seine

3. What is the name of the writer _____ wrote *Hamlet*?

    a. Charles Dickens   b. William Shakespeare   c. Ernest Hemingway

4. What's the name of the country _____ capital city is Buenos Aires?

    a. Mexico   b. Spain   c. Argentina

5. What is the name of the man _____ was the first to walk on the moon?

    a. Neil Armstrong   b. Frank Sinatra   c. John Kennedy

6. What is the name of the man _____ home was called Graceland, in Memphis, Tennessee?

    a. John Lennon   b. Mick Jagger   c. Elvis Presley

13E | Adjective Clauses with Prepositional Phrases

Form/Function

A measuring tape is something you measure things **with**.

1. The relative pronouns *who* (*whom*), *that*, and *which* can be the objects of prepositions in an adjective clause.

    I was sitting on a chair. It was uncomfortable.

    The chair **that I was sitting on** was uncomfortable.

2. There are two structures for prepositional phrases with relative pronoun objects. In informal English, we also use different relative pronouns.

The Relative Pronoun Refers to a Thing			
Rules	**Main Clause**	**Adjective Clause**	**End of Main Clause**
Informal English The preposition goes at the end of the adjective clause.	The chair	**that** I was sitting **on** **which** I was sitting **on** I was sitting **on**	was uncomfortable.
Formal English The preposition goes at the beginning of the adjective clause. The relative pronoun must be *which*.	The chair	**on which** I was sitting	was uncomfortable.

The Relative Pronoun Refers to a Person			
Rules	**Main Clause**	**Adjective Clause**	**End of Main Clause**
Informal English The preposition goes at the end of the adjective clause.	The woman	**that** I was talking **to**	was interesting.
		who I was talking **to**	
		I was talking **to**	
Formal English The preposition goes at the beginning of the adjective clause. The relative pronoun must be *whom*.	The woman	**to whom** I was talking	was interesting.

3. The choices of relative pronouns are the same as for other kinds of objects. In informal English, you can omit the relative pronoun because it is an object.

> The woman **that/who** I was talking **to** was interesting.
>
> OR The woman I was talking **to** was interesting.

But when we use formal English and put the preposition first, we must use the relative pronoun.

CORRECT: The woman **to whom** I was talking was interesting.

INCORRECT: The woman ~~to I was talking~~ was interesting.

8 Practice

First complete the definitions using informal English. Then write the definitions again using formal English. Use the phrases in the list.

care for   drink from   travel in   work toward   write with

1. INFORMAL: A pen is something you _write with._

   FORMAL: _A pen is something with which you write._

2. INFORMAL: A cup is something you _____

   FORMAL: _____

3. INFORMAL: A goal is something you _____

   FORMAL: _____

4. INFORMAL: A car is something you _____

   FORMAL: _____

5. INFORMAL: A sick person is someone you _____

   FORMAL: _____

Form

Carlos is happy **because he passed the test**.

1. A main clause has a subject and a verb and can stand alone as a complete sentence.
   Carlos is happy.
2. An adverb clause also has a subject and a verb, but it is not a complete sentence. We must use it with a main clause.

Main Clause			Adverb Clause			
Subject	Verb		Conjunction	Subject	Verb	
Carlos	is	happy	because	he	passed	the test.

3. *Because* is a conjunction that can begin an adverb clause.
4. An adverb clause can come at the beginning or at the end of a sentence. It has the same meaning. If the adverb clause comes at the beginning, we put a comma after the adverb clause.
   Carlos is happy **because he passed the test**.
   Because Carlos passed the test, he is happy.

Function

We use the conjunction *because* to give a reason for something or to say why something happens. *Because* answers the question *why*.
   Carlos is happy. **Why** is he happy? He's happy **because he passed the test**.

Combine the sentences with *because*. Use correct punctuation.

1. Pete failed the test. He didn't study.

   <u>*Pete failed the test because he didn't study.*</u>

   OR <u>*Because Pete didn't study, he failed the test.*</u>

2. Pete didn't have time to study. He was working.

   _____

3. Pete worked. He needed money.

   _____

4. Pete needed money. He needed to help his family.

   _____

5. Pete's family had problems. His father lost his job.

   _____

6. Today, Pete is happy. His father found a new job.

   _____

13G Adverb Clauses with *Although* and *Even Though*

Form

Although he has a car, Matthew uses a bicycle in the city.

1. *Although* and *even though* are conjunctions that can begin an adverb clause.
2. Like clauses with *because*, clauses with *although* and *even though* can come at the beginning or end of a sentence. If they come at the beginning of a sentence, we put a comma after the clause.

   He went to work **although he was sick.**   OR   **Although he was sick,** he went to work.

Function

1. We use *although* and *even though* to show contrast or an unexpected result.

   Even though it was snowing, the road was clear.

   Although it was cold, he wasn't wearing a coat.

2. *Although* and *even though* have the same meaning.

   Although he was sick, he went to work.

   Even though he was sick, he went to work.

---

10 Practice

Complete the sentences using *who* for people, *that* for things, *because*, and *although*. Add commas where necessary. Then listen to check your answers.

CD3, 18

J. Paul Getty became a millionaire when he was 24. ___Although___ his father was

rich he did not help his son. Getty was a hard worker _____ made his money

from oil. _____ Getty was a millionaire he wasn't happy. _____ he

married five times he was not happy. _____ he had five children he didn't

love them.

For a man _____ was the richest man in the world at one time, he was

tight with his money. _____ he was an American he loved to live in England. He

bought a house in England _____ had 72 bedrooms, but it had pay phones in

the bedrooms _____ Getty wanted to save money on phone bills. _____

he was very rich he wrote down every dollar he spent every evening. _____ he

could eat anything he wanted he ate simple food.

_____ Getty didn't like to spend money he bought beautiful and

expensive pieces of art. _____ he loved art he didn't care about the price.

Today, the wonderful pieces of art _____ he bought are in a museum. It is a

museum _____ is in California. It is one of the most famous museums in the

United States. It is called the J. Paul Getty Museum.

THE PRINCESS AND THE PEA

Once upon a time, there was a prince who wanted to marry a princess, but she had to be a "real" princess. He traveled the world but couldn't find what he wanted. He was sad because he wanted a real princess.

One night, there was a terrible storm. Knocking was heard at the castle door. There stood a young girl whose hair and clothes were all wet. She said she was a princess. Although no one believed her, she was invited in to stay for the night. The queen, who wanted to find out if she was a real princess, went into the bedroom, took off all the bedding, and put a pea on the bottom. Then she took twenty mattresses and put them on top of the pea. She put twenty eiderdowns, or feather quilts, on top of the mattresses. On this the girl had to sleep all night. In the morning, the queen asked her, "How did you sleep?"

"Oh, very badly!" she said. "I couldn't close my eyes all night. The bed on which I slept had something hard. And because of that, I am black and blue all over. It's horrible!"

The queen immediately ordered a wedding. Only a true princess could have such delicate skin to feel a pea through forty layers of bedding.

1. What kind of girl did the prince want to marry? _____

2. Why was the prince sad? _____

3. Who was at the door of the castle? _____

4. Who did the girl say she was? _____

5. Why did the queen take off the bedding? _____

6. Why did the girl sleep badly? _____

7. Why was the girl a real princess? _____

A Listen and check the correct answer.

☐ A. palm tree

☐ B. oak tree

☐ C. pine tree

B Discuss your answer with your classmates.

C Now listen again and write the sentences you hear.

CD3, 20

A Before You Read

Answer the questions.

1. What talents do you think Leonardo da Vinci had?
2. Who do you consider a great artist of the past or present?

B Read

LEONARDO DA VINCI

DID YOU KNOW ... ?
Leonardo da Vinci was left-handed and a vegetarian.

Leonardo da Vinci was an artist who most people think of as a genius. He was not just a painter but also a sculptor, musician, poet, scientist, architect, and engineer. He was born in 1452 near Florence, Italy. At age 15, he went to work for a famous artist who taught him painting, music, mathematics, and science.

Da Vinci started many painting projects that he never finished. Although he finished only a few paintings, the ones he completed were **unique**. He created a new realistic style of painting. At that time, people in paintings looked flat. When da Vinci painted people, they looked real. His famous painting, the *Mona Lisa*, is an example of this. Another of his great works is the wall painting *The Last Supper*.

Although da Vinci was a great painter, he was interested in other subjects. Many people think of him as the first scientist because he observed things and looked for explanations. He wrote his observations in notebooks that are filled with more than 5,000 drawings of plants, animals, and the human body. Da Vinci wrote his notes backwards, which some people think is a little mysterious.

Da Vinci designed nearly 1,000 inventions. He drew a flying machine nearly 400 years before the airplane was invented. He also designed an air conditioner, an alarm clock, a reading lamp, a submarine, a bridge, and many other things. Many of his ideas were not developed because the technology to make them did not exist.

C Notice the Grammar

Underline all adjective and adverb clauses.

Choose the best answer.

D Look for Main Ideas

1. What is the main topic of this reading?
   - (A) Leonardo da Vinci was a mysterious man.
   - (B) Leonardo da Vinci was a man of many talents.
   - (C) Leonardo da Vinci was a great painter.
   - (D) Leonardo da Vinci was an inventor.

2. What is the main idea of paragraph 2?
   - (A) Da Vinci didn't finish many of his painting projects.
   - (B) Da Vinci's most famous paintings were the *Mona Lisa* and *The Last Supper*.
   - (C) Da Vinci painted in a different style than other painters of his day.
   - (D) Da Vinci painted one of his great works on a wall.

E Look for Details

3. Leonardo da Vinci _____ .
   - (A) learned to paint from a famous artist
   - (B) was born in Venice, Italy
   - (C) made thousands of drawings on walls
   - (D) painted hundreds of famous paintings

4. All of the following are true of da Vinci EXCEPT
   - (A) He invented the first airplane.
   - (B) He painted people to look real.
   - (C) He wrote his notes backwards in notebooks.
   - (D) He was an engineer as well as an artist.

5. In which paragraph does the author describe da Vinci's scientific interests?
   - (A) paragraph 1
   - (B) paragraph 2
   - (C) paragraph 3
   - (D) paragraph 4

F Make Inferences

6. We can infer from the reading that da Vinci _____ .
   - (A) was a better scientist than an artist
   - (B) had only a few great interests
   - (C) had abilities beyond others in his time
   - (D) could predict the future

7. Da Vinci studied plants, animals, and people. What can we infer from this?
   - (A) He wanted to understand the world around him.
   - (B) He liked to collect things.
   - (C) He liked to travel to the countryside.
   - (D) He wanted to complete many projects.

G Look for Vocabulary

8. The word *unique* in the reading is closest in meaning to _____ .
   - (A) the best of all
   - (B) similar to others
   - (C) different from any other
   - (D) newer than others

Writing: Write a Description

Describe a photo of your family or friends.

STEP **1**

Bring a photo of some of your family and/or friends to class. Tell your partner about the photo.

1. Who is in the photo?
2. Where was the photo taken?
3. How are the people related to you/how do you know the people?
4. What are their physical characteristics?
5. What are their personalities like?
6. What are they studying, or what do they do for a living?

STEP **2**

Write a sentence or two about the place in the photo.

Example

The photo shows the house that I grew up in. Although it is small, we all like it.

STEP **3**

Write a sentence or two about each person in the photo. Use *who*, *whom*, *whose*, *that*, *which*, *because*, or *although*.

Example

There is a cake because it is my birthday. The person who is next to me is my aunt. That's the aunt whose husband is a doctor.

STEP **4**

Write a paragraph about the photo. Write a title in three or four words.

STEP **5**

Evaluate your paragraph.

Checklist

_____ Did you give your paragraph a title?

_____ Did you indent the first line of your paragraph?

_____ Did you describe the people and the place in the photo?

STEP **6**

Work with a partner or your teacher to correct grammar, spelling, and punctuation.

STEP **7**

Write your final copy.

Self-Test

1. Beethoven was a great composer _____ deaf for much of his life.

   A. who was   Ⓐ Ⓑ Ⓒ Ⓓ
   B. whose
   C. who's
   D. whom was

2. The largest animal _____ on land is the elephant.

   A. that live   Ⓐ Ⓑ Ⓒ Ⓓ
   B. that lives
   C. who lives
   D. whom live

3. Louis Pasteur was a French professor _____ showed that germs cause many diseases.

   A. whom   Ⓐ Ⓑ Ⓒ Ⓓ
   B. who was
   C. whose
   D. who

4. The panda is an animal _____ only food is the bamboo plant.

   A. that   Ⓐ Ⓑ Ⓒ Ⓓ
   B. which is
   C. whose
   D. which

5. People _____ money to charity are called donors.

   A. whom give   Ⓐ Ⓑ Ⓒ Ⓓ
   B. who gives
   C. which give
   D. who give

6. A barometer is an instrument _____ air pressure.

   A. who measures   Ⓐ Ⓑ Ⓒ Ⓓ
   B. that measures
   C. which measure
   D. whose measures

7. The blue whale is the largest animal _____ .

   A. who lives   Ⓐ Ⓑ Ⓒ Ⓓ
   B. that live
   C. that lives
   D. whom lives

8. Biographies are books _____ the stories of people's lives.

   A. that tell   Ⓐ Ⓑ Ⓒ Ⓓ
   B. whom tell
   C. that tells
   D. who tells

9. Thomas A. Watson was the first person _____ Alexander Graham Bell talked on the first telephone call.

   A. whom   Ⓐ Ⓑ Ⓒ Ⓓ
   B. who to
   C. to whom
   D. whom to

10. We have seasons _____ the Earth goes around the sun.

    A. although   Ⓐ Ⓑ Ⓒ Ⓓ
    B. because
    C. who
    D. that

1. There are many flowers who close up
   A   B   C
   at night.
   D
   Ⓐ Ⓑ Ⓒ Ⓓ

2. Because he was famous and talented,
   A   B
   Mozart died poor and alone.
          C   D
   Ⓐ Ⓑ Ⓒ Ⓓ

3. When people get older, their lungs get
                          A
   darker although they breathe dirty air.
          B   C   D
   Ⓐ Ⓑ Ⓒ Ⓓ

4. Picasso was a Spanish artist whom is the
                 A   B   C
   best known 20th century painter.
              D
   Ⓐ Ⓑ Ⓒ Ⓓ

5. Egypt is a country in Africa who's capital
   A   B   C
   is Cairo.
   D
   Ⓐ Ⓑ Ⓒ Ⓓ

6. Mark Twain was an American writer whom
                   A   B
   real name was Samuel Clemens.
   C   D
   Ⓐ Ⓑ Ⓒ Ⓓ

7. African elephants have large ears who help
                     A   B   C
   them to keep cool in the hot climate.
   D
   Ⓐ Ⓑ Ⓒ Ⓓ

8. The holiday who is on the fourth Thursday
               A   B
   in November is Thanksgiving Day.
   C   D
   Ⓐ Ⓑ Ⓒ Ⓓ

9. Because so much of the Amazon forest has
   A
   been destroyed, it is still the biggest forest
                   B   C
   in the world.
   D
   Ⓐ Ⓑ Ⓒ Ⓓ

10. Palm trees are not like other trees although
               A   B   C
    they do not grow side branches.
         D
    Ⓐ Ⓑ Ⓒ Ⓓ

Unit 14

Reported Speech and Conditional Clauses

I wish I **were** on vacation.

14A | Quoted Speech

Form

Elvis said, "I don't know anything about music. In my line*, you don't have to."

line = type of work

Quoted (direct) speech tells who said something and what they said.

1. We can put the name of the speaker at the beginning of the sentence.

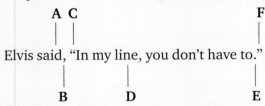

A. Mention the speaker and use a verb like *said*.

B. Put a comma after the verb.

C. Open the quotation marks (").

D. Write the quotation. Capitalize the first word.

E. End the quotation with a period, a question mark, or an exclamation point.

F. Close the quotation marks (").

2. We can also put the name of the speaker at the end of the sentence.

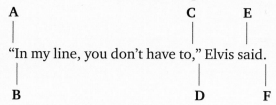

A. Open the quotation marks.
B. Write the quotation. Capitalize the first word.
C. If the original quotation ended in a period, use a comma at the end. If it ended in a question mark or an exclamation point, use those punctuation marks.
D. Close the quotation marks.
E. Mention the speaker and use a word like *said*.
F. End the sentence with a period.

3. We can also put the name of the speaker after *said*.

"In my line, you don't have to," said Elvis.

4. If there is more than one sentence in the quotation, we put quotation marks only at the beginning and at the end of the whole quotation. We do not use separate quotation marks for each sentence.

CORRECT: My mother said, "Elvis was my favorite singer when I was young. He changed my world."

INCORRECT: My mother said, "Elvis was my favorite singer when I was young ⊗ He changed my world."

5. We can also divide a quote.

"Elvis was a famous singer," my mother said. "He changed my world."

"Elvis was famous," she said, "and he changed my world."

Function

We use quoted speech for the exact words someone uses. We use quoted speech in novels, stories, and newspaper articles.

Source	Example
A newspaper article	"I'm retiring at the end of the season," the star player said.
A story about Thomas Edison	Edison said, "I have not failed. I've just found 10,000 ways that won't work."

1 **Practice**
Nasreddin Hoca (Hodja) is a character in Turkish folktales. Write quoted
speech for the speaker's words in this story. Use the verb *said* and the
correct punctuation.

*Nasreddin had a leaky ferryboat and used it to row people across the river. One day, his
passenger was a fussy teacher. On the way across, he decided to give Nasreddin a test to see
how much he knew.*

1.   TEACHER: Tell me, Nasreddin, what is eight times six?

   The teacher said, "Tell me, Nasreddin, what is eight times six?"

2.   NASREDDIN: I have no idea.

   _____

3.   TEACHER: You see, you can't multiply, and I know you cannot spell, either. You
   never studied anything at school. In that case, half your life is lost.
   (*Just then, there was a very bad storm, and the boat began to go down.*)

4.   NASREDDIN: Tell me, teacher, did you ever learn to swim?

   _____

5.   TEACHER: No.

   _____

6.   NASREDDIN: In that case, your whole life is lost.

   _____

14B   Reported Speech

Form

Muhammad Ali said that he was the greatest.

1. Reported (indirect) speech has a main clause and a noun clause.
2. We use reporting verbs such as *say* or *tell* in the main clause.

Main Clause		Noun Clause	
Speaker	**Reporting Verb**	**(That)**	**Reported Speech**
Muhammad Ali	said	(that)	he was the greatest.
Mary	says	(that)	she is happy.

3. We can leave out *that*.

    Muhammad Ali said **that** he was the greatest.

    OR Muhammad Ali said he was the greatest.

4. If the reporting verb is in the present, there is no change in the verb form in the noun clause.

    QUOTED SPEECH: Mary says, "I **am** happy."

    REPORTED SPEECH: Mary **says** that she **is** happy.

5. If the reporting verb is in the past (for example, *said*, *told*) the verb form in the noun clause changes when we report it. Some modal auxiliaries change, too.

    QUOTED SPEECH: Muhammad Ali said, "I **am** the greatest."

    REPORTED SPEECH: Muhammad Ali **said** that he **was** the greatest.

This chart shows the changes in verbs.

Quoted Speech		Reported Speech	
Verb Form or Modal	**Example**	**Verb**	**Example**
Simple Present	He said, "I **do** the work."	Simple Past	He said that he **did** the work.
Present Progressive	He said, "I **am doing** the work."	Past Progressive	He said that he **was doing** the work.
Simple Past	He said, "I **did** the work."	Past Perfect	He said that he **had done** the work.
Past Progressive	He said, "I **was doing** the work."	Past Perfect Progressive	He said that he **had been doing** the work.
Present Perfect	He said, "I **have done** the work."	Past Perfect	He said that he **had done** the work.
Future with *Be Going To*	He said, "I **am going to do** the work."	Simple Past for *Be (Going To)*	He said that he **was going to do** the work.
Future with *Will*	He said, "I **will do** the work."	*Would*	He said that he **would do** the work.
Can	He said, "I **can do** the work."	*Could*	He said that he **could do** the work.
Have To	He said, "I **have to do** the work."	*Had To*	He said that he **had to do** the work.
Must	He said, "I **must do** the work."	*Had To*	He said that he **had to do** the work.

6. There are many possible pronoun changes in reported speech. We use the logic of each situation to decide on the changes.

QUOTED SPEECH:	Bob said to Alice, "**You** gave me the wrong book."
REPORTED SPEECH:	Bob said that **she** had given him the wrong book.
QUOTED SPEECH:	Bob said to me, "**You** gave me the wrong book."
REPORTED SPEECH:	Bob said that **I** had given him the wrong book.

The following are some pronoun changes.

Pronoun Changes		
Subject Pronouns	I, you (singular)	he, she, I
	we, you (plural)	they, we
Object Pronouns	me, you (singular)	him, her, me
	you (plural)	us, them
	us (plural)	them

7. Time expressions can change in reported speech.

QUOTED SPEECH:	Jim said, "**Tomorrow** is my birthday."
REPORTED SPEECH:	Jim said that his birthday was **the next day**.

Time Expression Changes	
Quoted Speech	**Reported Speech**
now	then, at that time
today, tonight	that day, that night
yesterday	the day before
tomorrow	the next day
this week	that week
last week	the week before
next week	the week after
two weeks ago	two weeks before

Function

We use reported speech when we report what someone says or said. We use it when we do not want to use the exact words. We use reported speech often in both speech and writing.

Rewrite the sentences as reported speech. Make the necessary changes to verbs and pronouns. In some cases, there is no change.

1. Ben says, "I love swimming."

   Ben says that he loves swimming.

2. Kate says, "I can't swim, but I can ride a bicycle."

   _____

3. The newspaper article says, "Swimming is an excellent sport."

   _____

4. Dr. Carter said, "You have to do some exercise every day."

   _____

5. He said, "Twenty minutes a day is enough."

   _____

6. My mother said, "I can walk a lot."

   _____

7. My father said, "I'll go to the gym tomorrow."

   _____

8. Alice said, "I can go with you."

   _____

9. Tony said, "I went to the gym yesterday."

   _____

10. Paul said, "I have been to the gym this week."

   _____

3 Pair Up and Talk

Make up two events that could happen in a country's government. They don't have to be true. They can be funny. Write them on a piece of paper and give it to the class. Then take another classmate's paper. Using reported speech, tell your partner what the headlines say.

The president's dog bit a reporter.

YOU: It says that the president's dog bit a reporter.

14c — *Say* or *Tell*

Form/Function

A: **Tell me**, Sandy, what did he **say** on the show?

B: He didn't **say anything**. He **said good evening**. Then he **said a few words** about how happy he was to be the host of the show. Then he **told us** a funny story about his girlfriend.

A: That's me, Sandy. That's me!

1. We use *say* with or without a prepositional phrase with *to*.

   CORRECT: Linda said that she was thirsty.

   CORRECT: Linda said **to me** that she was thirsty.

   INCORRECT: Linda ~~said me~~ that she was thirsty.

2. We always use *tell* with an object. We do not use a prepositional phrase with *to* after *tell*.

   CORRECT: Linda told me that she was thirsty.

   INCORRECT: Linda ~~told that~~ she was thirsty.

   INCORRECT: Linda ~~told to me~~ that she was thirsty.

3. We use *say* and *tell* with some special expressions.

Say	Tell
say something/anything/nothing	tell the truth/a lie
say one's opinion	tell a story/a secret
say a few words	tell the time
say good morning/good afternoon/etc.	tell the difference

4 Practice

Complete the sentences with *say* or *tell* using the correct verb form. Then listen to check your answers.

CD3, 21

A

"No talking, Jimmy," the teacher _____*said*_____ . "I didn't _____
 1   2
anything," Jimmy _____ the teacher. "Don't _____ lies," the teacher
               3   4

352   Unit 14   *e-Workbook 14C*

_____ . "I can _____ the difference when someone talks and when
            5   6
someone doesn't talk," the teacher _____ the class. "Now, I don't want to hear a
                                                      7
sound. Is that clear?" the teacher _____ .
                                              8

B

      "Yesterday Meg _____ she was moving to Alaska," Karen _____ .
                                        1   2
"She _____ me that she had found a good job there."
           3

      "I don't believe that," Mike _____ . "Last month she _____ me
                                               4   5
she was going to Paris. She doesn't _____ the truth all the time, you know."
                                                6

C

      Today, my neighbor _____ good morning to me as usual. Then she
                                        1
_____ me a story about a mouse in her bedroom last night. She _____
        2   3
that the mouse had run out of her apartment and into my apartment. Did she

_____ me the truth or did she _____ me a story again?
        4   5

5   Pair Up and Talk

**Work with a partner. Tell your partner a short sentence. It does not have to be
true. Your partner tells the class what you told him or her.**

YOU: I have six children.

YOUR PARTNER: My partner told me she had six children.

14D Reported Questions

Form/Function

The president of the company **wanted to know why** everybody was sitting so far from him.

1. Reported questions have a main clause and a noun clause.

Main Clause		Noun Clause		
Subject	Reporting Verb	Wh- Word	Subject	Verb
He	asked	why	everyone	had left.

2. We use verbs like *ask*, *inquire*, and *wonder* or the expression *want to know* to report questions. We do not use *say* or *tell*.

   "Where do you live?" she **asked** me.

   She **asked** me where I lived.

   She **wanted to know** where I lived.

   She **wondered** where I lived.

3. When the question begins with a *wh-* word like *who*, *what*, *where*, *when*, and *how*, the noun clause in the reported question begins with the same word.

   He asked me, "**What** do you want?"

   He asked me **what** I wanted.

4. When the question is a *yes/no* question, we begin the noun clause in the reported question with *if* or *whether*. *If* and *whether* have the same meaning here.

   "Are you coming?" he asked.

   He asked **if** I was coming.   OR   He asked **whether** I was coming.

5. In reported questions, the words are in statement form. They are not in question form. We do not use question marks.

   He asked me, "How are you?"

   He asked me how I was.

   "Are you happy?" she asked us.

   She asked us if we were happy.

   "Where is your backpack?" she asked.

   She asked me where my backpack was.

6. Reported questions use the same rules as reported speech for changing verb forms, modal auxiliaries, and other words. Review these rules on pages 349–350.

6 Practice
I was a tourist in London last summer. I met a woman who asked me some questions. Write her questions as reported questions.

1. Can you speak English?

   She asked me if I could speak English.

2. Where do you come from?

   She asked me where I came from,

3. Where do you want to go?

   She asked me where I wanted to go,

4. Do you have a map?

   She asked me if I had a map,

5. Have you seen Buckingham Palace?

   She asked me if I had been seen Buckingham Palace.

6. Did you visit the British Museum?

   She asked me if I visited the the Britsh museum.

7. Is this your first time in London?

   She asked me if My first time was in london.

8. Are you traveling with your family?

   She asked me if I was traveling with your family.

9. What is your name?

   She asked me what my name was?

10. Are you on vacation here?

    _____

11. How long are you going to stay here?

    _____

12. Would you like to have a cup of tea with me?

    _____

7 Practice

Yesterday you saw a man who was lying on the sidewalk. You went to help him and asked some questions. Listen and underline the correct reported question for each question you asked.

1. a. I asked if he are OK.   b. <u>I asked if he was OK.</u>

2. a. I ask if he needs help.   b. I asked if he needed help.

3. a. I asked how he fell.   b. I asked if how he fell.

4. a. I asked if he can stand up.   b. I asked if he could stand up.

5. a. I asked if he was on his way to work.   b. I asked he was on his way to work.

6. a. I asked where it hurt.   b. I asked where hurt it.

7. a. I asked what his name was.   b. I asked what is his name.

8. a. I asked did he want me to call   b. I asked if he wanted me to call
    an ambulance.   an ambulance.

8 Pair Up and Talk

Write five questions to ask your partner. Your partner will answer your questions. Later, your partner will report to the class what you wanted to know and the answer.

YOU: Where do you live?

YOUR PARTNER: I live on Elm Street.

YOUR PARTNER: My partner wanted to know where I lived. I said that I lived on Elm Street.

Form/Function

> The man said, "Stop."
> The man **ordered me to stop**.

To report commands, requests, and advice, we can use reporting verb + someone + *(not)* infinitive.

1. We can report commands with the reporting verbs *tell* or *order* + someone + *(not)* infinitive.

   "Don't talk!" the teacher said to us.

   The teacher **told us not to talk**.

   OR The teacher **ordered us not to talk**.

   "Stay in the car," the police officer said.

   The police officer **ordered me to stay** in the car.

   OR The police officer **told me to stay** in the car.

   We can also use the reporting verb *warn* to report commands. We use *warn* to show that something is dangerous.

   "Don't go near the fire!" she said to the little girl.

   She **warned the little girl not to go** near the fire.

2. We can report requests with the reporting verb *ask*.

   "Wait a minute, please," Ted said.

   Ted **asked me to wait** a minute.

   "Would you help me?" he asked.

   He **asked me to help** him.

3. We can report advice with the reporting verb *advise*.

   The doctor said, "Helen, you should lose ten pounds."

   The doctor **advised Helen to lose** ten pounds.

4. There are other verbs that can use the verb + someone + *(not)* infinitive pattern. Here are some of them.

Verb	Example
beg	"Please help me," he said. He **begged me to** help him.
invite	"Will you come to the party?" she said. She **invited me to** come to the party.
offer	"Shall I carry your suitcase?" he said. He **offered to** carry my suitcase.
allow	"You can go early," the teacher said. The **teacher allowed us to** go early.

5. We can use two different structures for reporting suggestions.

Suggest + Verb + -ing				
Quoted Speech	Subject	Suggest	Verb + -ing	
"Let's start early," he said.	He	suggested	starting	early.
Suggest + Noun Clause				
Quoted Speech	Subject	Suggest	(That)	Subject + a Base Verb
"Let's start early," he said.	He	suggested	(that)	we start early.

When we use *suggest* + a noun clause, we always use a base verb in the main clause, even for the subjects *he*, *she*, and *it*.

CORRECT: The doctor suggested that she **get** more exercise.

INCORRECT: The doctor suggested that she ~~gets~~ more exercise.

The verb *recommend* also uses these structures:

The doctor **recommended drinking** a lot of water.

The doctor **recommended that she drink** a lot of water.

9 Practice
Complete the sentences with one of the verbs in the list. Use the past form of the verb. In some sentences, there is more than one correct answer.

advise   allow   ask   invite   warn

1. "Don't sit on that chair!" the teacher said. "It might break," he added.

   The teacher ___*warned*___ her not to sit on the chair.

2. "Would you like to have a cup of coffee with me after class?" Tony said to Nancy.

   Tony _____ Nancy to have a cup of coffee with him after class.

3. "You can use your dictionaries to write the essay," the teacher said.

   The teacher _____ us to use our dictionaries to write the essay.

4. "You should write a title for the essay," Tony told Kate. "The teacher likes us to write titles."

   Tony _____ Kate to write a title for the essay.

5. "You should check the spelling for these words," Kim said to Suzy.

   Kim _____ Suzy to check the spelling of those words.

6. "Do you need any help?" the teacher said to Suzy.

   The teacher _____ Suzy if she needed any help.

7. "You can finish the essay at home," the teacher said.

   The teacher _____ us to finish the essay at home.

10   Practice

Paul is going on vacation for two weeks. He wants people to help him take care of things. Choose a reporting verb and report the speaker's words.

1. Paul said to John, "Can you take care of my bird?"

   Paul asked John to take care of his bird.

2. Paul said, "Don't give the bird any cookies." .

   Paul warned John not to give the bird any cookies

3. Paul said to Linda, "Will you water my plants for me?"

   Paul asked Linda to water his plants for him

4. Paul said to Linda, "Don't water too much."

   Pauld told Linda not water too much

5. Paul said to his mother, "Please do my laundry."

   Paul ordered to his mother to do his laundry

6. Paul said to his mother, "Don't touch my CD player."

   Pauld warned to his mother don't touch my CD

7. Paul said to his mother, "Don't clean my apartment."

   Paul told his mommy not to clean his apart

8. Paul said to Matt, "Will you give these papers to my boss?"

   _____

11 Pair Up and Talk

Work with a partner. Say four things you ask people to do for you when you go away. Say three true things and one false thing. See if your partner can guess which one is false.

YOU:	When I go away, I ask someone to take my mail into the apartment. I ask someone to feed my cat. I ask someone to water my plants. I ask someone to answer my phone.
YOUR PARTNER:	You don't ask someone to answer your phone.
YOU:	Right!

14F Wishes about the Present or Future

Form/Function

I **wish** I **were** on vacation.

1. We use *wish* + the simple past to say that we would like something to be different in the present.

   I **wish** I **had** a credit card. (But I don't have a credit card.)
   I **wish** I **made** more money. (But I don't make more money.)

Main Clause		Noun Clause	
Subject	**Wish**	**(That)**	**Subject + Simple Past Verb**
I	wish		I **had** a car.
My brother	wishes		he **spoke** Thai.
She	wishes	(that)	she **didn't need** to borrow money.
My parents	wish		they **didn't live** in a small town.
Laura	wishes		she **could go** to Florida for her vacation.*

* We use *could* after *wish* to express ability.

2. For the verb *to be*, we use *were* for all subjects.*

Main Clause		(That)	Noun Clause	
Subject	*Wish*		Subject	*Were/Weren't*
I	wish	(that)	I	**were** on the beach now. **weren't** in class now.
You			you	
He/She/It	wishes		he/she/it	
We	wish		we	
They			they	

* In informal English, many people use *was* for the subjects *I*, *he*, *she*, and *it*.

---

12   Practice

Look at the information in the box. Then write sentences about Carol Brown's wishes.

Reality	Wish
1. has curly hair	have straight hair
2. is short	be tall
3. is a student	be a model
4. makes little money	make a lot of money
5. shares a small apartment	live in a big house
6. rides a bicycle	drive a sports car
7. stays home on weekends	go out with friends on weekends
8. wears regular clothes	wear designer clothes

1. *Carol wishes she had straight hair.*

2. _____

3. _____

4. _____

5. _____

6. _____

7. _____

8. _____

13   Practice

A   Nick is a famous soap opera star on television. Listen to him talk about his life. Write the missing words.

CD3, 23

Photographers _____ me everywhere. Newspapers write untrue
                    1

_____ about me. I _____ have privacy. People touch me and
    2   **3**

_____ my clothes. I have to sign autographs _____ the time. I have to
    4   **5**

_____ all the time. I can't _____ anything I want. I _____ go to
    6   **7**   **8**

the store to get groceries.

B   Nick doesn't like the way his life is now. He wishes it were different.
Work with a partner. Look at Part A to write at least six things Nick wishes.

Example

I wish photographers didn't follow me everywhere.

1. _____
2. _____
3. _____
4. _____
5. _____
6. _____

14   Pair Up and Talk

Do you wish things were different? Give two examples for each wish. Then share your answers with a partner.

YOU: I wish I had a million dollars. I wish I had my own television show.

YOUR PARTNER: I wish I had a house on the beach. I wish I had a boat.

1.   I wish I had …

2.   I wish I could …

3.   I wish I were …

14G Wishes about the Past

Form/Function

I **wish** I **had called** yesterday!

We use *wish* + the past perfect to make a wish about something in the past that we regret. We cannot change what happened.

I **wish** I **had listened** to you. (I didn't listen to you.)

I **wish** I **had studied** for the test. (I didn't study for the test.)

15 Practice

John went for an interview yesterday. He thinks he didn't get the job. Write sentences about what he wishes about the past.

1. I was so nervous.   *I wish I had not been so nervous.*

2. My hands were sweaty. _____

3. I didn't look the interviewer in the eye. _____

4. I asked about the pay. _____

5. I didn't look confident. _____

6. I didn't smile. _____

7. I forgot the name of my last boss. _____

8. I didn't tell the interviewer about my computer skills. _____

16 Pair Up and Talk
What did you do or not do last week? Are there things you wish you had done or hadn't done? Tell your partner at least three things.

I wish I hadn't spent so much money.
I wish I had seen that program on TV.

14H Present Real Conditional and Future Conditional Sentences

Form

If you **see** a koala bear outside of a zoo, you **are** in Australia.

1. We use two clauses in a conditional sentence: an *if* clause and a main clause. The *if* clause contains the condition, and the main clause contains the result.

Type of Sentence	Form	*If* Clause	Main Clause
Present Real Conditional	Simple present in both clauses	If you **see** a koala bear outside of a zoo,	you **are** in Australia.
		If the temperature **falls** below 0°C (32°F),	water **freezes**.
Future Conditional	*If* clause: Simple present **Main clause:** Future	If I **miss** the bus,	I **will be** late.
		If he **doesn't study**,	he **won't get** a good grade.

2. We can put the *if* clause first or the main clause first. There is no difference in meaning. When we put the *if* clause first, we put a comma after it.

      If I miss the bus, I will be late.

      OR I will be late **if I miss the bus**.

3. In the main clause of a future conditional sentence, we can use any verb form that refers to the future.

      If I finish my homework soon, I **can go** to bed.

      If my sister visits me, we**'re going to travel** around the country.

Function

1. We use the present real conditional to talk about what happens when there is a definite situation.

      If I have a big lunch, it makes me sleepy.

      If she hears his name, she gets angry.

2. We use the present real conditional to talk about general facts that are always true.

      If an elephant has big ears, it comes from Africa.

      If you mix oil and water, the oil stays on top.

3. We use the present real conditional to talk about habits or things that happen every day.

      If I go to work by car, it takes 35 minutes.

      I always walk to the store if it doesn't rain.

4. We use the future conditional to make predictions about what will happen in the future.

      If it rains tomorrow, we'll visit a museum.

      If he comes early, we'll go out.

17   Practice

Complete the sentences with the correct form of the verbs in parentheses.

1. If people sneeze, they (close)_____*close*_____ their eyes.

2. If you (exercise) _____ a lot, you lose weight.

3. You die if you (not/get) _____ oxygen.

4. If you (break) _____ a nail, it grows back again.

5. People (sweat) _____ if they exercise.

6. If you (cut) _____ your finger, it bleeds.

18   Practice

What will happen if…? Sandra's mother always worries about her when she is away from home. Match the sentence parts. Then write the sentences below. Use the correct punctuation.

___c___ **1.** lie in the sun   **a.** feel better

_____ **2.** drink too much coffee   **b.** catch a cold

_____ **3.** don't eat breakfast   **c.** get sunburned

_____ **4.** go without a coat   **d.** not sleep

_____ **5.** take her medicine   **e.** be hungry

1. _If she lies in the sun, she will get sunburned._ _____

2. _____

3. _____

4. _____

5. _____

19   Practice

René's parents are coming to visit him in the United States. Complete the sentences about their visit. Use the verb form for a present real conditional (simple present) if it is possible in the sentence. If it is not possible, use the verb for the future conditional (future).

1. My parents are coming for a visit next week. If we have enough time, we (visit) __will visit__ the art museum.

2. If they don't like the art museum, we (go) _____ shopping at a mall.

3. If it doesn't rain, we (rent) _____ a boat and row on the lake.

4. My father likes boats. If he is on a boat, he (be) _____ happy.

5. As for me, if I don't take a pill, I (get) _____ sick when I'm on a boat.

6. There is a concert at the university. If I can get tickets, we (go) _____ .

7. If we go to Chinatown, they (love) _____ the food there.

8. My parents like trying new food. If they have a choice, they (eat) _____ food from different countries.

9. If they have a good time this year, they (come) _____ back next year.

10. If I get to see my parents once a year, I (be) _____ lucky.

Form

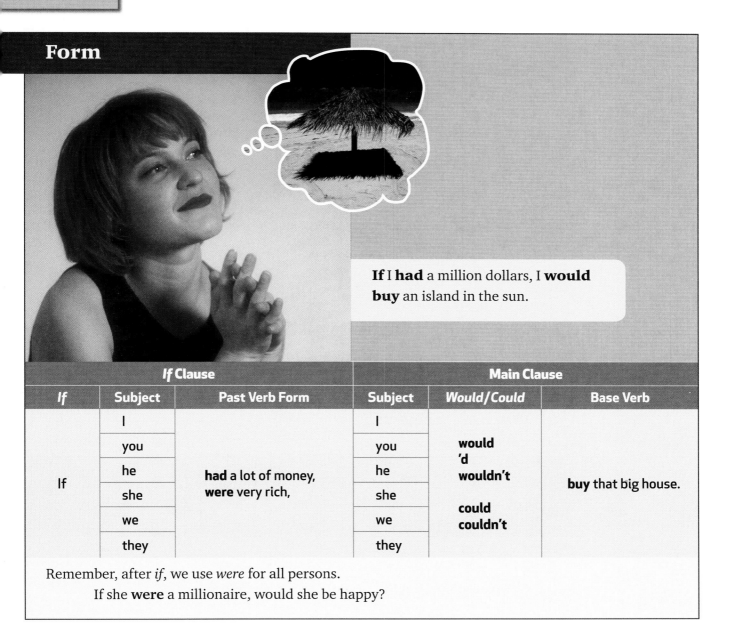

If I **had** a million dollars, I **would buy** an island in the sun.

If Clause			Main Clause		
If	**Subject**	**Past Verb Form**	**Subject**	**Would/Could**	**Base Verb**
If	I you he she we they	**had** a lot of money, **were** very rich,	I you he she we they	**would** **'d** **wouldn't** **could** **couldn't**	**buy** that big house.

Remember, after *if*, we use *were* for all persons.

If she **were** a millionaire, would she be happy?

Function

We use *if* + simple past + *would/could* + a base verb for an unreal situation in the present. The statement is contrary to fact. We imagine a result in the present or future.

If I **had** a million dollars, **I'd be** very happy. (I don't have a million dollars.)

If you **wrote** things down, you **wouldn't forget** them. (You don't write things down, and you always forget them.)

Practice
Complete the sentences with the correct form of the present unreal
conditional verbs in parentheses.

A

If my car (break) ___*broke*___ down on the highway at night, I
                    1
(lock) _____ the doors. Then I (call) _____ for emergency services on
        2   **3**
my cell phone. If I (not/have) _____ a cell phone, I (walk) _____ to the
                               4   **5**
nearest emergency call box. If the emergency call box (be) _____ too far away,
                                                          6
I (wait) _____ in my car with my doors locked.
         7

B

If I (see) _____ a big spider in my bed, I (scream) _____ .
           1   **2**
If I (be) _____ alone, I (find) _____ a friend or neighbor to do
          3   **4**
something about it. If I (not/find) _____ anyone, I (sleep) _____ in
                                    5   **6**
another room or maybe not sleep at all!

21 **Your Turn**
What would you do if these things happened to you? Write your own
sentences. Then share your answers with a partner.

1. If someone called you in the middle of the night
   If someone called me in the middle of the night,
   I'd get out of bed and answer the phone.

2. If you found a snake in your closet
   _____
   _____

3. If you saw a strange person breaking into your neighbor's house
   _____
   _____

4. If you smelled smoke in your house
   _____
   _____

22 Read

Read the story. Then write questions for the answers.

THE SHEEP AND THE DOG

A flock of sheep complained to the shepherd. They complained that the shepherd didn't give them the same treatment as his dog.

"Your behavior," they said, "is very unfair. We give you wool and lambs and milk. You give us nothing but grass, and even that we find for ourselves. You get nothing at all from the dog, but you give him food from your own table."

The dog heard this and immediately said,

"Yes, and quite right, too. Where would you be if it weren't for me? Thieves would steal you! Wolves would eat you! If I didn't keep watch over you night and day, you would be too terrified to even eat your grass!"

The sheep accepted that what the dog said was true. They never again said anything about how their master treated the dog.

1. _____ ? The sheep complained to the shepherd.
2. _____ ? The sheep said that the shepherd didn't give them the same treatment as the dog.
3. _____ ? The sheep gave lambs and wool to the shepherd.
4. _____ ? According to the sheep, the shepherd got nothing from the dog.
5. _____ ? According to the dog, thieves would steal them and wolves would eat them if it weren't for him.
6. _____ ? According to the dog, they would be too terrified to eat grass if he didn't watch over them.
7. _____ ? The sheep accepted that what the dog said was true.

23 Pair Up and Talk

Ask and answer the questions with a partner. Then ask two questions of your own.

YOU: If you could be someone else, who would you like to be? Why?

YOUR PARTNER: I'd be Bill Gates because I love computers, and I want to be rich.

1. If you could be someone else, who would you like to be? Why?

2. If you could live somewhere else, where would you like to live? Why?

3. If you could interview someone, who would you like to interview? What questions would you like to ask?

4. _____

5. _____

14J | Past Unreal Conditional Sentences

Form

If we **had lived** one hundred years ago, we **would have dressed** differently.

If	If Clause		Main Clause	
If	**Subject**	**Past Perfect**	**Subject**	***Would/Could/Might + Have + Past Participle***
If	I/you	**had lived** 100 years ago,	I/you	**would have worn** different clothes.
	he/she/it	**hadn't driven** so fast,	he/she/it	**would have passed** the driving test.
	we/they	**had been** here,	we/they	**might have gotten** the job.

Function

1. We use the past unreal conditional to talk about what might have been the result if things had been different in the past.

    If I **had studied** harder, I **would have passed** the test.
    (I didn't study harder, and I didn't pass the test.)
    If it **hadn't snowed**, we **might not have had** the accident.
    (It snowed, and we had the accident.)
    If they **had sent** the letter, it **would have arrived** last week.
    (They didn't send the letter, and it didn't arrive last week.)

2. We can use *would*, *might*, and *could* in the main clause.
    We use *would have* + past participle in the main clause if we think the past action
    was certain.

    If I had heard the telephone ring, I **would have answered** it.
    (I think I would definitely have answered it.)

    We use *might have* + past participle in the main clause if we think the past action was possible.

    If you had paid more attention, you **might not have burned** the food.
    (I think it's possible that you wouldn't have burned it.)

    We use *could have* + past participle to say that someone would have been able to do something in the past.

    If you had brought your CDs, we **could have danced**.
    (We would have been able to dance.)

---

24 Practice

Complete the sentences with the correct form of the verbs in parentheses.

1. If I (not/get up) _**hadn't gotten up**_ late, I (not/miss) _**wouldn't have missed**_ the train.

2. If I (not/miss) _____ the train, I (not/be) _____ late for work.

3. If I (not/be) _____ late for work, my boss (not/get) _____ angry with me.

4. If my boss (not/get) _____ angry with me, he (not/yell) _____ at me.

5. If I (not/yell) _____ back at him, I (not/lose) _____ my job.

Practice

Harold is thinking about his past. There are things in his life he wanted to do but did not do. Write sentences about what he would, might, or could have done if things had been different. Use *would, might,* or *could*.

1. I wanted to go to the university, but my parents didn't have the money.

   If his parents had had the money,

   he could have gone to the university.

2. I asked Nina to marry me, but she didn't like my nose.

   _____

   _____

3. I wanted to work for my uncle, but he died.

   _____

   _____

4. My uncle left a will, and I became a millionaire.

   _____

   _____

5. I became a millionaire, and Nina married me.

   _____

   _____

26 **Your Turn**

Think about your past. Do you wish things had been different? Write sentences with *wish* and sentences using the unreal past conditional.

Example

I wish I had learned to play the guitar.

If I had learned to play the guitar, I could have joined a band.

1. _____

   _____

2. _____

   _____

3. _____

   _____

A   Listen and check the correct answer.

❏   *A. Victoria Falls*   ❏   *B. Niagara Falls*   ❏   *C. Iguazu Falls*

B   Discuss your answer with your classmates.

C   Now listen again and write the sentences you hear.

CD3, 25

Reading Challenge

A Before You Read
Answer the questions.
1. What is Albert Einstein most famous for?
2. How might being a genius affect someone's life?

B Read

ALBERT EINSTEIN

If it weren't for Albert Einstein, we wouldn't have such things as computers, television, and space travel today. Albert Einstein was born in 1879 in Germany. He was a slow learner, and
5 his grades in school were poor. *The principal of his school told his father, "Your son will never make a success of anything."*
10 However, he was good at math and science and was able to go to college and later become a teacher.

Einstein was always interested in math and
15 physics. In 1905, he published his ideas, and soon his theory of relativity changed the world. When asked about his research, he said, "If we knew what it was we were doing, it wouldn't be called research." He was very humble about his
20 work and said, "It's not that I'm so smart, it's just that I stay with problems longer."

DID YOU KNOW ... ?
Einstein's brain was removed after he died and is preserved in a laboratory in Kansas, U.S.A.

Einstein became world famous. In 1922, he received the Nobel Prize for physics. When asked about his life, he said, "If I had to live my
25 life over again, I'd be a plumber." When Hitler came to power, Einstein, who was Jewish, left Germany and went to the United States. Just after he moved there, people told stories about him because he was **absent-minded**. Once, he
30 called the secretary where he worked and asked for his address. He whispered, "Please don't tell anybody, but I am Einstein. I am on my way home and I have forgotten where my house is." He lived in Princeton, New Jersey, for 22 years
35 until he died in 1955.

C Notice the Grammar
Underline all forms of the conditional.

Choose the best answer.

D Look for Main Ideas

1. What is the main topic of this reading?
   - Ⓐ Albert Einstein's youth
   - Ⓑ people's opinions of Albert Einstein
   - Ⓒ Einstein's problems
   - Ⓓ Einstein's personality and accomplishments

2. Paragraph 1 is mostly about Einstein's _____ .
   - Ⓐ contributions to the world
   - Ⓑ years as a student
   - Ⓒ parents and teachers
   - Ⓓ place of birth

E Look for Details

3. Einstein received the Nobel Prize for _____ .
   - Ⓐ math
   - Ⓑ physics
   - Ⓒ science
   - Ⓓ astronomy

4. What did Einstein's principal think about him?
   - Ⓐ He thought Einstein would change the world.
   - Ⓑ He knew Einstein would be a good mathematician.
   - Ⓒ He hoped Einstein would receive the Nobel Prize one day.
   - Ⓓ He believed Einstein would be a failure.

5. Einstein was interested in _____ .
   - Ⓐ computers and television
   - Ⓑ math and science
   - Ⓒ math and physics
   - Ⓓ space travel

F Make Inferences

6. What can we infer from paragraph 1?
   - Ⓐ Children who are good in math and science will probably become teachers.
   - Ⓑ Einstein didn't have very good teachers in his school.
   - Ⓒ A child's performance doesn't accurately determine adult achievement.
   - Ⓓ It's easy to predict whether a child will succeed in adulthood.

7. What can we infer about Einstein?
   - Ⓐ His genius didn't help him in ordinary life.
   - Ⓑ He knew he was a genius and he liked it.
   - Ⓒ His genius made life easier for him than it is for most people.
   - Ⓓ He was a genius in all aspects of his life.

G Look for Vocabulary

8. The word *absent-minded* in the reading is closest in meaning to _____ .
   - Ⓐ forgetful
   - Ⓑ uninterested
   - Ⓒ uncaring
   - Ⓓ stupid

Writing: Write a Personal Narrative

Write a diary entry about your mistakes.

STEP 1   **Imagine that you didn't pass your classes. Think about these questions.**

1. Would you have passed if you had studied better?
2. Why didn't you study harder? What do you regret?
3. What would happen if your parents knew? What would you say to them?
4. What do you wish you could do?

STEP 2   **Write your answers to these or other questions.**

STEP 3   **Look at the following diary entry. Use your answers in Step 2 to write your diary entry. Use some past unreal conditional sentences in your diary entry.**

December 22, 20XX

13 *Dear Diary,*
      I feel terrible. Everything has gone wrong in the last few months.
14 *I wish I had studied harder for my class. If I had studied harder, I would ...*
      Yours Truly,
15 *Yvonne*

STEP 4   **Evaluate your diary entry.**

Checklist

_____ Did you write a date for your diary entry?

_____ Did you start your entry with "Dear Diary" followed by a comma?

_____ Did you indent your paragraphs?

_____ Did you use some past unreal conditional sentences?

_____ Did you end your entry with a closing such as "Yours truly" and a comma?

_____ Did you sign your name at the end?

STEP 5   **Work with a partner or your teacher to edit your diary entry. Check spelling, punctuation, vocabulary, and grammar.**

STEP 6   **Write your final diary entry.**

Self-Test

1. I wish the sun _____ .

   A. is shining   Ⓐ Ⓑ Ⓒ Ⓓ
   B. was shining
   C. were to shine
   D. were shining

2. Kim _____ a funny story last night.

   A. said me   Ⓐ Ⓑ Ⓒ Ⓓ
   B. to me said
   C. told me
   D. tell me

3. Ben said that he _____ with us next week.

   A. will go   Ⓐ Ⓑ Ⓒ Ⓓ
   B. would go
   C. is go
   D. will to go

4. He asked _____ .

   A. whether   Ⓐ Ⓑ Ⓒ Ⓓ
      I am coming
   B. if I am coming
   C. whether I was coming
   D. if I come

5. If I could afford the plane ticket, I _____ on the next plane to Hawaii.

   A. would be   Ⓐ Ⓑ Ⓒ Ⓓ
   B. could have been
   C. will be
   D. were

6. If my father _____ the opportunity, he would have gone to college.

   A. have   Ⓐ Ⓑ Ⓒ Ⓓ
   B. had
   C. had had
   D. have had

7. She _____ happy, but I wasn't.

   A. asked to me if I was   Ⓐ Ⓑ Ⓒ Ⓓ
   B. asked me if I were
   C. said to me if I was
   D. told me if I was

8. He suggested _____ .

   A. going early   Ⓐ Ⓑ Ⓒ Ⓓ
   B. to going early
   C. to go early
   D. us going early

9. I didn't give him my card. I wish I _____ him my card.

   A. give   Ⓐ Ⓑ Ⓒ Ⓓ
   B. had give
   C. had given
   D. had given to

10. If you don't have air to breathe, you _____ .

   A. would die   Ⓐ Ⓑ Ⓒ Ⓓ
   B. die
   C. would have died
   D. died

B Find the underlined word or phrase, A, B, C, or D, that is incorrect. Darken the oval with the same letter.

1. If I had <u>a</u> car, I <u>will</u> not <u>use</u>
   A   B   C   D
   public transportation.
   Ⓐ Ⓑ Ⓒ Ⓓ

2. The teacher <u>warned</u> <u>to us</u> not <u>to talk</u> during
     A   B C   D
   the test.
   Ⓐ Ⓑ Ⓒ Ⓓ

3. If we had <u>lived</u> a hundred years <u>ago</u>, we
     A   B
   wouldn't <u>had</u> problems with air <u>pollution</u>.
     C   D
   Ⓐ Ⓑ Ⓒ Ⓓ

4. When I was a child, my father <u>told</u> <u>me</u> to
     A   B
   <u>always</u> <u>say</u> the truth.
     C   D
   Ⓐ Ⓑ Ⓒ Ⓓ

5. The doctor recommended <u>to</u> using <u>less</u> salt
     A   B
   and <u>sugar</u> and <u>drinking</u> more water.
     C   D
   Ⓐ Ⓑ Ⓒ Ⓓ

6. I <u>will have</u> health problems <u>if</u> I <u>won't</u> follow
     A   B   C
   <u>this diet</u>.
     D
   Ⓐ Ⓑ Ⓒ Ⓓ

7. My manager <u>said</u> me <u>that</u> he <u>was going</u> on
     A   B   C
   <u>vacation</u> next week.
     D
   Ⓐ Ⓑ Ⓒ Ⓓ

8. The school counselor <u>advised</u> <u>me</u> <u>taking</u>
     A   B   C
   <u>an</u> English writing class next semester.
     D
   Ⓐ Ⓑ Ⓒ Ⓓ

9. I didn't study English when I <u>was</u> in high
     A
   school, but now I <u>wish</u> I <u>have</u> studied <u>it</u>.
     B   C   D
   Ⓐ Ⓑ Ⓒ Ⓓ

10. <u>If</u> I knew how <u>to speak</u> French, I <u>will</u> go
    A   B   C
    <u>to France</u> with you.
      D
    Ⓐ Ⓑ Ⓒ Ⓓ

Audio Script

Unit 1, Practice 4, Page 5 (CD 1, 2)

1. John gets up at noon.
2. He eats breakfast.
3. He watches television.
4. He meets his friends for lunch.
5. He tries to find a job.
6. In the evening, he goes out with his friends.
7. John comes home at four o'clock in the morning.
8. On Sundays, he stays home.
9. He washes his clothes.
10. He cleans his apartment.
11. He calls his mother.
12. His mother worries about him.

Unit 1, Practice 7, Page 7 (CD 1, 3)

1. Ann: On weekdays, I *usually* get up at 3:30 in the morning.
2. Ann: I *never* eat breakfast.
3. Ann: I *always* leave the house at 4:15.
4. Ann: I *usually* get to the studio at 4:30.
5. Ann: "Good Morning" *always* starts at 7:00.
6. Ann: I *often* leave the studio at 10:00.
7. Ann: I *usually* go to the gym after work.
8. Ann: I *sometimes* go shopping after the gym.
9. Ann: My husband and I *usually* stay home in the evening.
10. Ann: We *hardly ever* go out on weekdays.
11. Ann: We *often* watch television.
12. Ann: I *usually* go to bed at 9:00.

Unit 1, Practice 10, Page 10 (CD 1, 4)

1. Juan is listening to a new album.
2. I am waiting for the bus.
3. They are studying for their English test.
4. I am staying in the U.S. for another year.
5. Bob is swimming in the ocean.
6. She is tying her shoelaces.
7. I am hoping to get a new job next year.
8. Joe is cutting the paper in half.

Unit 1, Practice 13, Page 12 (CD 1, 5)

Detective Roberts is watching a house. He's talking to Detective Jason on his cell phone.

Detective Roberts: A tall woman with dark hair is coming out of the house.

Detective Jason: That's Mrs. Johnson. She lives there. She's a housekeeper. It's 8:00. She usually leaves the house at 8:00. She goes to the store to do the grocery shopping.

Detective Roberts: Wait! A car is stopping in front of the house. A man in a uniform is getting out. He is tall and thin and has gray hair.

Detective Jason: I know he doesn't live there.

Detective Roberts: He is ringing the doorbell. He is looking at the house carefully. He is going to the back of the house. He is jumping over the wall.

Detective Jason: Go get him, Roberts!

Narrator: *Detective Roberts runs after the man and then returns to his car.*

Detective Roberts: No luck. He says he is looking for the gas meter. He works for the gas company.

Unit 1, Practice 19, Page 20 (CD 1, 6)

Woman: Excuse me, are you taking the flight to London at 10:00?
Man: Yes, I am. Do you live in London?
Woman: No, I don't. At the moment, I'm studying at Cambridge University. What about you? Do you often go to London?
Man: Yes, I go there on business.
Woman: Oh. What kind of work do you do?
Man: I work for the marketing department of a company. We publish dictionaries.

Unit 1, Listening Puzzle, Page 21 (CD 1, 7–8)

This fruit grows in a lot of countries because it adapts very well to the weather and the soil. In cold countries, the snow protects the fruit from extreme temperatures because it grows close to the earth. We eat this fruit today thanks to a French sailor named Frezier. He brought this plant from South America to Europe, and from there it went to other countries. The fruit has a special sweet smell. Thirty-five different chemicals make this smell. It is round and is in the shape of a heart. It has its seeds on the outside. We eat it raw or cook it or make it into jam or jelly. It comes from South America originally, but people all over the world enjoy it.
What is the name of this fruit?

Unit 2, Practice 1, Page 30 (CD 1, 9)

1. Yesterday I listened to the radio.
2. Bob waited for the movie.
3. I studied for my test all night.
4. She died at the age of 86.
5. They stayed all afternoon.
6. Sam admitted the truth.
7. It rained last week.
8. The movie started at 8:00.
9. It happened this morning.
10. Catherine tied her shoelaces.
11. She opened the door.
12. We hoped to see you.

Unit 2, Practice 10, Page 37 (CD 1, 10)

1. Last night, television and radio stations were warning people about the tornado.
2. It was getting closer.
3. People were running for shelter.
4. The tornado was destroying everything in its way.
5. We weren't watching television.
6. We were studying in the library.
7. Suddenly the librarian started shouting.
8. She was telling us to run to the basement.

Unit 2, Practice 12, Page 38 (CD 1, 11)

Susan was walking on the beach. She noticed that the wind was blowing very hard. The waves were crashing on the sand. Black clouds were coming toward the land very fast. When she got back to the house, her husband was covering the windows with wood. A hurricane was coming!

Unit 2, Listening Puzzle, Page 45 (CD 1, 12–13)

From 1661 to 1710, a king built this palace in a country in Europe. He was the most important king in Europe at the time. The palace took 47 years to build. The people of this country paid a lot of taxes because the king needed money to build this palace. It is a very luxurious palace with hundreds of rooms including a hall of mirrors. The palace became a model for palaces throughout the continent. The palace was in a huge park and had more than 1,400 fountains. Today, millions of tourists visit this palace every year. There is an emblem of the sun on the main gate of the palace. The king who built the palace called himself the "Sun King."
Do you know the name of this palace?

Unit 3, Practice 1, Page 53 (CD 1, 14)

In a minute, the astronauts are going to enter the spacecraft. The air in the spacecraft is different. The astronauts are not going to have any weight. They are going to do everyday things in a different way. They are not going to sleep in regular beds. They are going to sleep in hanging beds. They are going to fold their arms when they sleep. This holds their arms in place. It is going to be difficult to take a shower. It is going to take a long time because they need special equipment.

Unit 3, Practice 2, Page 54 (CD 1, 15)

1. Is she going to call her boss?
   No, she is going to call her family.
2. Is he going to listen to a baseball game?
   No, he is going to listen to music.
3. Is she going to watch television?
   No, she is going to look at the Earth from the window.
4. Is he going to take a walk inside the spacecraft?
   No, he is going to take a walk in space.

5. Is she going to rest tomorrow?
   No, she is going to rest today.

Unit 3, Practice 13, Page 62 (CD 1, 16)

1. This afternoon, I am watching television. The big game starts at noon.
2. The final exam starts at 10:00 tomorrow and ends at 12:00.
3. My flight arrives at 3:30 tomorrow, and then I am taking a taxi to the hotel.
4. I am having dinner with Ben tonight. We are meeting after work.
5. I am buying a new car this week. Then I am driving to Canada for my vacation.

Unit 3, Listening Puzzle, Page 67 (CD 1, 17–18)

All the ground in this place is frozen. The land is 98% ice, and the rest is bare rock. Scientists visit this place, but no one lives here. The weather is very extreme. There are freezing temperatures and strong winds. Water surrounds this land. Whales, penguins, seals, and birds live here. It is a beautiful wilderness. People worry about the future of this place. They are afraid global warming will change it. They think the ice will melt, and this will affect the animals there. Some will disappear. The land will melt, too. There are minerals and oil there. People will come to drill and mine. They will spoil this amazing place.
What is the name of this place?

Unit 4, Practice 3, Page 77 (CD 1, 19)

babies	dresses	ladies	potatoes
birds	feet	leaves	radios
bushes	foxes	mice	sandwiches
categories	halves	oxen	sheep
cherries	heroes	peaches	thieves
children	keys	photos	tomatoes
cities	knives	pianos	wolves

Unit 4, Practice 4, Page 77 (CD 1, 20)

Don: Did you go shopping yesterday?
Carla: Yes, I did. I bought a lot of things because they were on sale.
Don: Oh, what did you buy?
Carla: I bought two dresses, two shirts, and three scarves.
Don: Did you buy anything for the house?
Carla: Yes, I bought two beautiful dishes, six knives, six forks, and six glasses.
Don: Wow! You sure bought a lot of things!

Unit 4, Practice 8, Page 79 (CD 1, 21)

1. Terry works in an office.
2. He drinks coffee every day.
3. Lois uses a computer at work.
4. It is sitting on her desk.
5. She sits next to Terry.
6. They are friends.

Unit 4, Practice 9, Page 82 (CD 1, 22)

1. water
2. apple
3. chair
4. rain
5. tree
6. English

Unit 4, Practice 16, Page 85 (CD 1, 23)

Mary: Did you see a lot of wild animals? How about koala bears?

Ted: No, we didn't see any koala bears, but we saw a lot of kangaroos. They were everywhere.

Mary: Did you stay in the cities or did you go to the countryside?

Ted: We didn't spend any time in the city. We drove into a desert area called the outback. You don't see any people for hours, and of course there isn't any traffic. There is a lot of sunshine, and there aren't any trees. There isn't much water in this area. Someone took us to a river where we saw a few crocodiles. I was really scared!

Unit 4, Practice 21, Page 89 (CD 1, 24)

1. I need to buy a box of …
   … toothpaste.
   … lettuce.
   … cereal.
2. Do we have a can of …
   … chicken soup?
   … chips?
   … bread?
3. Could I have a cup of …
   … spaghetti?
   … cheese?
   … coffee?
4. When you go to the store, can you get a pound of …
   … potatoes?
   … water?
   … soap?
5. I just bought two loaves of …
   … cheese.
   … chocolate.
   … bread.
6. Can you pick up a roll of …
   … fruit?
   … toilet paper?
   … juice?

Unit 4, Practice 23, Page 90 (CD 1, 25)

Rita: Where did you take this photo?

Laura: At my friend's house. My friend's name is Carla. That day was the twins' birthday party. This is Cindy, my brother's wife. And that is Cindy's sister.

Rita: Who are the two boys?

Laura: The boys' names are Ken and Dave. They are Cindy's sons. And that's the boys' teacher, Mrs. Parkinson.

Unit 4, Listening Puzzle, Page 95 (CD 1, 26–27)

These boats first appeared about 1,000 years ago. People use eight different types of wood to make them. Scientists believe their design is very sophisticated. There used to be several thousands of these boats, but today there are only a few hundred. These boats are long and narrow. A boatman stands at the back of the boat and pushes with one oar. A lot of these boats now have engines. Today these boats are expensive to make. Only tourists take them.

Do you know the name of this boat?

Unit 5, Practice 4, Page 106 (CD 1, 28)

A.

Paolo: Is this your wallet?

Lillian: No, it's not mine. I thought it was yours.

Paolo: No, I have mine in my pocket. Maybe it's Ingrid's.

Lillian: If it is hers, she will be very worried. She went to the airport with her husband. They're going to Canada to visit her parents.

B.

Our television is not working. Our neighbors have an extra television, and they're going to give it to us. We have to fix ours or get a new one. They're expensive, you know. Our neighbors don't mind, so we may watch theirs for a long time.

C.

The Parkers are our neighbors. They're very rich. They have two cars in their garage, and the Porsche parked in front of our house is theirs, too. Everybody thinks it's ours, but ours is an old Honda. We park it in front of our other neighbor's house. We like to leave it there.

Unit 5, Practice 7, Page 108 (CD 1, 29)

1. Johnnie and Jenny are trying to make breakfast by …
   … himself.
   … themselves.
2. Johnnie got the box of cereal from the shelf by …
   … himself.
   … herself.
3. When Johnnie wants cereal, he helps …
   … myself.
   … himself.
4. Jenny was trying to cut a bagel and cut …
   … herself.
   … yourself.
5. Then she tried to toast the bagel and burned …
   … himself.
   … herself.
6. In the end, Johnnie and Jenny made and ate breakfast by …
   … ourselves.
   … themselves.

Unit 5, Practice 12, Page 113 (CD 1, 30)

1. I'm sorry, but I broke this glass. I dropped it.
2. I'm making a sandwich. Would you like one, too?
3. If you need change for the parking meter, I have some.
4. She bought some cookies and ate all of them.
5. I am throwing away the old magazines and keeping the new ones.
6. We need to call a taxi. I'll call for one.

Unit 5, Listening Puzzle, Page 115 (CD 1, 31–32)

This sport lets you fly like a bird. First you must jump off a cliff. That's pretty scary. Soon you are in the air and moving over land or water. The flight is slow and gentle. You can do this for hours. You are attached to a huge wing. A German engineer designed the first wing in 1889. Everyone forgot about it when airplanes came along. In 1948, an American invented a wing made of fabric. He made it for space capsules that returned to Earth, but people never used it for that. Finally, in 1960, an American named Palmer made a wing for people, and it became very popular. This sport is very dangerous. Some people crash. Many pilots carry a parachute for themselves.
What is the name of this sport?

Unit 6, Practice 2, Page 125 (CD 2, 2)

1. Have Jim and Sofia gone to the Empire State Building?
2. Have they seen the Statue of Liberty?
3. Have they walked in Central Park?
4. Has Jim been shopping?
5. Have they bought tickets for a Broadway show?
6. Have they visited the Metropolitan Museum of Art?

Unit 6, Practice 4, Page 125 (CD 2, 3)

Sue: I haven't seen Sofia and Jim all week. Where are they?
Pete: You didn't know? They've gone away on vacation.
Sue: Really! Where have they gone?
Pete: They've gone to New York.
Sue: How long have they been in New York?
Pete: They've been in New York for four days now.
Sue: Have they eaten in any interesting restaurants?
Pete: Oh, yes. They've eaten in Chinese, Korean, Greek, and Indian restaurants.
Sue: Have they visited the Metropolitan Museum of Art?
Pete: No, but they're going to visit the Metropolitan Museum of Art tomorrow.

Unit 6, Practice 5, Page 126 (CD 2, 4)

Armando: Daniel, I'm sorry, but it's time for you to find another place to live.
Daniel: Why? What's wrong?
Armando: What's wrong? You have been a terrible roommate. For example, today you have eaten my food, and you have broken my CD player.
Daniel: Don't be so sensitive, Armando. I'll replace those things for you.
Armando: That's not all. You have not paid the rent for two months. You have insulted my sister, and you have tried to steal my girlfriend. I have been very patient, but now I want you to go.
Daniel: Well, OK. I'll leave if you want. But … um, I have spent all my money. Could you lend me $500?

Unit 6, Practice 11, Page 129 (CD 2, 5)

Interviewer: Have you ever been married?
La La: Yes, I have. I've been married eight times.
Interviewer: Have you ever been to Hollywood?
La La: Yes, I have. I've been there many times.
Interviewer: Have you ever driven a Ferrari?
La La: No, I haven't. I never drive. I have a chauffeur.
Interviewer: Have you ever given an interview on television?
La La: Yes, I have. I've given interviews to famous journalists.
Interviewer: Have you ever written a book?
La La: No, I haven't. Other people write about me.
Interviewer: Have you ever sung in a movie?
La La: No, I haven't. I can't sing.

Unit 6, Practice 17, Page 133 (CD 2, 6)

1. I saw Karen yesterday.
   Oh, really? I haven't seen her for weeks.
2. What did you do last Saturday?
   I stayed at home.
3. Have you written your essay yet?
   Yes, I finished it an hour ago.
4. Have you been to the United States?
   Yes, I went to Miami last summer.

Unit 6, Practice 24, Page 141 (CD 2, 7)

Rob: Hi, honey, I'm back. It's almost five o'clock. Have you cleaned the house yet?
Linda: No, I haven't cleaned the house yet. But I've washed the dishes and changed the sheets. How about you?
Rob: Well, I've bought food and developed the photographs of Sophie, but I haven't rented any interesting movies.
Linda: Have you done the laundry?
Rob: No, I haven't. I also haven't made dinner. Can you help me with it?
Linda: Sure. We'd better hurry because they're going to be here soon.
Rob and Linda: Uh-oh.

Unit 6, Listening Puzzle, Page 143 (CD 2, 8–9)

This sports event did not exist at the time of the ancient Olympics in Greece. It became a part of the Olympics in 1896 and has been part of it ever since. In the first Olympics, only men could take part in this sport. However, today both men and women can take part in the sport in the Olympics. Outside the Olympics, thousands of people of all ages and abilities take part in this sport all over the world every year. This sport is the longest race in the Olympics. It is over 26 miles long and is usually the last event. Do you know the name of this event?

Unit 7, Practice 2, Page 152 (CD 2, 10)

1. Is New York City the capital of the United States?
2. Was Elvis Presley a scientist?
3. Do they speak English in Australia?
4. Did Edison invent the computer?
5. Was Cleopatra Italian?
6. Does rice grow in China?
7. Can monkeys climb trees?
8. Are there pyramids in Turkey?

Unit 7, Practice 5, Page 154 (CD 2, 11)

A.
1. When was she born?
   She was born in 1961.
2. Who did she marry?
   She married a prince.
3. What was she famous for?
   She was famous for her fashionable clothes.
4. When did she die?
   She died in 1997 in a car accident.
5. Where did the accident happen?
   The accident happened in Paris.
   The person is …
   … Diana, Princess of Wales.

B.
1. When was he born?
   He was born in 1975.
2. Where was he born?
   He was born in Florida, in the United States.
3. When did he start to play golf?
   He started to play golf when he was three.
4. What did he study in college?
   He studied economics in college.
5. Why is he famous?
   He is famous because he is already one of the best players of all time, even though he is young.
   The person is …
   … Tiger Woods.

Unit 7, Practice 8, Page 157 (CD 2, 12)

There was an accident this morning. It was 10:00, and it was raining. Bob saw a woman jogger crossing the street. Then he heard a loud bang. A white truck had suddenly stopped, and a red car had crashed into the back of the truck. Bob called 911 for the police and an ambulance. At about 10:15, the police and ambulance came. A police officer asked him questions.

Unit 7, Practice 10, Page 159 (CD 2, 13)

Nina: Which countries did you visit in Europe?
Claudia: I went to France and Italy.
Nina: Which did you like better?
Claudia: I loved France.
Nina: What did you buy?
Claudia: I bought some clothes and perfume.
Nina: Which country had the best clothes, France or Italy?
Claudia: Italy had the best clothes.
Nina: Which one had the most perfumes?
Claudia: France had the most perfumes. Tourists buy them tax free.
Nina: What cities did you visit in France?
Claudia: I went to Paris, Lyon, Nice, and Cannes.
Nina: Which city was the most beautiful?
Claudia: Paris, of course.
Nina: What is a good time to visit Paris?
Claudia: Anytime is good. I prefer spring.
Nina: Which month, April or May?
Claudia: I prefer May; it's warmer.
Nina: Which country was cheaper, France or Italy?
Claudia: They are about the same. My company paid for the trip; it was for business, you see.

Unit 7, Practice 18, Page 169 (CD 2, 14)

Karen: I feel so tired!
Jenny: Sit down for a few minutes. Why are you so tired?
Karen: I stayed up until midnight last night.
Jenny: Why so late?
Karen: Because I didn't get back from the library until 10:00.
Jenny: Well, when did you get up this morning?
Karen: At 7:00. Then I had to walk to school.
Jenny: Why?
Karen: Because my car broke down two blocks from my house.
Jenny: Oh no! Maybe you shouldn't sit down. Maybe you should lie down!

Unit 7, Listening Puzzle, Page 177 (CD 2, 15–16)

This place is a very mysterious place in a southern continent. It has giant stone statues. There are many questions about them. Who carved them? Why did they carve them? How did they move them? There is some evidence about the first people. What lessons can we learn from them? We know that they arrived around 400 A.D. and

set up a mysterious culture. They had dance and music, and they made wood carvings. They also had a written language. Eventually there were around 10,000 people. They cut down all the palm trees and used up all the resources. They fought among themselves. They tore down all the statues. The society almost became extinct. Today this is a fascinating place to visit. The statues have been put up again. There is a museum about the lost culture.
What is the name of this place?

Unit 8, Practice 10, Page 193 (CD 2, 17)

1. You are speaking to your brother.
   Can you hold this for me?
   Sure.
2. You are speaking to a bank teller.
   Could you give me the balance of my checking account, please?
   Certainly. It's $506.25. Is there anything else I can do for you?
3. You are speaking to your boss.
   Would you look over this report, please?
   I can't do it now, but I'll do it as soon as I can.
4. You are speaking to a flight attendant.
   Could you bring me some water, please?
   Certainly.
5. You are speaking to a doctor.
   Would you give me the same prescription as last time, please?
   Of course.

Unit 8, Practice 12, Page 195 (CD 2, 18)

Ann: What's for dinner?
Betty: We are having chicken. It's in the oven.
Ann: When will it be ready?
Betty: I'm not sure. It may be ready in half an hour.
Ann: What time is John coming?
Betty: I don't know. It depends on the traffic. He may be late.
Ann: Is Ted coming at 7:00?
Betty: Yes. He called. He's on his way. He will be here at 7:00 for sure.
Ann: Are we having dessert?
Betty: Yes, we are. It's in the refrigerator.
Ann: It's the doorbell. Who can it be?
Betty: I don't know. It may be Ted.

Unit 8, Practice 13, Page 196 (CD 2, 19)

George: Could his flight be late?
Carla: Maybe, or he may be caught in traffic.
George: I don't think so. There isn't much traffic at this time.
Carla: There might not be a lot of traffic, but perhaps he got lost.
George: Could we call him?
Carla: I tried. He didn't answer. His cell phone might not be on.

George: Let's call the airline. They may have some information about the flight.
Carla: Good idea. Oh! I see the lights in the driveway. Could that be his car?

Unit 8, Practice 15, Page 197 (CD 2, 20)

1. Her name is Angelica. Maybe she's French.
2. He doesn't know what she does. Maybe she's a dancer.
3. Yes, she may be a ballet dancer.
4. He saw Angelica for the first time yesterday. Why didn't he see her before? She may be from out of town.
5. He said, "Hello," and asked, "What's your name?" She didn't say anything. At first Antonio thought, "She may be from another country." So he said slowly, "My name is Antonio. What is your name?"
6. She looked at him strangely. Maybe she thought he was impolite.
7. Then she said, "Angelica." Maybe it wasn't her real name. Then she ran away.

Unit 8, Practice 28, Page 209 (CD 2, 21)

1. All students have to register and pay fees.
2. All students have to register before taking courses.
3. Every student has got to take an English placement exam.
4. Every new student has to attend orientation during registration week.
5. Students have got to present registration forms on the first day of classes.

Unit 8, Listening Puzzle, Page 217 (CD 2, 22–23)

Many animals live on the edge of the Arctic ice. This one is large and noisy. It can grow to 14 feet long and can weigh up to four tons. This animal couldn't fit in your bathtub! Its skin is very thick to protect it from most of its enemies. But thick skin can't protect this animal from polar bears and killer whales. It must run from these killers. This animal mainly lives in the water. It can swim fast in the water and move fast on land. It eats clams and other small animals on the sea floor. It has big whiskers that help it find food in the sand. Then this animal blows the sand to get the food loose. It isn't able to dig up food because its long tusks get in the way. If you cut a tusk, you can tell how old this animal is. The tusk has rings just like a tree. This animal lives about 50 years in the wild.
What is the name of this animal?

Unit 9, Practice 3, Page 226 (CD 2, 24)

I would like to discuss moving to a new city by the ocean. I can imagine living in a place where we could go sailing on the weekends. I know that you dislike swimming, but wouldn't it be fun to go walking on the beach in the mornings? You might also like to go fishing or golfing while I go shopping in the tourist shops nearby. When friends come to visit us, we could go sightseeing up the coast. Will you think about leaving this cold, depressing city? I don't want to keep on paying these awful heating bills.

Unit 9, Practice 11, Page 232 (CD 2, 25)

1. a. Liz and Ben want to go on vacation this year.
   b. Liz and Ben want going on vacation this year.
   c. Both are correct.
2. a. I don't mind to wait for you.
   b. I don't mind waiting for you.
   c. Both are correct.
3. a. Teresa enjoys to visit new places.
   b. Teresa enjoys visiting new places.
   c. Both are correct.
4. a. Greg loves to listen to music.
   b. Greg loves listening to music.
   c. Both are correct.
5. a. I promise to go with you next time.
   b. I promise going with you next time.
   c. Both are correct.
6. a. The rain continued to fall all day.
   b. The rain continued falling all day.
   c. Both are correct.
7. a. Let's go to dance tonight!
   b. Let's go dancing tonight!
   c. Both are correct.
8. a. Don't put off to call him.
   b. Don't put off calling him.
   c. Both are correct.

Unit 9, Practice 16, Page 236 (CD 2, 26)

1. You buy …
   a. English.
   b. some clothes.
2. You cash …
   a. a check.
   b. breakfast.
3. You eat …
   a. lunch.
   b. a credit card.
4. You learn …
   a. a computer.
   b. Spanish.
5. You mail …
   a. some letters.
   b. a truck.
6. You rent …
   a. a hat.
   b. a car.
7. You reserve …
   a. a pizza.
   b. a flight.
8. You send …
   a. an email.
   b. a seat.

Unit 9, Listening Puzzle, Page 243 (CD 2, 27-28)

Would you like to travel in your home? This vehicle lets you do that. You don't have to pull it behind you. This vehicle is a car and a home in one. It has all the comforts of home. It has beds and a kitchen and a shower for bathing. Many people like to go camping in this vehicle, but it isn't a tent. Some people like going on vacation in it. Others like living in it full time. They like to travel from place to place. More and more people are doing this. These vehicles are at tourist spots around the world. There are special places to park them. There is water and electricity available, and sometimes there is a swimming pool. Some of the vehicles are huge and elaborate. They cost as much as some houses. Others are more modest. Do you have one of these?
What is the name of this vehicle?

Unit 10, Practice 6, Page 255 (CD 3, 2)

1. Ann isn't happy today. She feels …
   … tell.
   … miserable.
2. She was cooking and cleaning for hours and hours. She got …
   … tired.
   … excited.
3. She forgot about the cake in the oven. The cake got …
   … clean.
   … burned.
4. She went out and it started to rain. She had no umbrella. She got …
   … wet.
   … warm.
5. The dog came in with muddy feet. The floor got …
   … clean.
   … dirty.
6. She put sugar instead of salt in the soup. The soup tasted …
   … sweet.
   … cold.
7. She tried on her new dress, but it seemed …
   … small.
   … dry.
8. Luckily, when her guests came, they had a good time. She felt …
   … jealous.
   … happy.

Unit 10, Practice 9, Page 258 (CD 3, 3)

1. Mary made a cake. The cake was as light as …
   … a feather.
   … a car.
2. This melon is sweet. It is as sweet as …
   … soup.
   … sugar.
3. Nobody noticed that Tina had come home. She was as quiet as …
   … a mouse.
   … a lion.
4. We left the children with my sister for the weekend. The children were happy and were as good as …
   … gold.
   … a tomato.
5. The coffee she made was very strong, and it was as black as …
   … water.
   … ink.

6. She had beautiful blue eyes.
   They were as blue as …
   … grass.
   … the sky.
7. He left home and moved to
   the city. Then he felt as free
   as …
   … a house.
   … a bird.

8. The fish I ate for dinner was
   bad, and I was as sick as …
   … a dog.
   … a child.

Unit 10, Practice 12, Page 262 (CD 3, 4)

Jane:	I want to fly to Los Angeles tomorrow morning. Are there any flights that are earlier than the one at 10:00?
Travel Agent:	Yes, there are. Flight 1620 is at 5:30. And flight 1535 is later than flight 1620. It leaves at 7:00.
Jane:	Are there a lot of people on the 5:30 flight?
Travel Agent:	No. The 7:00 flight is usually much more crowded than the 5:30 flight.
Jane:	I think the 5:30 flight will work better than the 7:00 flight. Will it be cheaper than the 7:00?
Travel Agent:	No. In fact, it's $10 more expensive than the other flights.

Unit 10, Practice 20, Page 268 (CD 3, 5)

Many people think that if they want to lose weight, they should just avoid desserts like ice cream. It is true that ice cream has a lot of fat and calories. Just one serving of ice cream has ten grams of fat in it. That's as much fat as a serving of pizza. On top of that, with 280 calories, a serving of pizza has more calories than a serving of ice cream, which has 190. Two other foods that also have more calories than ice cream are bread and rice. A serving of bread has 200 calories, and a serving of rice has 225 calories. One food that has fewer calories than ice cream is pasta, but with only two grams of protein in it, pasta also has less protein than ice cream, which has four grams. Looking at carbohydrates, with 52 grams of carbohydrates, rice has the most from this group of foods. This is notably more than the 14 grams of carbohydrates that you get in a serving of pasta. Even though this is true, pasta, bread, and rice all have less sugar and fat than ice cream, so they are still a better choice for dieters.

Unit 10, Listening Puzzle, Page 273 (CD 3, 6–7)

This place is vast and beautiful. There are mountains all around. The highest mountain is over 11,000 feet high. The air is cooler up there. The mountain is covered with snow in winter. It is home to mountain lions, deer, and sheep. They live among the trees. But the land below the mountain is very different. It is almost 300 feet below sea level. It is the lowest point in the Western Hemisphere. It is one of the hottest places on earth. Less than two inches of rain fall each year. So it is also one of the driest places.

Many animals live in this extreme environment. They have adapted. Native Americans once lived there, too. They knew where to find water and how to survive there. In the 1800s, white settlers went there to look for gold. There were 30 people in the first group, but only 18 survived. The survivors killed their oxen for food, burned their wagons, and walked over the mountains. Other people came to look for gold here but were not any luckier. They left ghost towns behind them.
What is the name of this place?

Unit 11, Practice 5, Page 284 (CD 3, 8)

German immigrants introduced the hamburger to the United States. The word *hamburger* comes from the German city of Hamburg. In 1904, at the St. Louis Fair, they served hamburgers on buns. McDonald's® made hamburgers a popular American food.

The McDonald brothers opened the first McDonald's® restaurant in California in 1949. The restaurant served only three things: hamburgers, French fries, and milkshakes. People waited outside the restaurant to eat. The business became too big for the McDonald brothers. The brothers sold McDonald's®. Ray Kroc bought the restaurant. Since then, the company has opened over 25,000 McDonald's® restaurants around the world. People eat more than 40 million hamburgers every day. Ray Kroc became a millionaire.

Unit 11, Listening Puzzle, Page 295 (CD 3, 9–10)

This crop is really grass. It is grown worldwide, and it is an important food source. It is used to make flour and other foods. Sometimes it is used to feed animals. This crop originated in Southwest Asia. The area is known as the Fertile Crescent. It is where agriculture started. Early people planted the wild grasses. They learned to choose the best ones. The idea of planting this grass for food spread and reached Africa, India, and Europe 5,000 years ago. A thousand years later, it reached China. Another thousand years passed. New farming equipment began to be used. Farmers increased their production. More land was used to grow this crop. Its berries were crushed into flour. Today the berries are used to make bread, cereal, crackers, and many other foods. It is grown in winter and in summer. For decades, there was more of this crop than people to eat it. But today there are more people eating this crop. There isn't enough of this crop being grown. There may be shortages one day.
What is the name of this crop?

Unit 12, Practice 4, Page 307 (CD 3, 11)

1.	Monica:	I love this kind of music.
	Ken:	So do I.
2.	Monica:	I haven't been to a party for a long time.
	Ken:	Neither have I.
3.	Monica:	I am very shy.
	Ken:	So am I.

4. Monica: I am not good at making conversation.
   Ken: Neither am I.
5. Monica: I love to read.
   Ken: So do I.
6. Monica: I live alone.
   Ken: So do I.
7. Monica: I came to this city a few years ago.
   Ken: So did I.
8. Monica: I don't have many friends.
   Ken: Neither do I.

Unit 12, Practice 6, Page 308 (CD 3, 12)

1. Judy: I haven't been here before.
   Laura: And I haven't, either.
2. Judy: I like the décor and atmosphere.
   Laura: And I do, too.
3. Judy: I don't like this dish.
   Laura: And I don't, either.
4. Judy: My food isn't fresh.
   Laura: And neither is mine.
5. Judy: My meal is cold.
   Laura: And mine is, too.
6. Judy: I don't have a napkin.
   Laura: And neither do I.
7. Judy: I am disappointed.
   Laura: And so am I.
8. Judy: I won't come here again.
   Laura: And I won't, either.

Unit 12, Practice 8, Page 311 (CD 3, 13)

1. Police Officer: What color was the car?
   You: I can't remember what color it was.
2. Police Officer: How many people were there in the car?
   You: I don't know how many people were in the car.
3. Police Officer: How fast was the car going?
   You: I don't know how fast the car was going.
4. Police Officer: What was the license plate number?
   You: I don't know what the license plate number was.
5. Police Officer: Where were you standing?
   You: I can't remember where I was standing.
6. Police Officer: How many other witnesses were there?
   You: I don't know how many other witnesses there were.
7. Police Officer: When did the accident happen?
   You: I am not certain when the accident happened.
8. Police Officer: Where was the pedestrian?
   You: I'm not sure where the pedestrian was.

Unit 12, Listening Puzzle, Page 319 (CD 3, 14–15)

This is the fourth planet from the sun. It is one of Earth's neighbors. It is like Earth in several ways. It has clouds in its atmosphere. It has ice at its north pole. It has a solid surface, and there are mountains and canyons. One difference is that it doesn't have liquid water. But evidence shows that water once flowed there. We don't know whether there was ever life on this planet. Some scientists think that life once existed there. From Earth, this planet looks dark orange. There is a large amount of iron in the soil. It gives this planet its orange color. The ancient Greeks and Romans said that it looked like blood. They named this planet after the god of war. We hope that this planet is always a peaceful place. Scientists want to build a space colony there. We don't know when they will do that. It is extremely cold, and there are fierce dust storms. There is less oxygen than on Earth. It will be a great challenge.
What is the name of this planet?

Unit 13, Practice 1, Page 327 (CD 3, 16)

1. A mechanic is a person who fixes cars.
2. A barber is a person who cuts men's hair.
3. A doctor is a person that helps sick people.
4. A coach is a person who trains athletes.
5. A waiter is a person that serves people in a restaurant.
6. A journalist is a person who writes for a newspaper.
7. A dentist is a person who fixes teeth.
8. A teller is a person that works in a bank.

Unit 13, Practice 7, Page 332 (CD 3, 17)

1. Who was the person who invented the light bulb?
   Thomas Edison.
2. What is the name of the long river that is in Africa?
   The Nile.
3. What is the name of the writer who wrote *Hamlet*?
   William Shakespeare.
4. What's the name of the country whose capital city is Buenos Aires?
   Argentina.
5. What is the name of the man who was the first to walk on the moon?
   Neil Armstrong.
6. What is the name of the man whose home was called Graceland, in Memphis, Tenessee?
   Elvis Presley.

Unit 13, Practice 10, Page 337 (CD 3, 18)

J. Paul Getty became a millionaire when he was 24. Although his father was rich, he did not help his son. Getty was a hard worker who made his money from oil. Although Getty was a millionaire, he wasn't happy. Although he married five times, he was not happy. Although he had five children, he didn't love them.

For a man who was the richest man in the world at one time, he was tight with his money. Although he was an American, he loved to live in England. He bought a house in England that had 72 bedrooms, but it had pay phones in the bedrooms because Getty wanted to save money on phone bills. Although he was very rich, he wrote down every dollar he spent every evening. Although he could eat anything he wanted, he ate simple food.

Although Getty didn't like to spend money, he bought beautiful and expensive pieces of art. Because he loved art, he didn't care about the price. Today, the wonderful pieces of art that he bought are in a museum. It is a museum that is in California. It is one of the most famous museums in the United States. It is called the J. Paul Getty Museum.

Unit 13, Listening Puzzle, Page 339 (CD 3, 19–20)

This tree began as long as 200 million years ago in the Northern Hemisphere. Today there are about 200 types worldwide. Only one species lives south of the equator. It is in Sumatra. This is a tree that grows from the edge of deserts to rainforests. It lives on mountaintops and at sea level. Even though the U.S. has many species, Mexico has the most. China has the third-largest number. Although this tree loves sun, it can grow in shade. There are two ways in which this tree is different from others. It has seeds in cones. It has narrow leaves that are called needles. This is a tree that lives hundreds of years. There is a species that lives for thousands of years. The place where they grow is high on mountains. Because of the cold temperature, they grow very slowly. The oldest tree lives in eastern California. It is in an ancient forest. It is known that this tree is almost 5,000 years old. In order to protect this tree, only scientists know where it is. What is the name of this tree?

Unit 14, Practice 4, Page 352 (CD 3, 21)

A. "No talking, Jimmy," the teacher said. "I didn't say anything," Jimmy told the teacher. "Don't tell lies," the teacher said. "I can tell the difference when someone talks and when someone doesn't talk," the teacher told the class. "Now, I don't want to hear a sound. Is that clear?" the teacher said.

B. "Yesterday Meg said she was moving to Alaska," Karen said. "She told me that she had found a good job there." "I don't believe that," Mike said. "Last month she told me she was going to Paris. She doesn't tell the truth all the time, you know."

C. Today, my neighbor said good morning to me as usual. Then she told me a story about a mouse in her bedroom last night. She said that the mouse had run out of her apartment and into my apartment. Did she tell me the truth or did she tell me a story again?

Unit 14, Practice 7, Page 356 (CD 3, 22)

1. Are you OK?
2. Do you need help?
3. How did you fall?
4. Can you stand up?
5. Were you on your way to work?
6. Where does it hurt?
7. What's your name?
8. Can I call the ambulance for you?

Unit 14, Practice 13, Page 362 (CD 3, 23)

Photographers follow me everywhere. Newspapers write untrue stories about me. I don't have privacy. People touch me and pull my clothes. I have to sign autographs all the time. I have to smile all the time. I can't wear anything I want. I can't go to the store to get groceries.

Unit 14, Listening Puzzle, Page 373 (CD 3, 24–25)

This waterfall is between two countries. It has two sections separated by an island. The waterfall on one side is in the shape of a horseshoe. This waterfall was formed by glaciers. As the glaciers melted, the water created the falls. It is an awesome sight. People travel far to see it, especially couples on their honeymoon. If it weren't for the falls, no tourists would come here. The falls don't only attract tourists. In 1829, a man jumped into the falls and survived. Since then, other daredevils have tried going over the falls. In 1901, a woman went over the falls in a barrel. She survived unharmed. But she said, "No one should ever try that again." Since then, 14 others have gone over. They were either in or on something. Some survived, others were seriously hurt, and a few died. Once, a seven-year-old boy was swept over the falls. Minutes later he popped out of the water below. Everyone said that it was a miracle. It is against the law to go over the falls. Survivors are fined or jailed. If people knew about this, maybe they wouldn't do it. What is the name of this waterfall?

Index

Photo Credits

Page xii: © BananaStock/JupiterImages; xiii: © image 100 Ltd.; 1: © Royalty-Free/Corbis; 2: © Photodisc/PunchStock; 3: © Royalty-Free/Corbis; 6: © Kevin Peterson/Getty Images; 8: © PhotoLink/Getty Images; 9: © Royalty-Free/Corbis; 11 (top): © Creatas/PictureQuest; 11 (bottom): © Royalty-Free/Corbis; 13: © Hyphen-Engineering Education (Thanos Tsilis); 14: © Roy McMahon/Corbis; 15 (left): © McGraw-Hill Companies, Inc./Gary He, photographer; 15 (right): © Brand X Pictures/PunchStock; 16: © Keith Brofsky/Getty Images; 18: © Ryan McVay/Getty Images; 21 (left to right): © Envision/Corbis, © Ingram Publishing/Alamy, © Stockdisck/PunchStock; 22: © Comstock/PunchStock; 27: © Royalty-Free/Corbis; 28: © Underwood & Underwood/Corbis; 29: © Geoff Caddick/epa/Corbis; 32: © Bettmann/Corbis; 35: © Hyphen-Engineering Education (Thanos Tsilis); 36: © Royalty-Free/Corbis; 40: © Royalty-Free/Corbis; 42: © Austrian Archives/Corbis; 44: © Joshua Ets-Hokin/Getty Images; 45 (left to right): © DAJ/Getty Images, © Royalty-Free/Corbis, © Royalty-Free/Corbis; 46: © Royalty-Free/Corbis; 51: © Stockbyte/Getty Images; 52: © Brand X Pictures/PunchStock; 55: © Royalty-Free/Corbis; 57: © McGraw-Hill Companies, Inc./Gary He, photographer; 58: © Hyphen-Engineering Education (Thanos Tsilis); 59 (left): © Rim Light/PhotoLink; 59 (right): Royalty-Free/Corbis; 60: © Steven Mason/Getty Images; 62: © image100 Ltd; 63: © Stockbyte/Getty Images; 65 (left): Michael Evans/Life File/Getty Images; 65 (right): Andrew Ward/Life File/Getty Images; 67 (all): © Hyphen-Engineering Education; 68: © J. Luke/PhotoLink/Getty Images; 73: © Brand X Pictures/PunchStock; 74: © Jess Alford/Getty Images; 78: © S. Solum/PhotoLink/Getty Images; 80: © Royalty-Free/Corbis; 83: © PhotoDisc/Getty Images; 84: © Royalty-Free/Corbis; 86 (left): © PhotoLink/Getty Images; 86 (right): © Royalty-Free/Corbis; 87: © Hyphen-Engineering Education (Thanos Tsilis); 88: © Photolink/Getty Images; 90: © Royalty-Free/Corbis; 92: © Doug Menuez/Getty Images; 94: © Brand X Pictures/PunchStock; 95 (left to right): © Medioimages/Superstock, © Karl Weatherly/Getty Images, © Philip Coblentz/Brand X Pictures; 96: © Galen Rowell/Corbis; 101: © Getty Images; 102: © Ryan McVay/Getty Images; 105: © Steve Cole/Getty Images; 107: © Getty Images; 109: © Hyphen-Engineering Education (Thanos Tsilis); 110: © Tom Grill/Corbis; 112: © Ryan McVay/Getty Images; 113: © Andrew Wakeford/Getty Images; 115 (all): © Brand X/JupiterImages; 116: © Bettmann/Corbis; 121: © Stefanie Aulmann/Getty Images; 122: © Tim Pannell/Corbis; 127: © C. Borland/PhotoLink/Getty Images; 128: © Royalty-Free/Corbis; 130: © Hyphen-Engineering Education (Thanos Tsilis); 131: © Buccina Studios/Getty Images; 133: © Andrew Ward/Life File/Getty Images; 135: © Stefanie Aulmann/Getty Images; 137: © BananaStock/PunchStock; 140: © BananaStock; 142: © Keith Brofsky/Getty Images; 143 (left to right): © Sean Thompson/Photodisc/Getty Images, © U.S. Air Force photo by Tech. Sgt. Tracy L. DeMarco, © Comstock/JupiterImages; 144: © Comstock/Alamy; 149: © Digital Vision Ltd.; 150: © Scott T. Baxter/Getty Images; 153: © Digital Vision/PunchStock; 156: © Steve Mason/Getty Images; 158: © BananaStock/PunchStock; 160: © Getty Images; 163: © Digital Vision Ltd.; 165: © Royalty-Free/Corbis; 167: © Comstock/PictureQuest; 168: © Jupiterimages/Imagesource; 170: © Hyphen-Engineering Education (Thanos Tsilis); 171: © Eric Audras/Photoalto/PictureQuest; 175: © Dynamic Graphics/PictureQuest; 177 (left to right): © Royalty-Free/Corbis, © Brand X Pictures/PunchStock, © R. Strange/PhotoLink/Getty Images; 178: © Digital Vision; 183: © Royalty-Free/Corbis; 184: © TRBfoto/Getty Images; 190: © Steve Mason/Getty Images; 192: © PhotoAlto; 194: © Royalty-Free/Corbis; 197: © Suza Scalora/Getty Images; 198 (top): © The Studio Dog/Getty Images; 198 (bottom): © Royalty-Free/Corbis; 199: © Royalty-Free/Corbis; 202: © Mel Curtis/Getty Images; 204: © Royalty-Free/Corbis; 207: © image100/PunchStock; 210: © D. Falcone/PhotoLink/Getty Images; 213: © Comstock/PictureQuest; 214 (all): © Hyphen-Engineering Education; 215: © Hyphen-Engineering Education (Thanos Tsilis); 216: © Royalty-Free/Corbis; 217 (left to right): © Digital Vision/PunchStock, © Brand X Pictures/PunchStock, © Digital Vision/PunchStock; 218: © Phil Schermeister/Corbis; 223: © Brand X/JupiterImages; 224: © Brand X/JupiterImages; 226: © Ryan McVay/Getty Images; 227: © Buccina Studios/Getty Images; 229: © Hyphen-Engineering Education (Thanos Tsilis); 230: © PhotoLink/Getty Images; 233: © Royalty-Free/Corbis; 235 (all): © Barbara Penoyar/Getty Images; 237: © Stocktrek/age fotostock; 238: © C Squared Studios/Getty Images; 240: © M. Freeman/PhotoLink/Getty Images; 242: © BananaStock/